TITANS OF HYDERABAD CRICKET

ABHIJIT SEN GUPTA

EDITOR
SANJAY SAXENA

INDIA • SINGAPORE • MALAYSIA

Copyright © Sanjay Saxena 2024
All Rights Reserved.

ISBN 979-8-89322-769-7

This book has been published with all efforts taken to make the material error-free after the consent of the author. However, the author and the publisher do not assume and hereby disclaim any liability to any party for any loss, damage, or disruption caused by errors or omissions, whether such errors or omissions result from negligence, accident, or any other cause.

While every effort has been made to avoid any mistake or omission, this publication is being sold on the condition and understanding that neither the author nor the publishers or printers would be liable in any manner to any person by reason of any mistake or omission in this publication or for any action taken or omitted to be taken or advice rendered or accepted on the basis of this work. For any defect in printing or binding the publishers will be liable only to replace the defective copy by another copy of this work then available.

Dedication

I would like to dedicate this book to all my family members who have always encouraged me and helped me in all my projects. But most of all, this book is for my granddaughter Sia. I hope she will enjoy reading it.

– Abhijit Sen Gupta.

Dedication

This book is dedicated to Guru Omkar Prasad, my parents Indira and Eshwar Raj. My lifelines Madhu, Kunal and Anoushka: Without you this would not be possible.

– Sanjay Saxena

Acknowledgements

We express our heartfelt gratitude to Siasat.com for granting us permission to use several articles published on their platform for use in this book. Their generosity in allowing us to incorporate the articles has greatly enhanced the information contained in this book. We are also grateful to Mr. P.R. Man Singh, former Secretary of the Hyderabad Cricket Association, who served as the manager of the victorious Indian team in the 1983 Prudential World Cup. He presented us with a copy of his book titled "Cricket Biryani: A History of Hyderabad Cricket". Many facts about the history of the game in the twin cities were found in his informative book.

Editor's Note

The main motivation for working on this book was that I would be able to reminisce on those days when I would watch Hyderabad cricketing giants and derive inspiration to do better.

Growing up, watching these cricketeers at such close quarters and dreaming of becoming like them seemed to be an important goal. Almost every Sunday I used to go and watch the Hyderabad cricket league matches (when we ourselves were not playing) and learn just by observing. Till today I remember their individual batting, bowling and fielding styles and their pursuit of excellence. I would like to mention that M.L. Jaisimha, one of the biggest titans of Hyderabad cricket addressed to as Chief by many cricketers has had a lasting impression on me and will continue to do so. He is one of the main reasons that the game of cricket is so close to my heart. The impeccable style in which he executed his on-drives are etched in my memory for ever. The way he bowled his off-spinners and used flighted deliveries to trick batsmen cannot be forgotten. He has a big fan following all over the world and I consider myself as one of the biggest fans of Jaisimha. Thank you Chief for creating your very own and distinctive cricketing style.

It was great working with Abhijit on this project and we have put our best into it. We go a long way back —those Osmania University days. I hope all of you will enjoy reading this book as much as we did in completing this work.

Contents

Introduction

Recently my friend and former Osmania University classmate Sanjay Saxena called me up one day and said: "Let us compile our memories and write a book about Hyderabad cricket." The moment I heard his words, I felt that it was a wonderful idea. Both of us are cricket fans and both of us love to discuss our experiences.

Besides, after following the fortunes of Hyderabad's cricketers for more than four decades, Sanjay and I feel that there are some unique aspects about the game and the players from Hyderabad that would be very interesting to analyse and write about. So that is the purpose of this book - to bring before the readers some unfamiliar and uncommon facts and stories which have enlivened the history of cricket in Hyderabad.

But our book is not only about cricket statistics and the achievements of the players. There is more to cricket than cricket alone. As the well known author, cricket lover and historian C.L.R. James, born in Trinidad and Tobago in the West Indies, said once: 'What does he know of cricket who only cricket knows.' Our book is about the ambience that surrounded the game and its players in the 1970s and 80s and continues to do in the present times. Decades ago, cricket was only a sport, not a commercial activity as well. There were no sponsors and no lucrative advertising contracts for the players. They played because they loved the sport and nothing else. Players had to procure a steady job to keep the home fires burning. Often the banks recruited cricketers and so the players managed to get along in life.

A bit about ourselves

Now to introduce ourselves - the men behind this book.

Sanjay was born and raised in Hyderabad. He holds a Bachelor's degree in Biology and Chemistry from Osmania University. He also holds a Bachelor's and Master's degree in Communication and Journalism also from Osmania University. In addition, he did Graduate work in Journalism at University of Alabama, USA.

But in one respect Sanjay and I were different from each other. While I entered the classroom only when I felt like it, Sanjay did not bunk classes and was an excellent student. His efforts fetched him the prestigious "Indian Herald Gold Medal" for standing first at Master's level. Soon he was teaching Communication and Journalism at Osmania University. He taught subjects like Advertising, Research Methodologies to name a few.

Sanjay's passion includes playing the Tabla. He started learning this instrument at a very early age and went on to perform at All India Radio and TV. He continues to perform and is a sought-after artist. His expertise is playing Tabla solo recitals and enjoys playing with many other instrumentalists, vocal and Kathak artists.

Sanjay was a good cricket player too. He played as an opening batsman and a leg spinner with and against the top names of Hyderabad cricket. He follows cricket with great interest, and this has led to collaborating on this book.

He is an entrepreneur, Business Development and Branding subject matter expert, founder of companies in the US, an advisor and a mentor. He lives in the US.

As for me, I lived in different parts of India before landing up in Hyderabad. In 1972, my father, who worked for the Survey of India, was posted to Hyderabad and our family moved here. I was then a boy of 17, fresh out of school in Mount Abu in Rajasthan where I had spent my boyhood. All I knew about the city of Hyderabad was that its most famous landmark was the Charminar.

But in school I had also read (newspapers and magazines were our only source of information since we did not have television back then) about the exploits of Hyderabad players like M.L. Jaisimha and the Nawab of Pataudi. Therefore, being a big cricket fan, I was looking forward to seeing them play in Hyderabad.

I went through the grind of higher education – at Nizam College, alma mater to Jaisimha, and later Azharuddin. However, my own modest skills were not good enough to get me a place in the college team but good fortune smiled on me later in life and I became a sports journalist.

That career gave me the opportunity to witness many memorable battles between some of the world's best players from the unique vantage point of the press box at the Lal Bahadur Stadium. Later the Rajiv Gandhi Stadium was constructed and is now the venue for international cricket.

Over the years, I developed a great fondness for Hyderabad, its easy going people, its food, and its language. The general attitude of the inhabitants of the city, not surprisingly, reflects strongly the attitude and approach of the players who represent Hyderabad.

Seeing how the culture influenced their approach to the game has always been fascinating for a sports lover like me.

Going only by results, Hyderabad may not have a record as impressive as Mumbai or Delhi in domestic cricket. But the city has been the birthplace of some of the most loved and most colourful cricketers to don the India cap.

There has always been a difference in approach between, for example, a cricketer from Mumbai, Kolkata or Delhi, and a player from Hyderabad. It may not be readily visible to a casual watcher but to anyone who has spent time studying teams and players from Hyderabad, it's quite self-evident.

Laid back Hyderabadis.

Hyderabad cricketers are traditionally often laidback people. It wouldn't be too much of a stretch to imagine that it has to do with the relaxed culture and traditions that the city of Nawabs has always been known for. The ambience has been changing in the last two decades – more on that later – but much of the old customs and attitudes have not yet completely vanished.

But that does not mean that Hyderabadi cricketers are casual in their approach to the game. In their own way, they take cricket seriously enough. Hyderabad too has produced some of the best players in the country. But they have achieved success by following a different path. The game is important for them but there is less anxiety in them, a greater sang-froid.

When a Hyderabadi says that he will get something done "parsoon", he doesn't really mean that he will do it the day after tomorrow. He means that he will not do it immediately. He may do it after one week, or after one month, or whenever he feels like doing it.

In the culture of old Hyderabad of the pre-independence days, the many Nawabs who used to be admired for their graceful manners and relaxed lifestyle, held the view that it was bad form to show anxiety or urgency about anything. And since the hoi polloi tried to imitate the aristocracy, it became a tradition in Hyderabad to take a relaxed view of life.

Besides, it has always been important for a true-blue old-time Hyderabadi not just to complete a task, but to do it with grace and style. A Hyderabadi should be able to do with ease – or at least appear to do so – what others struggle to accomplish.

In many ways, M.L. Jaisimha personified that attitude in the 1960s and '70s. Not only was he a fine all-rounder and an astute captain, but he had a flair for doing things differently. His swaggering walk, upturned collar, and insouciant demeanour, both on and off the field, earned him a legion of fans all over India and especially in Hyderabad. In many ways he was the first glamorous star of Indian cricket, along with his good friend Mansur Ali Khan, the Nawab of Pataudi.

The Nawab of Pataudi, who was then at loggerheads with the cricketing authorities in his then home state of Delhi, transferred to Hyderabad in 1966, after Jai put the idea into his mind. Both had the same attitude to cricket and to life. Pataudi was a man of many artistic passions, and Jai gave him the right kind of support to indulge them.

Jeffrey Archer on Pataudi.

The best selling novelist Jeffrey Archer knew Pataudi well and had a high opinion about him. Archer said once that Pataudi had the blood of a Maharajah but was a man of the masses. When asked to explain this dichotomy the author used the words of Rudyard Kipling in the poem IF. Kipling had written a line in his famous poem which stated "Or walk with Kings nor lose the common touch."

Jeffrey Archer used that line to explain why he felt Pataudi had the blood of royalty in his veins but was also a man of the masses. "When he had that car accident when he was a student at Oxford University, we were all very worried. He lost one eye. But with one good eye he became a fantastic cricketer. He scored 203 not out against England. I ask you to consider what he could have achieved with two good eyes," said Archer.

To return to the subject of Hyderabad, in the 1980s, Jai was living in a beautiful house in a quiet corner of the locality of Marredpally. The house had huge doors opening onto a spacious lawn where parties were held frequently.

Jai's house - a favourite haunt.

It was a favourite haunt for players and celebrities, who often gathered there to discuss cricket and exchange gossip, with the revelries lasting till the early hours of the next day. Jai was an excellent raconteur and had a razor sharp memory. He could keep audiences spellbound for hours with his stories of unusual incidents on and off the field of cricket.

Along with Pat and Jai, there was the scintillating Abbas Ali Baig. He was a batsman with prodigious talent who at the age of

20, scored a century on debut when he was selected to play for India. But that was not his only distinction. He was also the first Indian cricketer to be kissed by a female fan on the field of play.

The 1970s were perhaps the best phase of Hyderabad cricket. In 1971 when the Indian team toured the West Indies, it included five players from Hyderabad – Syed Abid Ali, D. Govindaraj, M.L. Jaisimha, K. Jayantilal, and wicket-keeper P. Krishnamurthy. That team made history by chalking up India's first-ever series triumph over the formidable islanders led by the legendary Sir Gary Sobers.

Quite often, a Hyderabad player needs something to shake him up, give him a jolt and get him going. Take V.V.S. Laxman, for instance. If a match was plodding along peacefully, his approach was equally placid. But put him in a difficult situation or give him a tough target, and he would start firing with all the weapons in his formidable armoury.

In the Kolkata Test of 2001, when India was following on against Australia, Laxman's knock of 281 (with 44 boundaries) is regarded by many experts as one of the best knocks ever played on the hallowed ground of the Eden Gardens. Australian captain Steve Waugh called it the greatest Test innings he had ever seen and confessed that he ran out of ideas about how to check the flow of runs that were cascading from Laxman's bat.

But to see the complete picture of Hyderabad's cricket culture and understand the approach of the players, it is necessary to also take a look at many other players, not just those who reached the topmost level. Players like Abdul Azeem, Shahid Akbar, Vijay Mohan Raj, P. Jyothiprasad, Mumtaz Hussain, Naushir Mehta, V. Ramnarayan, Kawaljeet Singh, Khalid Abdul Qaiyum, Narenderpal Singh and many others who achieved outstanding feats but were unlucky not to have represented India. They should be written about too.

Nowadays at the Rajiv Gandhi International Stadium in Uppal where matches are held, there is a different atmosphere from the one that once existed at the Lal Bahadur Shastri stadium. There is more excitement and more noise now. The crowd wants cricket to be colourful and thrilling. The days of quiet appreciation of the technique and determination of the players have gone. The fans nowadays want instant gratification. They want cricket to be served like fast takeaway meals. Not like fine dining with all its style and elegance.

The Rajiv Gandhi stadium in Uppal is the venue where IPL matches are conducted. The IPL has been a great success and young people decked out in the orange colours of the Sunrisers Hyderabad team throng the venue, vociferously lending their voices to the din.

One success that the IPL has achieved is also to bring many female fans to the stadiums – this would have been a rare thing in the stands at the Lal Bahadur Stadium back in the 1970s and 1980s.

Winds of change.

In the past couple of decades, though, the winds of change have blown hard across Hyderabad. There have been efforts to change its image from a city of old etiquette and relaxed ways, into a modern, bustling, fast-paced city. When Chandrababu Naidu was the Chief Minister of undivided Andhra Pradesh during the late 1990s and early 2000s, he enticed many software companies to set up offices in Hyderabad by offering good infrastructure and tax breaks.

Offices and industries mushroomed, and the city grew in size and population. The boom provided many young people much-needed jobs and good incomes. Efficiency and punctuality improved. But the old ways of leisure gradually vanished.

The decline of the Moin-ud-Dowlah Gold Cup reflects the decline in Hyderabad cricket. The tournament was begun in the early 1930s by Nawab Moin-ud-Dowlah Bahadur, one of Hyderabad's main patrons of sport.

Players like Jack Hobbs and Herbert Sutcliffe, the England openers who were then regarded as the best opening pair in the world, played in the tournament. So too did the infamous Douglas Jardine, inventor of bodyline along with Indian stalwarts like C.K. Nayudu, Lala Amarnath, Mohammad Nissar to name a few.

The tournament used to be classified as a first-class fixture when it started but has not even been conducted in recent times. To add to that, the original gold-plated trophy donated almost a century ago by Nawab Moin-ud-Dowlah Bahadur mysteriously vanished in 2011. Its disappearance seemed to symbolize the passing of the era of the Nawabs of Hyderabad cricket.

Chapter 1

Hyderabad's Cricket History

Cricket is one of the most popular sports in India, and Hyderabad, the capital city of Telangana, has a rich history of cricket. The sport was introduced to Hyderabad during the British Raj, and since then, it has grown in popularity to become a favourite pastime for people of all ages.

The game was introduced to the people of Hyderabad by British army units which were stationed in the area before independence. Around 1880 cricket started to take roots in the city. Raja Lochan Chand was one of the pioneers who worked hard to promote cricket throughout the Nizam's territory. In the late 19th century and early 20th century Masood Ahmed, Ahmed Ali, Nazeer Baig and Khurshid Baig were few cricketers to distinguish themselves.

First recorded match in Hyderabad.

The first recorded cricket match in Hyderabad was played in 1885 between the British Army and a team of local players. The match was played on the grounds of the Hyderabad Gymkhana, which was established in 1884. The Hyderabad Gymkhana was one of the earliest sports clubs in India, and it played a crucial role in the development of cricket in Hyderabad.

The Oxford University Authentics that toured India in the 1902- 1903 season was the first foreign team to visit and play in Hyderabad. However, since the matches they played in Hyderabad were not deemed first class cricket, there is no official record for reference.

Thereafter, in the 1920s and 1930s quadrangular tournaments between the Hindus, Muslims, Europeans and Parsees were instrumental in popularizing the game throughout India and Hyderabad was no exception. Despite appeals by Mahatma Gandhi to end the concept of teams selected along communal lines, the Quadrangular and Pentangular tournaments continued to thrill the fans until 1947 and encouraged youngsters to take up the sport seriously.

In Hyderabad the educational institutions like Nizam's College, Madrasa-E-Aliya and other schools also promoted the game by encouraging students to play it. Nawab Moin-ud-Dowlah, Maharaja Kishan Pershad, Nawab Salar Jung Bahadur were among those who patronized the game and initiated matches for schools and clubs. Private Clubs like HUCC and SUCC, were formed by cricket enthusiasts and became prominent and cricket leagues were established.

Nawab Moin ud Dowlah, an important patron.

One of the leading patrons of the sport of cricket in the 1920s and 1930s was Nawab Moin ud Dowlah Bahadur. He was a man with an immense passion for the game. It was his commitment and boundless energy which gave Hyderabad cricket the push that it greatly needed back then. His love for all sports was immense. He loved riding horses, shooting, tennis, billiards and cricket. But among all these, his greatest devotion was to cricket.

It has been recorded in the book "Cricket Biryani" written by P.R. Man Singh, one of the most knowledgeable personalities in Hyderabad cricket, that sometimes when the Nawab was traveling in his car along the road and happened to see school boys playing cricket in any open space beside the road, he would instruct his driver to stop for a few minutes while he watched them playing. Such was his love for cricket that he could hold back all his important engagements just to watch children playing a makeshift game of cricket with sticks and a bat and ball.

The Nawab had two palaces, one in Saroornagar and another in Basheerbagh where he lodged his guests and outstation cricket teams for the many tournaments that he organised. His generosity was well known. But sometimes, quite unfortunately, some players took advantage of his generous nature. It started many years ago, when one player complained to the Nawab that his playing kit had been stolen or lost during his journey to Hyderabad.

The Nawab instantly bought him a new bat, and a new pair of pads and gloves. Thereafter, some other unscrupulous players also claimed that they had lost their belongings and the Nawab had no hesitation in buying new clothes and playing equipment for them. In the cricket season of 1933-1934, a cricket team from England put together by the prestigious Marylebone Cricket Club toured India from 15th December 1933 to 4th March 1934. It played three Test matches in India before going on to Ceylon (as Sri Lanka was then called).

Before the start of the tour, there was a discussion about the venues where the three Tests would be played. The Nawab made an offer to the cricket control board that he would host one Test match in Hyderabad and promised to pay to the board the required amount of guarantee money if the match was awarded to Hyderabad.

Hyderabad's first international match.

But after considering all the offers that had been received, the board decided to allocate the Tests to Bombay (now Mumbai), Calcutta (Kolkata) and Madras (Chennai). But so as not to disappoint the Nawab, one first class match was given to Hyderabad. That was how Hyderabad got the chance to host its first ever international first class fixture.

For his team, the Nawab picked up the cream of the Indian cricketers. They included legendary names such as Syed Mushtaq Ali, Lala Amarnath, C.K. Nayudu and his brother C.S. Nayudu, Hyderabad's two most talented players of the time, S.M. Hussain and his brother S.M. Hadi and India's topmost fast bowling all-rounder L. Amar Singh.

On the MCC side the most famous player was Hedley Verity. He was England's most effective spin bowler and had the distinction of dismissing Don Bradman eight times in Test matches – more often than any other bowler. The visiting side also had Bryan Valentine who had scored 136 in the first Test at Bombay. In Stanley Nichols they also had a tireless fast bowler who could bowl for long spells with great hostility.

When the match began, the MCC side batted first but were bundled out for a surprisingly low score of 112. The credit for this went to Amar Singh and Mushtaq Ali. The former, as usual moved the ball beautifully off the pitch and took 4 wickets for 33 runs while Mushtaq Ali who was more famous for his strokeplay, did well with the ball by taking 5 wickets for 37 runs.

In reply the Nawab's team scored 194 and thus took a first innings lead of 82 runs. Amar Singh performed well with the bat too and top scored with 58 before he was caught by Gregory of the bowling of Townsend.

In its second innings the touring MCC side approached their task with greater determination and scored 303. It was not a very big total but good enough under the circumstances. Nichols top scored with a half century in the lower order. They set the Nawab's team a victory target of 222 runs.

If batsmen like Mushtaq Ali, Lala Amarnath or C.K. Nayudu had found their form, the target could easily have been achieved. But luckily for MCC, the big guns of the Indian side did not fire their salvos. Mushtaq scored 26 before he was stumped by Levett off Townsend while Lala was caught by Nichols off Townsend for a duck.

Only C.K. Nayudu came up with a hard hitting knock of 79 before he was caught by Mitchell off the bowling of Nichols. But it was not enough to guide his team to a win. The match ended in a draw as the Nawab's men took their total to 188 for nine when the match ended. Townsend who captured four wickets for 76 runs and Verity with three wickets for 78 runs were the bowlers who prevented a victory for the Nawab's team. Thus ended the first ever international cricket match played on Hyderabad soil.

Beginning of the Moin ud Dowlah trophy.

First class cricket began with the advent of the Moin ud Dowlah trophy which began in 1930-31. Thanks to the patronage and efforts of Nawab Moin ud Dowlah Bahadur, first class cricket came to Hyderabad in 1930 - 1931 with the first ever Moin ud Dowlah

Gold Cup tournament. Three teams participated in the tournament. They were Hyderabad XI, the Maharaj Kumar of Vizianagaram's XI and Nawab of Moin ud Dowlah's XI. The people of Hyderabad had the opportunity to watch some of the legendary names of the sport such as Jack Hobbs and Bert Sutcliffe, then considered to be the best opening pair in world cricket.

In the year 1934, the Ranji trophy national cricket championship was begun in India. So there was an immediate need for an authorised and recognised body to administer the game in Hyderabad. In April 1934, the Hyderabad Cricket Association was formed by Nadir Shah Chenoy, D.N. Dittia, Ganesh Rao, Hussain Ali Khan, S. Ali Raza, Mahmood Hussain Khan, Dattatreya and Rangannath. They elected Nawab Turab Yar Jung as its first President and Syed Mohammed Hadi as Secretary.

Under the leadership of S.M. Hadi and Nawab Turab Yar Jung, the HCA organized tournaments, maintained cricket grounds, and trained young cricketers. The association has produced several cricketers who have gone on to represent India at the international level. In conclusion, the history of cricket in Hyderabad is a rich and colourful one. The city has produced several world-class cricketers who have made significant contributions to Indian cricket.

Two Brothers of Rare Merit

Over the decades Hyderabad has produced many exceptionally talented cricket players whose exploits on the field made them famous throughout the land. But due to various reasons they were unable to find a place in the Indian teams. At first the only opening was the Test team but later there was also the ODI team after limited overs cricket was introduced.

S.M. HUSSAIN

Nawab Syed Mohammed Hussain was a very gifted batsman of his days. He was selected for the Indian team when it toured England in 1936. He was born in Hyderabad on 8th December 1902 and did his schooling at the famous Madrasa-E-Aliya and later at the Nizam College.

He belonged to a well to do Nawabi family of Hyderabad and was the elder brother of S.M. Hadi who became the first player to score a century in the Ranji trophy and also represent India in the Davis Cup. Hadi had so many sports talents that he was dubbed Rainbow Hadi because he had as many talents as a Rainbow has colours.

The elder brother Mohammed Hussain was a very disciplined man and in keeping with his mental outlook he joined the Hyderabad state army before later shifting to the Hyderabad police department. For this he had to undergo specialized training at the police academy in Mhow in Madhya Pradesh. Such was his reputation in the police department that he rose rapidly up the ranks in the later stage of his police career he became the Director General of Police.

As a cricketer he played for the Hyderabad army team and later also for the police team. When he was a young man the All India level cricket tournaments that were most popular were the Quadrangular and then the Pentangular tournaments.

In these tournaments, the teams were divided according to the religious affiliation of the players and for this reason these tournaments were later abolished after many people including Mahatma Gandhi objected to this system of selecting teams according to religion.

However, when Hussain was a good player, the tournaments were still being played and Hussain represented the Muslims team. He also had the distinction of leading the first ever Hyderabad team when it played in the Ranji trophy championship. This happened in the year 1934.

His good batting and fielding in the Ranji trophy championship that year caught the eye of the experts and he was included in the Indian team which was selected for a tour of England in 1936. Although the Nawab was not included in any of the Test matches, he did get to represent India in the first class matches against the English county teams. In these matches he performed well and kept India's colours flying high.

This was the tour which became infamous due to the spat between the Maharaja of Vizianagaram and Lala Amarnath following which Lala was sent back to India.

But back then international matches were rarely held. By the time he got his chance to play the first international series of his life, he was already 34 years old. About a year later he decided to stop being an active player and took up the role of a coach.

Hussain as a coach.

He moulded the careers of the Hyderabad police team's players and could be seen daily at the nets encouraging them and correcting their technique. Being a strict disciplinarian, he insisted that the players conduct themselves in a sportsman like manner not only on the field but also off the ground in their regular police duties.

According to P.R. Man Singh, former Secretary of the HCA, the Nawab was a very reserved man and rarely spoke. But on occasions he would tell the stories about his tour of England in 1936 and also the dismissal of Lala Amarnath by Vizzy and many other tales about his own experiences. These stories about the famous players of his days could hold audiences spellbound. One of the most glorious moments of his cricket career was when he led Hyderabad to its very first Ranji trophy victory. He passed away on 8th July 1982.

In his first class career he represented Muslims XI and Hyderabad XI. In first class cricket he played 44 matches and scored 1724 runs at an average 24.62 per innings. He did not score any centuries but on 14 occasions he scored more than 50 runs with a highest score of 94. He was distinctly unlucky to miss that century in first class cricket.

S.M. HADI

Now to talk about the other brother Syed Mohammed Hadi also known as Rainbow Hadi. He excelled at cricket, football, hockey, tennis, table tennis, polo and chess.

In cricket he was the first player to score a century in the Ranji trophy championship after it was started in 1934. In tennis he represented India in the Davis Cup tournaments. He also represented India in tennis at the Olympic Games in 1924.

Hadi's father was an officer in the army in the then Nizam's Hyderabad State. Tragically the gentleman passed away when his son Syed Mohammad Hadi was only two years old. The family was able to get along but as the baby grew into a boy it was felt that his schooling and education should be under able hands.

That is when the family of Sir Asman Jah, former Prime Minister of Hyderabad State, came to the rescue. Perhaps the family members had known that the boy's father was an able and dedicated officer and felt that the little boy should be given all possible help to fulfil his potential. No doubt their motives were charitable and the little boy profited from it.

When he was a little older, Hadi was sent to Nizam College – then the leading education institution in Hyderabad. It was when he was studying at Nizam College that he developed a love for horse riding and took up the game of Polo.

He was already showing his amazing skills at various sports. He was playing cricket and football for the Nizam college team and his remarkable skills drew the attention of the teachers as well as the coaches and his fellow students. Realising that his destiny lay beyond the confines of Hyderabad, the family of Sir Asman Jah decided to send the boy for further studies to England.

The decision proved to be the right one and when he reached England Hadi joined Cambridge University.

Cambridge Blue.

It was while studying at Cambridge that Hadi's abilities came to be noticed at an international level. He represented the University against arch rivals Oxford. Hadi helped Cambridge to win tennis tournaments against Oxford and also university teams from the USA.

That was not all. He went on to represent Cambridge University in hockey, football and table tennis. The media came to know about this extremely talented lad from Hyderabad in India and his skills caught the eyes of the sports fans and patrons in England. But it was not smooth sailing all the time. He could have become the captain of the University team but was denied the position probably because he was from India.

In a magazine in England, it was reported: "The wardrobe in his (Hadi's) room at Peterhouse must have been bursting with light blue jackets, as he shone at polo, tennis, soccer, field hockey, cricket and table tennis.

A particularly fine tennis player, it is at the racket game that his sporting career perhaps hit its greatest heights, as he played at Wimbledon five times, reaching the doubles quarter final in 1926. He also represented India at the 1924 summer Olympics and in the Davis Cups of 1925 and 1926. The run of representative appearances for his country must have more than made up for his frustration at being denied the Light Blues' tennis captaincy on account of his nationality."

Playing at the Wimbledon championships.

But the denial of captaincy did not discourage his fighting spirit. He continued to develop his tennis game and was selected to represent India at the Davis Cup on two occasions. His game was good enough to get him a place in the Wimbledon championships five times where he played in the doubles events. And then he also represented India in the Olympic Games.

After returning to India he played cricket for Hyderabad. His first class career lasted ten years during which he scored more than 1000 runs at a healthy average of 32.59 per innings with two centuries. His highest score was 132 not out. He was already an established player in the national scene when the Ranji trophy began and he was the first player to score a century in the championship.

First century scorer in the Ranji trophy.

It came in the third match of the inaugural season of the Ranji trophy. The first two matches did not see any century being scored. The third match was played between Hyderabad and Madras at Secunderabad. The match saw the hosts Hyderabad, led by Syed Mohamad Hussain while the Madras team was led by M Venkataramanujulu.

Hyderabad won the toss and decided to bat first. The team scored 256. In reply to which Madras scored 301. In its second innings Hyderabad was in disarray when Hadi walked out to bat. Three wickets had fallen with the total only 12 at that stage. But

Hadi turned the game around with a sparkling knock. He scored an unbeaten 132 even as wickets fell at the other end.

Hadi thus became the first ever centurion in the Ranji trophy championship. Needless to say, his batting helped Hyderabad to win the match.

In his first class career Hadi fought duels with legends such as C.K.Nayudu, Cotah Ramasamy, A.G. Ram Singh, Mushtaq Ali and others. Hadi represented the Maharajkumar of Vizianagaram's team in the Moin ud Dowlah Gold Cup cricket tournament at the Gymkhana ground in Secunderabad. Back then the tournament was designated as a first class event.

His brother Asghar Ali was a talented cricketer too who played first class level. So, sports talent probably ran in the family. It was not just Rainbow Hadi alone. It is not known now who gave him the nickname of Rainbow. But it may have been a name that was mentioned in the media and was widely accepted after that.

An able administrator.

After he left his active sports career, he took up sports administration along with his other duties. In addition to his degree from Cambridge University he had also acquired a master's degree from the University of Pennsylvania. His educational qualifications and his great knowledge were needed in the government and he served as an administrator. He rose up the ranks to become Joint Secretary in the Education Department in the Government of India.

In Hyderabad he used his contacts and influence to spread the development of sports. He was one of the founder members of the football association along with the famous coach Syed Abdul

Rahim and others. He was also a founder member of the Hyderabad Cricket Association and the Tennis Association.

As a sports administrator, Hadi served as the treasurer of the Indian cricket team on their tour of England in 1936 when his brother was a team member. When the All-India Council of Sports was formed in 1959, Hadi was its first secretary. The multitalented sportsman developed lung cancer in later life and passed away in 1971. He left behind a legacy that inspired and served the interest of sports in and around Hyderabad for many decades.

Chapter 3

Ghulam Ahmed

The contribution of Ghulam Ahmed to cricket in Hyderabad and India is extremely difficult to quantify in mere words. He was a legendary player, inspirational leader, far thinking administrator and a very capable manager. Whichever role he played, he did so with a measure of excellence that was unmatchable. The Greek philosopher of ancient times Aristotle, once said: "Excellence is never an accident. It is always the result of high intention, sincere effort and intelligent execution. Choice, not chance, determines our destiny." The words can be applied most aptly to the life and career of Ghulam Ahmed.

He meant more to Hyderabad than W.G. Grace meant to English cricket. Perhaps the only person who can be likened or compared to Ghulam Ahmed was Plum Warner (Pelham Warner) the man who made his Test debut in 1899, then led England's team and finally also served the game as an administrator.

Ghulam Ahmed did the same for Hyderabad. He was like a father figure. Speaking symbolically, the cricketing home that he built later housed several generations of players and provided them shelter and a place to flourish. Ghulam Ahmed's efforts paved the way to their success.

For Indian cricket too, he contributed immensely. As a player, captain, administrator and selector he put in untiring efforts to see that Indian cricket prospered and surged ever ahead. Born on 4th July, 1922, he became one of the best off spinners in the country. As a child his nickname, known only to close family members, was Aijaz. But to most others he was known as Ghulam. When he grew up, he became a superb bowler. Those who had seen him play, used to say that his bowling action was like poetry in motion.

But any person who knows about the family from which Ghulam Ahmed emerged, will not be surprised by the fact that this gentleman cricketer achieved so much in his lifetime. In a way, this illustrious family can be called the first family of Hyderabad sports.

Family of sportspersons.

Among those who are connected to the family are Pakistan's former captain Asif Iqbal, India's former captain Mohammed Azharuddin and tennis champion Sania Mirza. So that makes it two captains of India (Ghulam Ahmed himself and Azharuddin), a captain of Pakistan and a tennis Grand Slam winner in doubles and mixed doubles, all belonging to or connected to one family.

We all know about the famous off spinner's exploits on the cricket field. But what was he like as a person? Was he a disciplinarian or was he indulgent? Was he a strict parent or a friendly person who could be addressed as Dad?

For an article in Siasat.com, on the occasion of his 100th birth anniversary in 2022, I had spoken to a few people who knew him well including Ghulam Ahmed's son Nisar Ahmed.

This is what I learnt:

Ghulam Ahmed was a person whose character and conduct were without blemish. It was his most outstanding trait. He was painstakingly honest and fair in his thought and judgement. If he made a decision, everyone would accept it because they knew his reputation for being impartial and equitable.

As a parent he was not the old-fashioned taskmaster. Instead, he obtained the love, affection and friendship of all his children. As a person he stuck to his principles but did so with a measure of kindness and tact that earned the willing cooperation of his colleagues.

He hailed from a family wherein the male members had mostly served in the civil services. Ghulam Ahmed himself chose the same path. He was the chairman of the A.P. Public Service Commission and then also the Hyderabad Race Club. He handled sensitive issues with graceful prudence.

He had a large group of friends and was well loved and respected by all. Often there would be large gatherings of his friends at his house. The men would play cards and sometimes go out on hunting trips which was a popular pastime among young men of those days.

Ghulam Ahmed studied at the famous Madrasa-E-Aliya and then at Nizam College. In his cricket career, his seniors were the well known brothers S.M. Hussain and S.M. Hadi. The latter was an all-round sportsman who excelled at many sports while the former was a member of the Indian cricket team. When he was a raw beginner, he once sought permission to bowl against Hussain. After he was allowed to do so, he bowled the experienced batter with his very first delivery leaving Hussain highly impressed.

Later Ghulam Ahmed grew up and became a very famous player himself. He grew to be very close to some of the most famous names of those days. They often dropped in at his house. Cricket administrators such as M.A. Chidambaram, M. Chinnaswamy and Kishan Rungta visited him regularly.

The legendary Lala Amarnath, Test cricketers C.D Gopinath, Hemu Adhikari and Polly Umrigar - all these people used to visit his house. Later, Ghulam Ahmed also served as a cricket administrator both in Hyderabad as well as the BCCI. Besides serving as the Secretary and Vice President of the BCCI, he was the Chairman of the BCCI selection committee which selected the Indian team that won the World Cup in 1983. He was also given honorary membership of the prestigious Marylebone Cricket Club (MCC).

This is what "The Independent" (UK) wrote about him: "His smooth action enabled him to bowl for long spells while his clever flighting and variations of pace, length and line brought him comparisons with Jim Laker.

First class debut.

Ghulam Ahmed made his debut at 17 for Hyderabad but the second world war interrupted his further progress and he did not appear in Test cricket until 1948 when he was chosen for the third Test against West Indies in Calcutta.

From his days as a student in the Madrasa-E-Aliya, Ghulam made his talent known. His inspiration in those days was his uncle Hamid Razvi, former Chief Secretary of the erstwhile Hyderabad state and it was this gentleman who encouraged young Ghulam to pursue cricket on a full-time basis.

As an off spinner, Ghulam was the best of his time. India has had the good fortune of being served by many famous off spinners such as Erapalli Prasanna, S. Venkataraghavan, Shivlal Yadav, Arshad Ayub, Harbhajan Singh and Ravichandran Ashwin.

The inspiration.

But all these bowlers had to have a leader who showed the way. Ghulam Ahmed was that inspirational pioneer who proved for the first time that the Englishmen, the Aussies and the dashing West Indians could be conquered by deceptive off spin.

Another Hyderabad star M L Jaisimha who was a teammate of Prasanna and Venkataraghavan, rated Ghulam as the best off spinner India has ever had. Although Jai was a great admirer of Prasanna, he had no hesitation in ranking Ghulam a notch above all the others.

Along with Vinoo Mankad and Subhash Gupte, he formed a deadly spin combination for the Indian team. He was a tall and graceful bowler with an easy action. Because of his easy action, he was capable of bowling long spells. He once bowled 555 balls for Hyderabad in a Ranji trophy match against Holkar XI in the 1950-1951 season which then became a record. His bowling analysis read 92.3-21-245-4.

In all, twenty times he captured five or more wickets per innings and six times he captured ten wickets in a match. According to an article in Cricinfo, he was absolutely unplayable during the third Test against Australia at Calcutta in 1956 when he finished with ten wickets for 130 runs including seven for 49 in the first innings.

There is a story that in one club match, Ghulam Ahmed found himself repeatedly bowling short pitched balls. He was so immaculate in his line and length that this was highly unnatural. Soon he became convinced that the pitch had not been properly marked. He forced the umpires to stop the game and measure the length from wicket to wicket. It was found that Ghulam was right. A careless groundsman had pitched the stumps one foot further than they should have been.

After he began playing for the country and went on to captain India, his leadership ability proved to be a boon for the team. He played first-class cricket for Hyderabad from 1939 to 1958. He made his Test debut for India against West Indies in 1948. Thereafter he represented India in 22 Tests between the years 1948 to 1958.

He toured England in 1952 and Pakistan in 1954-1955. He captained India in one Test against New Zealand in 1955-1956 and two Tests against West Indies in 1958-1959.

He was the leading bowler on the 1952 tour and ended up with 80 wickets in first-class matches at an average of 21.92. In the four Test matches that he played, he took 15 wickets at an average of 24.73. According to Wisden he looked world class on days when he was in form. But when he was off his game, his bowling lacked bite. However, that is the case with many bowlers and players.

One of his memorable performances came in the first innings of the First Test when he bowled 63 overs and took 5 wickets conceding 100 runs. In another match against Oxford University, he took 8 wickets for 84 runs and then followed it up with 5 for 66 in the second innings. It was a marvelous display of controlled off spin bowling. He had that knack of hitting the right line and length for each and every batsman.

In the First Test against Pakistan in 1952-53, which was the inaugural Test between the two countries, he took five wickets, and scored a half century. With his partner Hemu Adhikari, he added

109 for the ninth wicket. It was a most unexpected fight back low down in the batting order. Both Adhikari and Ghulam Ahmed were known to be gutsy players who never gave up without a fight.

But Ghulam Ahmed's best Test performance was yet to come. That was seen in the Third Test against Australia in Calcutta in the 1956-1957 series. His superb bowling had the strong Australian batting line up all at sea. He snapped up 7 wickets for 49 runs and then followed it up with 3 for 81 to record his best innings and match figures in Test cricket.

At the domestic level too he was often unplayable. His best match and innings figures in first-class figures came in the Ranji trophy match against Madras in the 1947-1948 season. His nagging length, line and deceptive flight enabled him to capture 5 wickets for 28 runs and then 9 for 53. Not only was he good in short spells he also had the stamina to bowl long spells without conceding too many runs.

After he had decided to retire from Test cricket, he was selected to tour England with the Indian team in 1959, Ghulam refused to go because he had already retired from first class cricket. But he continued to play club cricket for the Deccan Blues in Hyderabad and was always available as a friend and guide to the youth of Hyderabad.

Role as an administrator in the HCA.

Long after his playing days were over, he continued to be associated with cricket at all levels both in Hyderabad and throughout India. In 1959 Nooh Abbassi, the then Secretary of the Hyderabad Cricket Association, coaxed Ghulam to take over the reins of the HCA. He was elected as Secretary of the HCA in

1959 and he continued to serve till 1975. He also served as Vice President and President of the HCA.

Ghulam Ahmed was appointed the team manager when India toured the West Indies in 1962. It was on that tour that India's captain Nari Contractor almost died when he was hit on the head by a bouncer bowled by the fiery West Indies fast bowler Charlie Griffith.

The young Mansur Ali Khan Pataudi who was a member of that team has written in his book "The Tiger's Tale", that Griffith's bowling was unplayable. The ball came down so fast that it was almost impossible to see it. On top of that, Griffith allegedly threw the ball on occasions. He was called for chucking a few times.

Later in the match Griffith was no-balled by umpire Cortez Jordan for throwing. It was the first of two times that he was called during his career. The other occasion was a tour match against Lancashire in 1966, when Griffith was called by umpire Arthur Fagg. Griffith was named Wisden's Cricketer of the Year in 1964 and was made a Knight of St. Andrew by the government of Barbados. But there are batsmen who swear by the fact that he throws the ball sometimes. Not every time, but some balls were definitely bowled with a bent elbow.

That fateful day when he bowled the bouncer at Nari Contractor, the Indian captain seemed initially, not to have picked up the line of the ball at all. According to Pataudi, he saw the ball too late and then ducked his head but there was no time to avoid it.

Saved the life of Nari Contractor.

The ball crashed into the batsman's head and the blow fractured Contractor's skull. But it was due to Ghulam Ahmed's timely intervention that a surgery was carried out which saved the life of the Indian captain. Years later, Contractor acknowledged the fact that Ghulam Ahmed's timely action had saved his life while talking to Ghulam Ahmed's son Nisar Ahmed.

Nisar Ahmed also recalled one more interesting incident that had happened once in Mumbai. On a visit to that city, Nisar Ahmed had met the legendary thespian Dilip Kumar at his house in a gathering with his relatives. At first the Bollywood star did not know the fact that Nisar Ahmed was the son of Ghulam Ahmed. But when Dilip Kumar came to know, he said: "Stand up at once young man and come and give me a hug. You are the son of the great cricketer and you have come to my house and you did not even hug me? Your father was one of the great players whom we admired. He was a Prince of Cricket."

In 1983 Ghulam Ahmed was the Chairman of the selection committee which selected the Indian team that ultimately won the Prudential World Cup. It was one of the greatest moments of Indian cricket and has been rated by experts as a turning point in the history of Indian cricket. It was the day which saw the birth of a new superpower of the game.

Ghulam's contribution was recognised by the prestigious MCC and he was given life membership. He served as BCCI Secretary from 1975 to 1980. He was also Chairman of the Hyderabad Race club in Malakpet and instrumental in setting up the Sultan-Ul-Uloom Education Society which established many reputed educational institutions in Hyderabad.

The memories of Ghulam Ahmed and his outstanding achievements can never fade from the minds of all those who knew him. Players and administrators who interacted with him remember his sterling qualities, good nature and impeccable conduct.

According to former India captain Mohammed Azharuddin

he was a towering personality and young players were tongue tied in his presence.

Azhar awed by Ghulam Ahmed.

Azharuddin told me once: "When I was in school, I was in awe of Ghulam Ahmed sir. Whenever I was at the Lal Bahadur stadium, I used to see him sitting at one end of the ground with his colleagues. I was so scared that I did not want to go close to them. From afar I would watch them with great respect," said Azhar.

"He was a shining beacon for us youngsters. We could realise the importance and value of everything that he had accomplished and it inspired us. When I began playing Test cricket, he was a selector and it was then that I had the courage to talk to him. He was always very kind and helpful. He gave me advice on so many matters, " said Azhar.

"His biggest asset was that he was a very knowledgeable person. It was not just cricket that he knew. He had a good grasp of many things in life," said Azhar.

"He was respected and revered all over India. We Hyderabadis should count ourselves lucky that we had a person like him among our midst to inspire us and guide us. It was Ghulam sir's blessings and guidance that helped me to become (after him) the second captain of India from Hyderabad. I am humbled whenever I think of that. I have immense respect and goodwill for Ghulam sir and spending time with him is an experience that I will never forget in my life," said Azhar.

Imran Mirza, father of Sania Mirza is distantly related to Ghulam Ahmed from his father's side but more closely so from his mother's side. He gave me a few wonderful glimpses into the life of Ghulam Ahmed.

Said Imran: "My father and Ghulam uncle were childhood friends. After my father passed away when I was in my late teens, he became like a father figure to me. His personality was like that. He was always there to support and guide youngsters. He did the same for M.L. Jaisimha too. When my daughter Sania began her tennis career, he encouraged her abundantly."

"When I was young, initially I was in awe of him but we soon became like friends. There was no generation gap. I used to spend a lot of time in his house, especially the weekends. He loved to watch movies and we used to go for night shows," said Imran.

He loved action films.

"The surprising thing is that he loved to watch action films. Especially the ones which had lots of fight scenes (what we used to call dhishum-dhishum scenes). It was so much against his normal character that it was funny. He was a very sober and disciplined man but when it came to films, he loved to watch the fighting and shooting," said Imran with a laugh.

"Then he was a connoisseur of good food. He never ate a lot but whatever little he ate, he wanted it to be cooked well. He relished dishes that were cooked with care and perfection. He had no favourite dish as such. It was not that he was excessively fond of biryani or anything. But all that he wanted was that the dish should be well cooked and tasty," said Imran.

"Another thing that I admired about him was that he always stayed true to his principles. If my friends and I visited him in his office, he would order tea and snacks for us. But he always paid from his own pocket, it was never at his office's expense. He was scrupulously honest in that way."

"His most significant asset was his helpful nature. If anyone was in any difficulty, they would go to him. Be it a family member or a cricket player, he would figure out a way to solve the problem. We don't see men like him nowadays. I miss him very much," said Imran.

Mr. P.R. Man Singh who is one of the most experienced administrators of cricket in Hyderabad and perhaps in all of India too, considers Ghulam Ahmed his guru.

Man Singh has written in his book that Ghulam Ahmed was his (Man Singh's) mentor and was a pillar of strength for all. "Ghulam sahib groomed me as a cricket administrator and saw to it that I got all the breaks. Thanks to his help I was able to get both domestic and international assignments which gave me the opportunities to prove my mettle," Man Singh has stated.

"I am proud to have had Ghulam sahib as my guru and mentor. The vast knowledge that he had gained as captain of the Indian team, Secretary and Vice President of the BCCI and Secretary and Vice President of the HCA, he imparted to me and I learnt everything from him," Man Singh has written.

All said and done, Ghulam Ahmed was a man of remarkable achievements and talents. His passing away in 1998 left a void in Hyderabad cricket and society that has never been filled.

Chapter 4

M.L. Jaisimha

Every sport needs a person like M. L. Jaisimha to pull the spectators into the stands. Jai had a unique style and panache in everything that he did. The spectators would be mesmerized by his presence. I have seen him knocking the ball around in the nets with a crowd of fans standing nearby just to watch him practice. I haven't seen it happening with any other player.

When I was a student my friends and I used to watch cricket matches at the Lal Bahadur Shastri stadium. Often the entry was free. As the word spread around the city that Jaisimha was batting, more students from nearby colleges would troop into the stadium. Every eye would be fixed on the hero of Hyderabad.

Every movement by him, even a gesture to another player, would be greeted with claps and cheers. If he hit a four, there would be impromptu celebrations in the stands. But the moment he got out, everyone would leave the stadium and the ground would become empty and quiet.

First meeting.

My first face to face meeting with M.L. Jaisimha took place after he had retired from playing cricket and was in charge of an advertising agency. The office was located opposite Asrani Hotel near the Paradise junction in Secunderabad. I was then a young and inexperienced sports reporter and he was a well known star who had carved out a great career in international and domestic cricket.

I still vividly remember that meeting even though it happened more than 40 years ago. He was about 16 years older than me but he treated me like an equal. He had no airs and no superiority complex. "Call me Jai. Don't call me sir or anything else," he told me with a welcoming smile and arranged a cup of tea for me. He had absolutely no airs of being a celebrity athlete. He was a man devoid of ego.

He could speak to teenagers, world famous cricketers, leading politicians and film stars in the same way without any change in demeanour. It was a unique quality that he possessed. Not only was he a very talented sportsman but also an extraordinary human being. I cannot think of any modern day cricket superstar who can be as humble and unassuming as Jaisimha.

Over the years I got to know him very well. Many enjoyable evenings were spent at his house in Marredpally. The house had a beautiful lawn and sometimes my fellow journalists and I sat on the lawn and listened to Jai's recollections of his experiences while playing against some of the legendary cricketers of the world.

Jai loved rock music.

He loved western music. His favourites were Elvis Presley and Harry Belafonte. The lively numbers of Presley such as "Jailhouse Rock" and "You're Nothing But A Hound Dog" as well as the softer melodies like "Love Me Tender" were among his favourites.

The songs of Harry Belafonte who popularized calypso music throughout the world had a special appeal for Jai.

In a book titled My Way - The Biography of M.L. Jaisimha, my friend A. Joseph Antony (former sports journalist in The Hindu), has written about the numerous interesting incidents that happened during his childhood. On one occasion the family dog prevented a Cobra from biting Jaisimha who was then a child. He was a pampered and beloved little boy who, from an early age, developed a love for sports.

The book mentions that during his schooldays, among Jai's closest friends was S.P. Misra who later became an internationally famous tennis player and captain of India's Davis Cup team for a few years. On one occasion when the Hollywood musical Rock Around The Clock (starring Bill Haley And His Comets), was being screened at the Tivoli theatre in Secunderabad, Jai and some of his friends climbed onto the stage to dance to the music. But the youngster himself had to face the music when his father came to know about it.

When Jaisimha was emerging as a cricketer, he was once tested by Lala Amarnath who was visiting Hyderabad to spot talent. During net practice, Ghulam Ahmed introduced Jaisimha as a future international prospect and so Lala decided to put him to the test. Lala took the ball himself and began bowling to Jai. The youngster was no match for the veteran and Lala frequently had him clean bowled. That experience taught Jaisimha to become more serious and work harder to improve himself. That day Jai realised that he still had a long way to go and it increased his motivation to polish his technique and sharpen his reflexes with constant practice.

Failed prank on Gary Sobers.

After Jai became a senior player, he and his teammates once tried to get the better of Gary Sobers with a prank one evening. They invited the great all rounder for a few drinks and began filling him with alcohol. If the hosts had one drink they would ensure that Sir Gary had three. The idea was to make him so drunk that he would not be fit to play the next day. But when the party ended, the Indian hosts were fully drunk. The West Indian captain was still fit and fine.

During another match, the famous leg spinner B.S. Chandrasekhar happened to comment to Jai that the shirt he was wearing was a lovely one. The next day, to his surprise, Chandra found the shirt was sent to him as a gift from the hero of Hyderabad.

Jai was a good storyteller and could remember facts and figures in perfect detail. He loved to give his stories a humorous touch. It was from Jai that I first heard the famous story of Pataudi arranging a "kidnapping" of some cricketers by a bunch of fake dacoits in the jungles of Madhya Pradesh. Pataudi loved to play such pranks.

More pranks.

On another occasion, during a trip to East Africa, Pataudi and Jai were put up in a lodge near a game reserve. In the lobby of the building there was a replica of a large alligator placed within a glass case.

In the dead of the night the two of them, Pat and Jai, came down from their rooms, took the alligator out of its glass case and carried it up to a teammate's room. There they placed it beside his bed and quietly crept away. In the morning the player woke up and stepped out of his bed, only to find himself standing on the back of what he thought was a live alligator!

Needless to say, it was a nasty shock for him while the rest of the players couldn't stop laughing. For many years that incident was recalled and the story retold at parties whenever the cricketers gathered. But although Jai loved having fun and enjoying himself, when it came to cricket, he took the game with great seriousness.

If any cricketer in his team played truant or was casual in his approach on the field, he soon got to see the other side of Jai's character.

Jai always gave his best effort into cricket and he demanded that the others did so too. A strict word from Jai was enough to make the errant player realise that he had crossed the limits. Jai had that stamp of authority over his team. He did not have to shout or display his seniority. One sharp word of caution could bring a rebellious player to his senses.

India's former captain and legendary all rounder Kapil Dev has written in a book that his first meeting with Jaisimha was in 1975 when he came to Hyderabad to participate in the Moin ud Dowlah Gold Cup tournament when he was in his teens. "I had heard many stories about him from Bishan Singh Bedi and Tiger Pataudi. The story I loved most was the one about his flying to Brisbane as a replacement player and entering the field directly from the airport without taking any rest. How he overcame jet lag I don't know. But he scored 74 and 101 against the top-class Test bowlers of Australia. How could he do that? He was amazing."

According to ace batsman G.R. Vishwanath, Jaisimha fully lived up to his name which meant Victorious Lion. For some reason,

Jai took an instant liking to GRV. The Hyderabad captain invested a lot of time and effort into developing GRV's technique and approach to the game. They were involved in only one international outing that was the tour of the Caribbeans in 1971 when India defeated the West Indies to register a series win for the first time in history.

"I was injured and missed the first two Tests," Vishwanath has written. "But I learned as much from the sidelines as if I had been playing, thanks to Jai's wisdom and his incredible propensity to share his thoughts and analysis of each game freely with others. On that tour in 1971, he was our teammate, guide, coach and mentor. His observations were put in such simple terms that you could instantly grasp the fundamentals. Jai was an expert at noticing small details and could offer simple solutions to complex problems. Very often his suggestions worked perfectly."

V.V.S. Laxman who was one of India's best middle order batsmen during his playing days, has written about Jai: "Growing up in Hyderabad, it was in the natural scheme of things that I would hear repeated references to Jai uncle and his commanding presence on and outside the cricket field. I first saw Jai uncle when I was a 12-year-old boy. There are few people who leave you in complete awe and he was one of them. He impressed me in so many ways. As a guru, mentor coach and a compelling personality. He was a man of impeccable taste, great panache, innate style and was a debonair gentleman."

In appearance Jai was every cricket fan's image of a dashing cricketer. Sharp features, slim but strong physique, immaculate dress sense and a ready smile and friendly attitude gave him an aura of confidence and grace personified. I have never seen him lose his cool. He was always courteous and chose his words carefully whenever he spoke.

Sunil Gavaskar's idol.

It is no wonder that he had so many fans. Sunil Gavaskar idolised him. When he was an upcoming player, Gavaskar thought Jai was his ideal of a cricketer. Jai was handsome, had a distinctive style on and off the ground and was also a very talented player. As a captain he had a sharp cricketing brain and could read the game perfectly.

Even Mansur Alli Khan Pataudi who was the captain of the Indian team, did not hesitate to play under the captaincy of M.L. Jaisimha when it came to representing Hyderabad. Pataudi himself was a very knowledgeable player and captain so if he had faith in Jaisimha's leadership and decision making ability, then Jai must have been really good.

It is said that Jai was the best captain who never led India. But Jai was not the man to feel let down or hold a grudge for not being appointed captain of India. He was always willing to share his thoughts and insights with whoever was leading the side. Often it was his good friend Pataudi. On numerous occasions his tips and guidance helped the Indian team to tackle a crisis.

He was always polite to a fault, warm and generous and also a source of great inspiration to many Hyderabad cricketers, including Mohammed Azharuddin. The latter often emulated many things of Jai, such as the turned-up collar. Many fans think that Azhar started that sartorial style but actually Azhar picked it up it from Jai.

As a batsman, Jai could open the innings or play a few places lower in the order. In both capacities he was excellent and could play according to the need of the hour. Former Test cricketer Chandu

Borde who played many matches with Jai once said that Jai was the first of his generation who did not hesitate to play lofted shots.

Sometimes he even played the reverse sweep which was then a crime under all situations. But if required, Jai could also bring down the shutters and block out the opponent. Once he put up a wall, there was no bowler who could breach his defence.

Jai's friend and teammate from Hyderabad, Abbas Ali Baig, said that Jai's audacious batting could light up a stadium with joy and excitement but if the team needed it, he could also shut down one end to prevent any loss of wickets. Jai was a superb player of spin because he had very nimble footwork. Not many people know that he was also a very good tennis player and won many tennis tournaments in Secunderabad and Hyderabad.

Jai could bowl medium pace or off spin and was a brilliant fielder too. He sometimes opened the bowling for India or Hyderabad. He made his debut in first class cricket when he was a teenager. At the young age of 15 he played his first Ranji trophy match in the 1954-1955 season representing Hyderabad against Andhra. He did well by scoring 90 runs and taking three wickets for 51 runs.

But he had to wait for two more years before he could score his first century. In fact, two centuries came close to each other when he slammed the formidable bowling attacks of Madras and Mysore which were then two of the top teams in the south zone. He also picked up 20 wickets and his all round performance earned him a place in the national squad which was to tour England in 1959.

Jai's Test debut was inconspicuous because the green and moist surface of pitches in England were vastly different from the dusty fields of hot and sunny Hyderabad. The ball swung a lot more and batting was not easy. But after he gained international experience, Jai blossomed.

The following Test matches saw Jai beginning to carve out a noteworthy career in cricket. In the last Test match against the visiting Australian team in 1959 at Kolkata (then Calcutta) Jai went in to bat towards the end of the first day and finished with 20 not out on the second day. He started his second innings just before stumps on the third day, batted throughout the fourth scoring only 59 runs, and was out on the final day for 74 This made him the first batsman to bat on all five days of a Test match.

The next year while playing against Pakistan at Kanpur he showed his stamina for a lengthy knock. As mentioned earlier, he could play his shots or he could put up a solid wall depending upon the requirements. In this match he was required to do the latter so he batted through a whole day for just 54 runs.

Multifaceted abilities.

In doing so, he displayed the flip side of his game and his character. The light hearted and fun loving Jaisimha could also transform himself into a dour and defensive batter who could not be evicted from the crease by the rival bowlers.

Later yet another aspect of Jaisimha's game emerged. He worked on his technique against fast bowling and converted himself into an opener. During this phase of Indian cricket, there was stiff competition between several players for the team's middle order.

But the career of the steady and experienced Pankaj Roy was nearing its end. India would soon need another reliable opener and Jai saw his opportunity in that slot. So he put in hours and hours of hard work at the nets to polish his technique against the swinging balls and the short pitched deliveries.

As expected, Jai's hard work and mental focus paid off. He was given the opportunity to open the innings and scored two centuries against England in successive years and another century against Ceylon (now Sri Lanka). In the 1963-1964 season against England he slammed an aggregate of 444 runs. Later he chose the middle order again while playing for Hyderabad in the 1964-1965 season and piled up a whopping 713 runs.

Inexplicably he was then dropped from the Test squad. Strange are the ways of those who control cricket in India and the selectors who choose the teams. Dropping Jai at this stage was yet one more decision which defied logic.

Sent to Australia as a replacement.

In 1967 the Indian team was sent on a tour of Australia. Jai was not initially selected to be a member of that team but when Chandu Borde was suddenly injured, the selectors decided to send Jai out as a replacement for Borde.

Jai went into action right away. He had no time to rest after the tiring journey because the third Test was about to begin. Again Jai showed everyone his pluck and determination. Tackling the ferocious Aussie fast bowlers with aplomb on a bouncy track Jai scored 74 and 101 and almost earned an improbable victory for India.

His last series was the tour of the West Indies in 1970–1971. That was a historic tour in many ways. Apart from Jai there were four other Hyderabad players in that team. India played five Test matches against the formidable West Indies led by Gary Sobers, considered by many to be the best all rounder in the history of cricket.

India ended up winning the series 1-0. The solitary victory came at Port of Spain. The series triumph was a watershed for Indian cricket in many ways. This was India's first ever Test victory and Test series victory over the West Indies. It was also India's first victory in the West Indies. The series saw the emergence of Sunil Gavaskar who would soon be acknowledged as the best opening batsman India has ever had and perhaps the leading openers in world cricket during his time.

Before the West Indies tour, the Indian selectors picked Ajit Wadekar to lead the team in place of the Nawab of Pataudi. Another notable player who was not in the team was Chandu Borde. In his place S. Venkataraghavan was named vice captain.

After the historic victory, skipper Ajit Wadekar mentioned that he got a lot of help in formulating tactics and strategy from Jaisimha. It was Jai's reading of the match situation that contributed to one of India's memorable triumphs in Test cricket.

Jai led Hyderabad for 14 seasons till 1977. Thereafter he retired even from first class cricket. In the domestic game he scored 13,516 runs in 245 matches. He scored 33 centuries and also took 431 wickets with seven for 45 being his best performance. He made his Test debut in 1959, played 39 Tests, scored 2056 runs at an average of 30.68. He scored three centuries and a dozen half centuries.

After leaving the game as a player Jai continued to be involved in many other ways. He served as a selector between 1977 and 1981. He also managed the Indian team on its tour of Sri Lanka in 1985–1986. Then Jai was also a TV commentator for some time and did commentary for the World Cup in 1987.

When Jai passed away in 1999, one of the best cricketers and gentleman to have emerged from the twin cities departed from the cricket fields leaving thousands of his fans disconsolate. Hyderabad cricket has sorely felt his absence since then.

Chapter 5

Abbas Ali Baig

Watching Abbas Ali Baig wielding the bat like a warrior wielding his scimitar, was a treat for all spectators. He was a natural athlete and came from a family of cricketers. His brothers Murtuza, Mazhar and Mujtaba were all good cricket players. Abbas and M.L. Jaisimha had many things in common and their careers began at the same time. Like Jai, Abbas too was born in March 1939. Only a few days separated the two of them, Jai being the older one.

When only 15 years old, Abbas Ali Baig made his debut in first class cricket in the 1954-1955 season of the Ranji trophy championship. His first match was against Andhra and right away he showed his talent. In his second match against Mysore he surprised all the experts with his ability to master both spin and pace alike by scoring 105 and 43 not out. It was a unique achievement for a 15-year-old schoolboy playing his first season in the Ranji trophy.

By the end of the season, he had emerged as one of Hyderabad's most significant discoveries. He became the team's second-highest run scorer having scored 187 runs in total.

Good at studies.

However, Abbas was not just a good cricketer. He shone in academics too. When traveling to participate in cricket matches, he used to carry his books with him. The moment he got an opportunity between practice sessions, he would open his books and study. The other players often ragged the studious Abbas by hiding his books. Sometimes they tucked away the books in the most unimaginable places and Abbas had a very tough time finding them again.

In the late 1950s, his studies took him to Oxford University in the UK and he commenced his studies there. When not busy with his books he continued to play cricket and went on to represent the University. In the year 1959, he played 15 first-class matches for the university team.

Playing for his University, Abbas scored 221 not out and 87 in one match against the Free Foresters. He also became the highest run getter for his team in a first-class match. But now luck was shining on Abbas. It deserted him later in his career but it shone brightly and strongly during this phase of his life.

It was during this time that the Indian team was on a tour of England. In the fourth match of the series, Baig was called up to play for India as a replacement for the injured Vijay Manjrekar. At the time he was just over 20 years of age and he seized the opportunity with both hands as the expression goes.

Century on debut.

In the second innings he became the youngest Indian cricketer to score a century on Test debut by scoring a well made 112 against an attack which had Fred Trueman among others in its ranks. It was a noteworthy match. England also had Ted Dexter and Ray

Illingworth in its ranks. Both became captains later. England batted first and scored 490 in its first innings. Opener Geoff Pullar and Mike Smith scored centuries and skipper Colin Cowdrey compiled a solid 67. Ken Barrington chipped in with 87 in the middle order. For India the main wicket taker was opening bowler Surendra Nath with five for 115.

India replied with 208. Only Chandu Borde (75) showed some resistance but the rest did not do well. Abbas at number three scored 26 before he was caught by Colin Cowdrey off the bowling of Ray Illingworth.

In its second innings Egland scored 265 for eight before declaring the innings. That left India with a massive target of 548 to win, which was beyond reach. India lost the match but it did reach 376 thanks to centuries by Abbas Ali Baig and Polly Umrigar. Both combined caution and aggression in the right measure and tackled the bowling capably. Abbas was run out when he had scored 112.

A word here about England's bowling attack would be apt. Opening the bowling was Fred Trueman who is considered one of the greatest fast bowlers that international cricket has seen. In the second innings when Abbas scored his century, Trueman bowled 23.1 overs with six maidens and took two wickets while conceding 75 runs.

Quite obviously both the century scorers had got the better of Trueman. The Yorkshire born Trueman was then 28 years old and at the height of his powers. He was acknowledged as one of the best bowlers in the world at the time. Trueman possessed genuine pace, could bowl a very deceptive outswinger and his yorkers were unplayable by the best batsmen of the world.

For the 20-year-old Hyderabadi Abbas Ali Baig who was playing his very first Test match to tackle the bowling of Trueman and reach the three figure mark spoke volumes for his ability and consistency.

Pleasure to watch.

When he was in form it was a pleasure to see Abbas timing his shots so perfectly. But the remaining portion of his Test career did not go very well for Abbas. He played only ten Test matches in which he scored 428 runs. That blazing century with 12 fours against bowlers like Fred Trueman, Ray Illingworth, Ted Dexter and Ken Barrington remained the only century he scored in Test cricket.

Abbas is also well known for another incident that happened during his cricket career. After his debut in England, he was selected for India's home series against Australia. In the third Test, in the first innings Abbas scored 50 and was involved in a crucial 133-run partnership with Nari Contractor. Then Baig followed that with another half-century in the second innings when he made 58. His half-centuries helped India secure a draw against the strong Australians.

In the second innings Abbas and Ramnath Kenny had added 109 runs for the fifth wicket. At the tea break, when Abbas was walking back to the pavilion along with batting partner Kenny, a woman ran out of the crowd and kissed Baig on the cheek. Then she ran back into the crowd. What prompted the young lady to do this was a mystery that has never been revealed. Was it some sort of bet that she had taken with her friends? Till today no one knows her identity nor the reason behind her act.

Abbas Ali Baig became the first Indian cricketer to be kissed on the field by a fan. Vijay Merchant who was one of the commentators during that match remarked: "I wonder where were all these enterprising young ladies when I was scoring my hundreds and double hundreds." To which another commentator replied: "Vijay you scored too many runs. They all fell asleep."

Many years later, history repeated itself. This time it occurred during a Test match between India and the West Indies. A woman in a black sari dashed onto the field along with a bunch of fans who were congratulating Brijesh Patel on his half-century. She gave a quick peck on Brijesh's cheek and returned to the safety of the teeming crowd after dodging the cops and security men.

The Three Musketeers of Hyderabad.

Abbas, Jaisimha and Pataudi were very good friends and teammates. It was surprising that Hyderabad did not win the Ranji trophy at any time during this period despite the presence of these three and other superbly gifted cricketers in its ranks. In the book "Pataudi, Nawab of Cricket ", Abbas has described how Pataudi came to play for Hyderabad.

He writes that one day during the 1965-1966 season the Hyderabad team members found Pataudi, the captain of India, sitting in the dressing room when he should have been busy representing Delhi in the North zone. It soon came to be known that Ghulam Ahmed who was a board official at the time, and Jaisimha, had both contrived to bring Pataudi to Hyderabad as a player.

Pataudi knew everything about the strengths and weaknesses of Hyderabad cricket and was also quite familiar with the city.

He had visited Hyderabad several times because his sisters lived in Hyderabad and he also had many friends living in the twin cities. It was great to have Pataudi in the team because he could entertain team members on long train journeys with his musical talents.

On the field Pataudi displayed great determination and did not hesitate to adopt unusual tactics. Like Jaisimha, he too loved hitting over the top and this double assault from Pat and Jai often took the rival teams by surprise. Before they could think of some new tactics to check the flow of runs, the damage would be done.

And on many occasions, after a home match, dinner at Jaisimha's house for all team members would be a sumptuous fare of south Indian dishes. Not only was there fun and laughter but also serious discussions about cricket strategy and the plans were formulated to get the better of rival teams. In those days Hyderabad had a star studded team. There were players like D. Govindaraj, K. Jayantilal, P. Krishnamurthy, Mumtaz Hussain, Pataudi, Syed Abid Ali and Habeeb Ahmed with M.L. Jaisimha as the captain.

On one occasion Hyderabad almost had the Ranji trophy in its grasp. That golden opportunity came when Hyderabad clashed with Bombay (now Mumbai) in the semi finals. Hyderabad took the first innings lead but later Ashok Mankad came up with a century to dash Hyderabad's hopes.

The day Abbas decided to leave cricket and stop playing for Hyderabad was, by coincidence, the same day that Pataudi also made the same decision. So it was a double blow for Hyderabad. Hyderabad cricket lost a lot of life and laughter as well as determination and dedication, all at one go.

——◆◆——

Chapter 6

Mansur Ali Khan Pataudi

According to the opinion of several of his contemporaries, Mansur Ali Khan Pataudi would have been the world's best batsman if he had not lost sight in one eye in a road accident at a young age. But even with that one good eye, Pat or Tiger as he was called by his friends could hammer the best fast bowlers of the world during his heydays.

I never had the good fortune to interact with Pataudi because he had stopped playing by the time I became a journalist. But when I was a student, I had watched him playing in first class matches at the Fateh Maidan ground in Hyderabad. My classmates and I used to bunk classes whenever players like Jaisimha and Pataudi were playing in action in first class matches against some of the visiting teams from West Indies and England.

In domestic cricket within India, although Pataudi initially represented Delhi, he later switched his allegiance to Hyderabad and played under the captaincy of his good friend M.L. Jaisimha.

Former Australian captain Ian Chappell has written that the first time he saw Pataudi in action was in the Test match at the Melbourne Cricket Ground during India's tour of Australia in 1967-1968. For Chappell it was a memorable introduction. According to the Aussie skipper, Tiger played two innings that would have been exceptional if he had all his faculties and full physical fitness.

On that occasion not only was Pat hampered by his usual handicap of one blind eye, he had also suffered an injury to his leg. Batting with one eye and standing on one leg, he scored 75 and 85 against some of the best bowlers in the world. Chappell was all praise for this effort and said that he had never seen anything like it before or after.

Pataudi was the captain of the team with Chandu Borde as his deputy. The match which Ian Chappell was talking about was the second Test of the series which was held at the MCG. India won the toss and decided to bat first. But the pace of the Aussie fast bowlers Graham (Garth) Mackenzie, Allan Conolly, David Renneberg was too hot to handle.

Mackenzie took seven for 66 and Renneberg captured two wickets for 37 runs to bundle India out for 173. Because of his injury, Pataudi came in at number seven and showed the others how to tackle the fast bowlers. Out of the 173 runs, he alone scored 75 with eight hits to the boundary before he was caught by wicketkeeper Barry Jarman off the bowling of Renneberg.

When Australia batted, centuries by the two openers Bob Simpson and Bill Lawry as well as by Ian Chappell in the middle order, helped the hosts to pile up a huge total of 529.

In its second innings India fared a little better by soring a respectable 352. Ajit Wadekar was unlucky to be dismissed for 99 while Pataudi again coming in at number seven, scored 85 with 12 boundaries. He was eventually caught by Ian Redpath off Bob Simpson. Australia won by an innings and four runs but Indian skipper Pataudi's fighting spirit was appreciated by all.

Such a display of quiet courage was not unusual for Pat. He faced many difficulties in his life but overcame them all. His father Iftikhar Ali Khan Pataudi passed away when Mansur was all set to celebrate his 11th birthday. He said in an interview that even though he was very young, his father's death was a big blow to him. Many of his family members did not even realize how severely it affected the little boy.

Pat tackled all of life's setbacks with quiet fortitude. At times he seemed aloof but one has to keep in mind that his personality and his traits were fashioned by the circumstances that he grew up in.

Iftikhar Ali Khan Pataudi.

His father Iftikhar Ali Khan was a very good sportsman. He excelled at cricket, hockey and polo and represented both England and India in Test cricket. At the same time Iftikhar was a man of principles and when Douglas Jardine employed bodyline tactics against the Aussies, Iftikhar was one of the few courageous men to raise his voice against the unfair methods of the domineering team captain. Little Mansur must have learnt many things by observing his father.

Jardine discloses his plan.

The story behind the bodyline series was that even before embarking on the tour, the captain of England, Douglas Jardine, had already formed a plan in his mind about how to tackle the Australian batsmen, in particular Don Bradman. He had not revealed his plan to anyone so as to prevent it from being leaked to the media. But after the team had begun the voyage on board the ship, he called his players together one day.

After lining up his players on the deck he revealed his strategy to them. He instructed them to develop a hatred for the Australians. "Our fast bowlers will attack on the leg stump line with short pitched deliveries and we will set a predominantly leg side field," he revealed. As he explained his plan in detail, most England players agreed with his policies except for two team members. One was fast bowler Gubby Allen and the other was Iftikhar Ali Khan Pataudi.

The latter spoke up immediately and told his skipper that the tactics would not be in keeping with the principles of good sportsmanship. When the Test matches began, the Nawab scored 102 in the very first Test. His teammates Herbert Sutcliffe and Wally Hammond also scored centuries which enabled England to win the Test by ten wickets.

Conflict between IAK Pataudi and Jardine.

But in the simmering tension between Iftikhar Ali Khan and his captain Jardine came to the forefront in the second Test. When the captain instructed Pataudi to take up a fielding position within the arc on the leg side, the Indian player flatly refused to do so. He told his skipper that he will not be a party to this unsportsmanlike conduct. Jardine sneered at him: "I see his Highness is a conscientious objector." But Iftikhar Ali Khan stood by his statement and did not budge.

It so happened that in that Test, Iftikhar could not get a big score and Australia won by 111 runs. That result provided Jardine with the excuse that he needed to drop the Nawab from the side. But the incident brought into sharp focus Iftikhar Ali Khan's love for fair play and courage to stand by his beliefs.

MAK Pataudi breaks Jardine's records.

After Iftikhar's son Mansur was sent to study in England, the young boy proved to be a batting prodigy for Winchester college. He captained the team in 1959 and by scoring 1,068 runs that season Pataudi broke the school record set in 1919 by Douglas Jardine, the man who had sacked his father Iftikhar. It was poetic justice in a way.

Iftikhar Ali Khan came from a long line of warriors and he showed his bravery by opposing his own captain when he felt that the spirit of sportsmanship was being blatantly disregarded. His family was the ruling house of Pataudi which is a small princely state that now lies in Haryana.

The Pataudi family's origins begin with Faiz Talab Khan who belonged to the Barech tribe of Afghanistan. Faiz Talab Khan became the first ruler of Pataudi in 1804. From his mother's side Iftikhar Ali Khan was related to the Nawab of Loharu who in turn was linked to several important personalities in history.

Iftikhar Ali Khan was educated at Aitchison College in Lahore and Balliol College, Oxford, before marrying Begum Sajida Sultan who was the daughter of Hamidullah Khan, Nawab of Bhopal. Iftikhar was an excellent cricketer and is the only player to have represented both England as well as India in Test cricket.

But not many are aware of the fact that he was also a top class hockey player and was named in the Indian squad before the 1928 Olympic Games. Back then India was the best team in world hockey so just being named in the list automatically meant that he was among the world's best hockey players too. However he could not take part in the Olympics due to various personal reasons.

He was also a very good polo and squash player. Later in his cricket career he was named captain of India on his tour of England in 1946. But by then he was past his prime and his performance did not have that earlier class.

Iftikhar's wit and humour often regaled many people, including the Englishmen. On one occasion, as captain of the Indian team, he was asked to give a speech after a formal dinner party which was attended by several dignitaries. Around the same time, a three member delegation of the British Government was scheduled to meet Jawaharlal Nehru and other Indian leaders for a discussion.

So Iftikhar Ali Khan began his speech by remarking that his task as captain of the Indian cricket team was even more difficult than the task faced by the political leaders of India. "They will have to deal with three Englishman while I will have to tackle eleven Englishmen," he said amidst roars of laughter.

Later when India became independent, the Nawab voluntarily acceded to India and his act was praised by many important personalities. The well known civil servant of that time Mr. V.P. Menon has mentioned his decision in the book "The Story Of The Integration Of Indian States" and referred to Iftikhar Ali Khan Pataudi as a great patriot.

Such was the personality of the man who was the father of Mansur Ali Khan who inherited the title of Nawab after his father died. Both father and son had many things in common. Both of them were good at several sports, not just cricket. Both shared a love for fair play and both had a dry sense of humour which often took their friends off guard.

MAK Pataudi and pranks went together.

Pataudi also had a liking for practical jokes and pranks. One of the most elaborate pranks that he played was when he arranged for a party of cricketers to be kidnapped during a trip into the forests of Madhya Pradesh.

Pataudi himself narrated the incident very briefly during a television interview with film actress Simi Garewal. But his friend M.L. Jaisimha, former Test cricketer and captain of Hyderabad, narrated the incident in more detail on one occasion at a gathering with journalists at his house in Marredpally in Secunderabad.

Pataudi had invited a group of young players over for a day of shikar (hunting) in the jungles of Madhya Pradesh. The region was notorious for the presence of dacoits (bandits). A day before the shikar was to take place, the "pitch was prepared" by Pataudi and his close friends.

The cricketers were told stories about the grave risk of going into the forest and that they should be careful during the trip. Dacoits often kidnapped celebrities and held them to ransom. They were desperadoes who stopped at nothing. Shooting and killing was an everyday affair for them.

So, the next morning, with some trepidation but also with a sense of adventure, the party of cricketers set off on Jeeps for a day of hunting. Pataudi was in the group too.

But when the vehicles reached a remote part of the forest, they found their path blocked. A gang of fierce looking and heavily armed dacoits stood in the way and ordered them to halt. Unknown to them, these were all Pataudi's men. They had been planted in the forest to carry out this stunt.

That morning they had been made to dress up like filmi dacoits and told to wait in the forests till the players turned up. The men had brought along a few kitchen knives and whatever looked dangerous. But they were all dressed like typical Hindi film dacoits complete with turbans and covered faces.

Only Pataudi and one or two more in the group knew what was going on. The rest thought they had really been kidnapped and were soon trembling with fear.

After a while a fake argument ensued following which E.A.S. Prasanna was led off deeper into the forest and then the captive players heard the sound of a gunshot. Thereafter they were informed that Prasanna had been shot dead. Leg spinner B.S. Chandrasekhar and Gundappa Viswanath broke into tears when they heard that the world's best off-spinner had been unceremoniously bumped off by dacoits. Viswanath who was tied to a tree was scared out of his wits. He thought it will definitely be his turn next.

Another player, V. Ramnarayan, has also written about the incident in his book "Third Man". According to Ramnarayan, the former Test cricketer Vijay Manjrekar, realizing that his life was in grave danger, did some quick thinking and came up with a ruse.

Manjrekar had retired from cricket by then and was working in Air India. But he told the dacoits: "I am a very poor man. Please let me go. I am only a clerk. My salary is only Rs.300 and my DA is Rs. 225 and my HRA is Rs. 150. My family lives on my meagre income. Please let me go."

Hearing him verbally rattling off an entire salary slip to the fake dacoits, cricket administrator Raj Singh Dungarpur, (who knew what was going on) could not contain himself any longer and ran away to hide his laughter. Seeing him run away, Manjrekar felt very hurt. "Dekho. Kaisa Rajput hai yeh. Darr ke bhag gaya," he said.

After several hours of stress and tension, Pataudi finally decided that the players had enough for one day and revealed that it was all a prank - a game which had been enacted by men who were following his orders. So they need have no fear. Nothing would happen to them and they would all return to their homes that night.

The players were so relieved that they didn't know whether to laugh or cry. Till today they remember the scare that they got that day with mixed feelings.

Loved classical music and good food.

Pataudi was a big lover of classical music and ghazals. His father who was an excellent sitar player introduced him to Hindustani classical music. The son learnt to play the flute, harmonium and tabla and became quite proficient at playing all these instruments. His favourite singers were Talat Mahmood, Lata Mangeshkar and Mohammed Rafi.

According to his wife Sharmila Tagore, Pataudi had a taste for good food and knew how to prepare several dishes. At home he often instructed the kitchen staff on how to go about preparing special food items.

Captaincy thrust upon him.

The captaincy of the Indian team was thrust upon him when he was least expecting it. During the Indian team's tour of the West Indies in 1962, skipper Nari Contractor was seriously injured by a bouncer bowled by Charlie Griffith. When it became certain that Contractor would not be able to play any more matches, the mantle of captaincy was draped around the shoulders of a 21-year-old Mansur Ali Khan Pataudi.

Pataudi was one of the junior most members of the side then. But he managed to get the cooperation of his senior teammates. As the years passed, Pataudi developed his own brand of captaincy and brought about a change in the attitude of the Indian players. Under Pataudi's captaincy, they grew in confidence and ability.

For many years the Indian team did not have a genuine fast bowler. This was a big handicap but Pataudi was used to overcoming hurdles. He encouraged the famous spin quartet of India and gave them a free hand. According to Bishen Singh Bedi who himself became the captain of India later, Pataudi was a very far sighted leader. In fact Bedi calls him a cricketing sage.

Not everyone appreciated his methods or understood what he was attempting to accomplish. It was only after many years that all the pundits of the game acknowledged Pataudi's contribution to Indian cricket as a leader and policy maker. He brought about unity in the team.

An excellent fielder.

As a fielder there were very few players anywhere in the world who could match Pataudi's swiftness in covering the ground in the outfield. His catching was always safe. If a lofted shot saw Pataudi getting under the ball, everyone knew that the catch would be taken. It was almost a certainty. No less a person that the famous commentator John Arlott once called him the best fielder in the world - an opinion seconded by former England captain Ted Dexter.

Once in an interview to The Hindu he talked about his life and career and explained: "I'm happy that I played for my country. Nobody thought that one day limited overs cricket would become so popular. When we played there was not much money in the game. We played because we enjoyed playing."

"I was not the only from a princely background in the sport. There were others like me such as Hanumant Singh, Fateh Singh Rao Gaekwad, the Maharajah of Udaipur, members of the Patiala royal family and so on. There were many players who were from a princely background."

"In my case it was not my background that was a disadvantage. It was because I did not understand the undercurrents in Indian cricket. I had not studied in India but abroad. But perhaps that was a good thing in some ways. I did not get involved in local politics and loyalties because I dd not understand these things. So there was a plus and minus aspect in everything."

"As a man I think I am a fairly private person. I do not make an issue of going to my ancestral place in Pataudi. I do go there sometimes. A lot of people came to my mother's funeral to pay their respects. So the connection is still there. I do some social work and run an eye hospital there."

In 2011 Pataudi was admitted to a hospital in New Delhi because he was suffering from an acute lung infection. He died in the hospital due to respiratory failure on 22nd September 2011. Thus ended the life of a wonderful cricketer, a wise captain and a fun loving human being. Hyderabad lost one of its legendary players that day

Chapter 7

Hyderabad's Famous Five

The 13th of January, 1971, was an important date in the history of Hyderabad cricket. For it was on that day that the BCCI announced the team which was scheduled to go on a tour of the West Indies that year. In the team list were no less than five players from Hyderabad. It was a phenomenon that had never happened earlier and has never happened since then. Never have five players from Hyderabad been selected at the same time for the Indian team.

The five Hyderabadis were M.L Jaisimha, Syed Abid Ali, P. Krishnamurthy, K. Jayantilal and D. Govindaraj. They quickly became known as the Famous Five of Hyderabad cricket. Had Pataudi and Abbas Ali Baig been selected for that tour, there would have been seven Hyderabadis in the team.

As is well known India won the second Test at Port of Spain and then held on to that slender lead by drawing all remaining Test matches. Thereby India chalked up a historic first ever win over the West Indies led by the world's greatest all rounder Sir Gary Sobers.

In the fifth and final Test, the West Indies had the chance to win the match. Batting in the fourth innings they needed only 262 to win and Clive Lloyd who came in at number three began firing with all the power in his sinewy arms. All he needed was a steady partner at the other end. It would have been all over if the number four (Rohan Kanhai) or number five (Gary Sobers) had given Lloyd the stand that he was looking for.

Abid Ali makes sure of India's win.

But Syed Abid Ali ensured that would not happen. Bowling with accuracy and moving the ball sharply off the pitch, he clean bowled Rohan Kanhai for 21 and then Sir Gary Sobers for a duck as Lloyd watched in shock from the other end. Eventually this match too ended in a draw and finally it led to the Indian team celebrating one of the greatest feats that it ever achieved overseas.

P. Krishnamurthy, a reliable wicket keeper.

Wicket keeper P. Krishnamurthy did well and showed that he had a reliable pair of gloves behind the wickets. In the first Test at Kingston, he took a good catch to dismiss Gary Sobers off Eknath Solkar for 93 when the all rounder was looking good for a century and more.

Pallemoni Krishnamurthy also known as Pochaiah Krishnamurthy played in all the five Test matches against the islanders in 1971 and also in one ODI match against New Zealand in 1976.

Later in 1971 he toured England as a deputy to Farokh Engineer. He was also selected for tours to New Zealand and West Indies as second choice to Syed Kirmani. Krishnamurthy played first class cricket for Hyderabad for most of the 1970s, after making his debut in 1967.

The unique feat that he achieved was that he batted at all 11 slots for Hyderabad in the Ranji Trophy. He is also the only batsman to be associated in a century partnership batting as an opener and also as a number eleven batter. Surely that is a feat which will not be easily replicated by any other player.

For a wicket keeper he was rather tall. Although there have been tall wicketkeepers in the game most Indian wicket keepers were of average or short height. Adam Gilchrist was one among the tall keepers in international cricket. Even Farokh Engineer was quite tall for a wicket keeper. But usually a tall person does not have the speed and agility of a shorter person stationed behind the stumps. But Krishanamurthy was adept at his task and he loved to stand near the stumps even to medium pacers.

As a keeper he was not flamboyant or showy but quiet and reliable. In first class cricket he snapped up 218 victims which included 68 stumpings. He was a quick stumper especially when the spinners were able to lure the rival batsmen out of the crease.

Kenia Jayantilal, a solid opener.

Hyderabad's Kenia Jayantilal was a solid opening batsman with sound technique. But he was selected to play only one Test match during that 1971 tour where he scored five runs. He was a substitute for Sunil Gavaskar when the Little Master was injured.

From 1967 to 1979 he played first class cricket for Hyderabad and had the distinction of scoring 153 in his very first Ranji trophy match which was against Andhra. In 91 first class matches he scored 4687 runs at an average of 33.36 per innings. His top score was 197 and he was unlucky to miss a well deserved double century that day.

In all he scored eight centuries and 22 half centuries so he was often the man who provided the backbone to the Hyderabad innings. Strongly built, he had a liking for the pull shot and had a good defence. He made his entry into the Indian team backed up by a series of good performances in domestic cricket. But he got only one opportunity in Test cricket and that was his misfortune.

The phenomenal and continuing success of Sunil Gavaskar in the West Indies in 1971 and for many years thereafter meant that the slot for one opener would always be occupied. All the other opening batsmen in India would have to fight it out for the single remaining slot.

Jayantilal's father's name was Hirjee and his mother's name was Ratna Behen. He was born on Jan 13th 1948 in the Sultan Bazar area of Hyderabad. From childhood he was surrounded by a cricketing atmosphere since his elder brother Premji was a good player. Premji made his mark and represented Hyderabad state teams in the junior category.

Jayantilal grew up to be a well built young lad like his elder brother and became an opening batsman as well as an opening bowler at his school Vivek Vardhini High school and later his game improved further when he joined Nizam college.

He was selected to represent Hyderabad in the inter state south zone under-19 cricket tournament and he gave a good account of his skills. In his second year he was the captain of the team and led Hyderabad to a victory. The south zone selectors then rewarded him with the job of captain for the South zone team as well.

Although at this time he was discharging the duties of an opening batsman and also opening bowler, he gradually began to ease himself away from bowling and focus on his batting because he felt he could excel at batting.

Not everyone agreed with his choice. There were those who felt that in batting he was too defensive and slow scoring. But the way he looked at it was that his primary job as an opener was to give the team a solid start. That would make things easier for the stroke players who would come in the middle order. When he did play shots, they were mainly cuts and pulls square of the wicket. He was particularly strong with his off side play.

The year 1967 was a watershed in his career. Playing for the Osmania University in the inter university Rohinton Baria trophy tournament, he piled up a massive accumulation of runs. For the first time Osmania University won the title when he was playing in the team and many people acknowledged that Jayantilal had played an important role in the victory. The other player who shone was Mumtaz Hussain with the ball.

He also did well in the south zone Vizzy trophy tournaments. He scored a double century against the strong West zone side packed with Bombay's best talent, in the Vizzy trophy.

Jayantilal made his Ranji trophy debut in 1968-1969 at Guntur against Andhra and as mentioned earlier he began with a bang by scoring a century in his very first match. Before him only S.M. Hadi had been able to accomplish this feat by scoring a century in his first match.

Over the next two years Jayantilal developed his repertoire as a batsman. He was no longer a defensive player only. He could play attacking shots whenever the need arose. In 1970-1971 against West Zone he scored a scintillating century in front of the national selectors. This innings is what earned him a spot in the Indian team which was selected to tour the West Indies in 1971.

At first his luck was on his side. Sunil Gavaskar who was slated to open the innings in the first Test match at Sabina Park stadium went down with an injury before the match began so Jayantilal was given the job. He opened the innings with fellow Hyderabadi Syed Abid Ali. But when India's total was on 10 and Jayantilal was on 5, the fearsome West Indies fast bowler Grayson Shillingford got him caught by Gary Sobers.

India scored 387 and then dismissed the West Indies for 217. Then India enforced the follow on and the home team scored 385 for five in its second outing when the match ended in a draw. So Jayantilal never got the chance to bat again. From the next Test onwards, Sunil Gavaskar cemented his place in the side as an opener which meant that Jayantilal got to play only one innings in his career.

When I was a journalist I had heard many experts in Hyderabad who were of the opinion that Jayantilal had what it takes to achieve considerable success at the international level. But he was not given the opportunity by the national selectors.

D. Govindraj, the unlucky pace bowler.

The other unlucky Hyderabadi in the 1971 team was seam bowler Devraj Govindaraj. The family was a large one and had seven sons in its fold so Govindraj had plenty of playmates when he was a child.

Govindaraj did his schooling at Keshav Memorial school and then joined New Science college for his degree course. The family lived in a house with a large compound so it was not surprising to see that the boys were always playing some game or the other. Most often it was cricket but they played with a soft ball. Govindaraj was the best of the lot. Even at an young age he could bowl at a ripping pace.

Later when he began playing serious cricket with a cricket ball, he decided to switch to off spin. But his coaches soon advised him to go back to bowling fast since he had the talent to do so. Moreover, he was tall and had long limbs so he had the physical requirements to bowl fast.

He had the good fortune to be coached by some of Hyderabad's best coaches including E.B. Aibara and A.R. Bhupathi. For some time, the West Indian fast bowler Roy Gilchrist had been brought over to Hyderabad to represent the side in the Ranji trophy and the tear away paceman from the Caribbean islands also provided Govindaraj with many helpful guidelines.

In the 1964-1965 season Govindaraj made his debut in the Ranji trophy for Hyderabad against Madras. In the 1960s, after Ramakant Desai had left the scene, there was a dearth of good fast bowlers in India. Govindaraj's career surged upwards under the leadership of M.L. Jaisimha who knew how to make best use of a pace bowler with Govindaraj's abilities. At this time many experts were of the opinion that Govindaraj would fulfil the role of a fast bowler for the Indian team.

In 1970-1971, his wonderful performances in the Ranji trophy and Duleep trophy tournaments saw him being selected for the Indian team to tour the West Indies under the new captain Ajit Wadekar who had replaced the Nawab of Pataudi. But in the series, Govindaraj was given a chance only in the preparatory matches and not in the Test matches.

In one of the matches against local sides, even Gary Sobers was impressed with his bowling so it is a mystery why he was not given a chance to prove his mettle in the Test matches. He was also in the Indian team for the tour of England later but there again he was not picked for any Test match. The fact that he was not given even a single opportunity to play in Test cricket despite being a good seam bowler, will no doubt remain a regretful aspect of his cricket career.

Chapter 8

Language Problems

If players from Hyderabad are different from others, so too is their language. Telugu is the most widely spoken language, but many residents of Hyderabad also speak the Deccani, which is also called Dakhni, dialect. It's a mixture of Hindi, Urdu, and words adopted from different languages spoken in the Deccan region. But there are some words and phrases which are spoken only in Hyderabad and nowhere else. All spoken with a typically Hyderabadi twist.

The differences in language sometimes lead to amusing incidents between players. Spinner Venkatapathi Raju was not only a player with plenty of talent but is also a top-class entertainer off the field. Blessed with a great sense of humour, he can make an audience laugh with his funny stories about his experiences.

Once, early in his international career, Raju was sharing a room with teammate Narendra Hirwani, the mercurial leg-spinner most remembered for his 16 wickets on debut. Hirwani was born in Gorakhpur in UP, but played for MP. He spoke a very chaste version of Hindi, and Raju couldn't understand much of what he was saying

Hirwani, in turn, was puzzled by the words and expressions that Raju used in his speech. Each was unable to understand what the other was trying to say. They decided to communicate with signs. "There we were – the two of us – speaking the same language but still unable to understand each other," an amused Raju recalled later.

This was not the only occasion when there was a difficulty in communication between Hyderabad players and those from the northern states although both parties felt that they were speaking Hindi.

The Deccani (also called Dakhni) dialect consisting of a mix of Hindi and Urdu which is spoken in Hyderabad came into existence as a lingua franca under the Delhi and Bahmani Sultanates during which period trade and migration from the people of the north saw Hindustani being introduced to the southern regions of India.

It is said that Muhammad Quli Qutub Shah, one of the rulers of the Golconda sultanate, wrote poetry in Deccani. His works were compiled into a Kulliyat (collection of poetry by a single author). It is widely considered to be the earliest Urdu poetry collection written in Deccani. Another royal personage namely Ibrahim Adil Shah of the Bijapur Sultanate wrote a book titled Kitab-e-Navras (Book of the Nine Rasas), which was a work of musical poetry written entirely in Deccani dialect.

In more recent times, films have been produced wherein the language used is largely the Deccani dialect. Shyam Benegal's film Mandi, which was released in 1983, has a story that is based in Hyderabad. In that film, one finds many of the characters speaking in the Deccani dialect.

Deccani differs from standard Hindustani due to archaisms retained from the medieval era, as well as confluence with local regional languages such as Telugu, Kannada and Marathi. Here again it must be mentioned that Telangana Telugu is a little different from the Telugu spoken further south in the Andhra region. But that is the beauty of India. There is unity in diversity.

Chapter 9

M.V. Narasimha Rao (Bobby Rao)

M.V. Narasimha Rao, better known in cricket circles as Bobby Rao or sometimes Bobjee, was one of the most exciting all rounders to emerge from Hyderabad. He was a player who could swing a match around with electrifying batting in the middle order, or by snapping up a handful of wickets at a crucial juncture and also pull off some breathtaking catches anywhere in the field.

As a journalist, I have covered many matches in which he played and he became a good friend. Although he now lives in the town of Strabane in Northern Ireland we are still in touch. He is a person who has no airs and has an easy going and friendly disposition. It is always a pleasure to talk to him because he has a wide perspective about different aspects of the game and the players.

As a leg spinner Bobby was included in the Indian team after B.S. Chandrasekhar had left the scene. It was going to be difficult to fulfil the role of Chandra but Bobby gave it his best effort. His plus point was that he was a very good batsman too.

He was selected to represent India against the West Indies in 1978–79, but after two Test matches, he was dropped. He was again brought back into the Indian team the following season for the series against Australia led by Kim Hughes. That Australian team had players like Alan Border, Andrew Hilditch, Graham Yallop, Bruce Yardley and Rodney Hogg. So it was a strong side.

However, Bobby Rao was given only two Test matches before being dropped again. It was difficult to say what was going on in the minds of the national selectors.

Hughes was surprised to hear that Bobby was dropped.

Reportedly when Kim Hughes heard that the clever leg spinner had been dropped, the Aussie skipper was surprised. "Why did they not include him? He had the ability to trouble our batsmen. But I have no complaints. The decision will help us."

In the same series, fifth Test at the Eden Gardens in Kolkata, Bobby played a crucial role in saving India from a looming defeat. India was facing an uphill task. The home team needed 247 to win on the last day. At one stage India was struggling to stay afloat and had scored 123 for the loss of four wickets.

The side's top batsmen like Sunil Gavaskar, Dilip Vengsarkar, Gundappa Vishwanath and Chetan Chauhan had all been dismissed. That was when Bobby Rao stood firm with Yashpal Sharma and the two of them saved India. Yashpal Sharma scored an unbeaten 85 and Bobby gave him excellent support by scoring an unbeaten 20 off 52 deliveries in 75 minutes stay at the crease. India ended up scoring 200 for 4 in 63.2 overs to draw the Test.

Sadly that was the last Test match played by Narasimha Rao. He continued to play with great commitment and enthusiasm for Hyderabad. He chalked up some superb performances in the Ranji trophy. But the national selectors had decided that they did not want him any more. He had been given very little opportunity to show his admirable skills.

In first class cricket his performance was impressive. He played 108 matches, scored 4845 runs at an average of 40 plus, with nine centuries and 30 half centuries. In bowling he took 245 wickets and on three occasions he took ten or more scalps per match.

On numerous occasions he helped Hyderabad to win or draw its matches. I remember watching one match at the Railway Recreation Club ground in Secunderabad where Hyderabad was playing against Saurashtra.

Bobby at his best.

The visiting team had a superb spin attack in the hands of Uday Joshi and Dhiraj Parsana. The latter played two Test matches as a member of the Indian team. On a helpful track these two spinners were making the ball behave in the most unexpected manner. It jumped, turned or stayed low and skidded.

All the batsmen were shackled by their own doubts and fears. But I watched in awe as two Hyderabad batsmen, one Bobby Rao and the other Shahid Akbar, played as if they were having a party. Strokes flowed from their bats as if they had not a care in the world. The tall and athletic Bobby was in marvellous form that day. His record in domestic cricket was very impressive both with the bat and with the ball.

A successful captain.

Bobby Rao has not been given sufficient credit for the fact that he was the most successful captain of Hyderabad. Under his captaincy Hyderabad won the Ranji trophy as well as the Irani trophy in 1987.

The 1986-1987 season was a memorable season for Hyderabad cricket. On several occasions Hyderabad came close to lifting the coveted Ranji trophy but that year it finally happened.

It would be pertinent to recall the details of that tournament for it was a glorious phase of Hyderabad cricket and in the cricket career of its captain Bobby Rao.

It so happened that March 26th, 1987 became a memorable day in the history of Hyderabad cricket. For it was on that day that Hyderabad won the prestigious Ranji trophy championship for the second time. Back then the team was a force to reckon with.

There were several extremely talented players in the line-up. M.V. Narasimha (Bobby) Rao, Shivlal Yadav and Arshad Ayub were Test cricketers. Arshad played Tests after this Ranji victory. Others like Vijay Mohan Raj, Khalid Abdul Qaiyum and Vivek Jaisimha were a formidable force in the batting line up.

Bobby Rao who was leading Hyderabad, was in great form with the ball and bat throughout this season. In the league phase he took ten wickets against Kerala and nine wickets against Goa. His century against Gujarat and 74 against Bihar were outstanding knocks.

Among the batsmen who performed well were Vijay Mohan Raj whose characteristic determination fetched him a century against Kerala and Tamilnadu in the league phase. Khalid Abdul Qaiyum was another batsman whose tons helped Hyderabad's cause.

Abdul Azeem in great form.

Against Tamilnadu, Abdul Azeem was in great form. His sparkling 303 not out tore the rival attack to shreds. As everyone knew, when the dashing Azeem was on song, the bowlers just had to sit back and hope that he would make a mistake. That day Azeem didn't make any mistakes. It was one of the memorable knocks seen by a home team batsman in Hyderabad.

Arshad's double century.

In Arshad Ayub, Hyderabad had another all rounder with awesome talent. Although he was known primarily as an off spinner in international cricket, in First-Class cricket he could also wield the willow with telling effect. He had two hundreds in domestic cricket and one of them was a double hundred.

It came against Bihar in Ranji Trophy semi-final. Ayub batting at No. 8, scored an unbeaten 206 to help Hyderabad take the first innings lead. Then in the final that came next, Ayub went in at 110 for five and struck 174 to help Hyderabad clinch the Ranji Trophy.

In the south zone league phase, Hyderabad began with a spate of drawn matches. But with each league match being of only three days duration, this was to be expected. However, Hyderabad qualified for the knockout stage after a victory against Goa.

In the quarter final, Hyderabad clashed with Gujarat. Hyderabad took the first innings lead thanks to Qaiyum (203) and Narasimha Rao (114) and Vivek Jaisimha (141). They guided Hyderabad to a mammoth 605 for seven declared. In the second innings V. Manohar (101) helped Hyderabad to set a victory target of 516 which was practically out of reach for Gujarat.

In the semi final, Hyderabad was up against Bihar on its home turf at the Gymkhana ground. Bihar did put up a good fight and scored 468 but Hyderabad replied even more strongly. Arshad Ayub's double century and centuries by Vivek Jaisimha and

M.V. Ramanamurthy and also a gutsy 93 by Vijay Mohan Raj saw Hyderabad reach 783 for eight declared.

Then came the grand final match against Delhi in Delhi. Batting first Hyderabad scored 457. Centuries were hit by Abdul Azeem and Arshad Ayub. Delhi failed to take the first innings lead and were all out for 433. Rajesh Yadav's haul of five wickets and Shivlal's three wickets helped to contain the Delhi batting line up. When Hyderabad batted again, Vijay Mohan Raj came up with an unbeaten double century to rub salt into the host's wounds.

The scenes of jubilation that followed when the team returned to Hyderabad had to be seen to be believed. Cricket fans, officials and players seemed to go crazy with delight. Never before or since have Hyderabad cricketers been feted and paraded like the champions of 1987.

Bobby moves to Northern Ireland.

Soon after that momentous victory Narasimha Rao moved to Northern Ireland which he had already visited on work assignments earlier. He decided to take up a job as a coach in Strabane and over time he settled down there. Initially it was a difficult experience but due to his affable nature he made friends easily and got along well with everyone.

It must also be mentioned that when in Hyderabad, Bobby had also set up the Sri Venkateswara cricket academy (which later changed its name to St. John's Cricket Academy) in Marredpally.

This academy which roped in the services of several well known coaches and former players produced some of the stars of Hyderabad cricket such as V.V.S. Laxman, Mithali Raj and Hanuma Vihari.

After Bobby departed, John Manoj did a splendid job of managing the academy.

It was when he was coaching in Strabane in Ireland that he met and fell in love with Josephine McElroy. Seven years later the couple married. Increasingly Bobby's coaching skills were noticed and he received praise from all quarters. Over more than three decades, Bobby Rao has lived, played for and coached the Irish squad.

Many of his trainees went on to achieve international fame for Ireland. He has helped to develop the skills of many of the nation's international team players such as the former Ireland captain William Porterfield, Andrew White, Boyd Rankin, Niall O'Brien and Craig Young.

Bobby also became the first Indian cricketer to be honoured with the MBE (Member of the British Empire) by the British government for his contribution towards promoting sport, harmony and community service by using cricket as a peace-making tool during difficult times faced by the ethnic Asian communities in Northern Ireland.

An article in The Derry Journal has written about Bobby Rao:

Since moving to Ireland, the man from Hyderabad has also made it his goal to help those from foreign lands who have left their homelands in search of a better life.

After being at the wrong end of racial abuse, Bobby established Strabane Ethnic Community Association, an organisation that has become a beacon of hope for thousands of families from all over the world.

Only Indian cricketer to receive an MBE.

In 2011 and in recognition of his community work, he was awarded the MBE by Buckingham Palace, the only Indian Test cricketer ever to receive such an award. More than 30 years after moving to Strabane, Bobby Rao continues to be a factor for positive change in Ireland and every detail of his incredible journey is captured in his newly published memoirs.

Bobby's autobiography.

His book titled Bobby: India and Ireland, A Love Story, traces the journey of Bobby Rao from playing as a budding young cricketer growing up in the lanes of Walker Town in Secunderabad to the topmost level of Indian cricket and his life and career in Strabane where he is now settled.

When the book was released in Secunderabad, a host of cricket stars, VIPs and celebrities were present on the occasion. Said VVS Laxman: "I first met Bobby Rao sir in the year 1987 after Hyderabad won the Ranji trophy. He helped me immensely in improving my game. Winning the Ranji trophy was a big achievement and we all looked up to him and our seniors in that team. Players of my generation and I myself tried our best to emulate them."

Bobby himself was ecstatic about bringing out the book. "This book is the result of more than two years of work between myself and Conor Sharkey (who helped him to write it). The book follows my life from my earliest days in Walker Town right up until this summer and the Covid-19 pandemic. The highs, the lows, the cups and the controversies, every detail of my journey has been left on the pages of this book," said Bobby Rao.

Chapter 10

Shivlal Yadav

Iused to see Shivlal Yadav practicing at the nets in the Osmania University ground when he was a student. That was when he and I were both students - a few years before Shivlal became a famous Test player. He was one of those hustling and bustling bowlers who could create problems for rival batsmen with plenty of variety in his bowling. The batsmen would have no time to settle down. Shivlal could force them into committing mistakes because of the assortment of angles, trajectories and speeds with which he sent the ball hurtling towards the batsmen. His faster delivery was particularly difficult to play. As a right arm off break bowler, he made his Test debut in 1979. That was when the Indian team was in a transitional phase. The famous spin quartet had departed and the Indian selectors were looking for a combination that could replicate the feats of Bedi, Prasanna, Chandra and Venkat. Obviously, that was not an easy task.

A successful debut series.

In his debut series, against Australia, Shivlal was quite successful. He took 24 wickets in the five Tests that he played. Thereafter except for a brief break, he played regularly for India until 1987, forming a new spin attack with Ravi Shastri and Dilip Doshi as his partners. His debut Test was at Bangalore against Australia. Right away he made his presence felt by taking seven wickets in the match. Australia won the toss, decided to bat and scored 333. Skipper Kim Hughes top scored with 86. But Shivlal dismissed opener Andrew Hilditch (62), Graham Yallop (12), and tailenders Jim Higgs (1) and Alan Hurst (nil) to finish with four wickets for 49 runs off 22.5 overs. He was India's top wicket taker in that innings.

Kapil Dev and Karsan Ghavri took two wickets each while Dilip Doshi and S. Venkataraghavan took one wicket each. Centuries by Dilip Vengsarkar (112) and Gundappa Vishwanath (161 not out) were the highlights of India's strong reply of 457 for five declared.

In its second innings Australia scored 77 for three when the match ended in a draw. All three wickets were captured by newcomer Shivlal Yadav. He scalped Hilditch, Graeme Wood and Alan Border to finish off with three for three for 32 off 15.4 overs. After the match ended, many of the experts and former players were of the opinion that India had found a spinner who would serve the nation well for the next few years.

Played a role in the tied Test in Chennai.

Another important match that Shivlal was involved in was the tied Test match at Chennai in 1986. It was the second ever tied match in the history of Test cricket. Once, in a casual conversation he told me that it was one of the most memorable matches of his career.

He is proud of the fact that he played well in that historic match and was India's leading wicket taker in the Australian first innings. "The last few minutes were enough to give anyone a heart attack. All of us were sitting on the edge of our seats. I was the penultimate batsman to be dismissed. I was the ninth person to be out with

India's score at 344. Skipper Kapil Dev was clearly not pleased that I was bowled by Ray Bright. But we were all shivering with tension," he told me.

Finally, Maninder Singh was trapped leg before by Greg Mathews and the match ended in a tie. Kapil Dev was declared Man of the Match. But it was Greg Mathews and Ray Bright, the two Aussie spinners, who earned a lot of respect with their lion hearted bowling. According to Australian cricket writer Mike Coward, the suspense was as much if not more than a Hitchcock thriller on the silver screen.

Against Australia in the 1985–1986 series Shivlal picked up 15 wickets in the three Test matches. This haul included career best match figures of eight for 118. His best innings figures came against Sri Lanka at Nagpur with a haul of five for 76. He took his 100th Test wicket in his penultimate Test, against Pakistan and his Test career ended with 102 wickets from 35 matches with five or more wickets on three occasions.

Friendship with Rod Marsh.

After having played against Australia so many times, Shivlal developed a good friendship with wicket keeper Rodney Marsh. When Marsh passed away in 2022, I called Shivlal to get his comments about Marsh and his recollections about his friendship with the famous wicket keeper.

I wanted to write an article for Siasat.com and this is what Shivlal told me: "Marsh was one of the legends of cricket and was a good friend of mine. Although we were rivals on the field, when we were not playing, we hit it off well. I often had a beer or two with him. It was very easy to get along with him because he had no airs and no complexes."

"During our Test match against Australia in Melbourne, when their fast bowler Len Pascoe broke my toe with a yorker, Rodney had warned me before that happened.

Look out mate, he is going to come down - Rodney told me. At the time I did not understand what Rod was talking about and in the heat of the match, there was no time to ask what he meant."

"But just a few balls later Pascoe hurled down a toe crushing yorker and it broke my toe," recalls Shivlal Yadav. "It was later that I asked Rodney about his remark and he told me that he was warning me about his teammate Pascoe's game plan to injure me. First Pascoe bowled bouncers and the ball hit my helmet, then my shoulders and arms and then came that high speed yorker which landed on my toe," said Shivlal.

The fact that Shivlal took painkillers and continued to bat with a broken toe is one of the stories of bravery that highlight the commitment of our cricketers. "A wicket keeper plays a crucial role in the performance of any team. In this respect Marsh was invaluable to his side. Had it not been for his excellence behind the stumps, the great bowlers of those days like Dennis Lillee, Jeff Thomson and Max Walker would not have been as effective as they were," said Shivlal.

"Coincidentally, in his Test career, Marsh ended up with a tally of 355 victims which was the same number of victims as Dennis Lillee. They were close friends. Marsh's trademark was his colourful personality and his acrobatic catches. Despite being a stocky and heavily built person, he could hurl himself in different directions to take stunning catches whenever the batsmen edged steeply rising deliveries from Thomson and Lillee. Needless to say, he was a much loved figure among Australian cricket fans," said Shivlal.

After leaving the game as a player Shivlal became an administrator. His sharp brain and his problem solving ability made him a successful administrator too. He takes a lot of pride in the fact that it was under his stewardship that the long delayed cricket stadium in Hyderabad finally came into existence at Uppal.

Chapter 11

Arshad Ayub

Arshad Ayub had immense talent both as a bowler and as a batsman. Most cricket fans remember him primarily as an off spin bowler with a nagging line and length. But they need to be reminded that he has also scored a double century in first class cricket which is a feat that only the very best all rounders can achieve.

The first thing that strikes you about him are his suave and polished speech and manners. But he is also a very competitive player with a keen cricketing brain. Arshad Ayub's Test career was not a very long one but within that short span he proved his mettle. When a fight back was required Arshad was a reliable presence in the lower batting order. When the need of the hour was a quick wicket or two, Arshad was the man who could pull it off.

As an off spinner he was always spot on. Rarely did his bowling deviate from the perfect line and length. He did not have a prodigious turn or tantalising flight but he captured wickets by playing a game of patience. Often it was the batsman who ran out of patience and lost the fight against Arshad.

One of Arshad's best ODI performances came against Pakistan in 1988. On one occasion Arshad shared with me his memories of playing matches against Pakistan. Contests involving India versus Pakistan have always caught the imagination of cricket fans on both sides of the border. There have been many unforgettable moments in these battles.

When I interviewed him for an article in the Siasat.com he said:

"Every India vs Pakistan series promotes development of cricket in both countries. Fans in India as well as in Pakistan love to see the two teams playing against each other and most of the time there is a feeling of camaraderie and mutual appreciation," he said.

Memorable India-Pak contests.

"There have been many other memorable incidents in India-Pak contests. There was one incident in a match in Peshawar when Mushtaq Ahmed was an upcoming leg-spinner in the Pakistan line up. After Sachin Tendulkar (who was then a young player himself) hit Mushtaq for a couple of sixes, the senior bowler Abdul Qadir told Sachin "Bachche ko kyun maar rahe ho? Dum hai to mujhe maar ke dikhao". That was enough for Sachin. He banged away with gusto and took 28 runs off Qadir's over," recalls Arshad.

"Over the years Pakistan has produced several fantastic players. I have played against Imran Khan, Wasim Akram, Javed Miandad, Salim Malik, Waqar Yunus, Abdul Qadir, Aquib Javed and others. Although the competition on the field is very intense, off the field we had some very good interaction with the Pakistani players," recalled Arshad.

Test debut against West Indies.

Arshad was given his first Test opportunity against the West Indies in 1987. Immediately he showed what he was capable of. It was a low scoring affair in the first innings. India was all out for only 75 and then the visitors were bundled out for 127. The second innings saw India reach a respectable total of 327 thanks mainly to a century by Dilip Vengsarkar (102).

West Indies needed 276 and ran into trouble as Arshad engineered a collapse. He dismissed the famous opening duo of Gordon Greenidge and Desmond Haynes. Then he picked up the wickets of Winston Benjamin and the diminutive Gus Logie. It needed a special knock by the master, Vivian Richards, who scored an unbeaten 109 to ensure a victory.

In a later Test match, he came good with the bat. Batting at number nine position, he scored a solid 57 to send a message to the top brass. "I can bat well too. I deserve a place higher up in the batting order," he seemed to be telling them.

Leading role for India.

In the next season he played a leading role as India defeated New Zealand in a Test series. Arshad's haul was a rich one - 21 wickets in three Tests at an average of seven wickets per Test.

When the Indian team toured the West Indies a few months later, Arshad took 14 wickets in four Test matches against a strong West Indian side in the Caribbean grounds. Astonishingly this included two five wicket hauls. But thereafter, when he was not so successful against Pakistan he was eased out of the Indian team.

However, one of his best performances came in an ODI match against Pakistan in the Asia Cup in 1988. Arshad ran through the Pak batting line up and dismissed five batsmen for 21 runs in his nine overs. At the time it was the best bowling performance by an Indian bowler in ODI cricket.

His scalps included Ramiz Raja, Aamer Malik, Shoaib Mohammed, Naved Anjum and Wasim Akram. Although Wasim Akram is most famous for his superb swing bowling, it must be remembered that he has a top score of 257 with the bat in Test cricket. So dismissing Akram is not a light task.

India won that match very comfortably by four wickets with 26 balls remaining. Much of that victory was due to Arshad Ayub's wonderful and incisive spell with the ball. He was at his best that day as an off spinner of real class.

While playing for Hyderabad his contributions were often invaluable. A clever captain, he was always alert to any opportunities that came along. In first class cricket he scored 3014 runs (highest score 206) and he took 361 wickets (best bowling performance being eight wickets for 65 runs).

Activities after retirement.

After retiring from the game as a player, Arshad continued to be involved with cricket as a coach and administrator. He was elected to the post of the President of the HCA in 2014. Arshad had also started the Arshad Ayub Cricket Academy which he runs nowadays.

The academy was founded in 1998 and over the years, it has produced several talented players at different age group levels ranging from under 14 to Ranji trophy. Several players established themselves in the Hyderabad team by making a start at Arshad's academy.

The academy teams have also taken part in tournaments outside Hyderabad so as to provide the trainees with greater exposure and experience against a variety of rivals. Arshad hopes that more talented players will emerge from the ranks and make Hyderabad's colours fly high again.

Chapter 12

Mohammed Azharuddin

The first time I covered a match in which Azharuddin was playing was during the Ranji trophy season of 1981. When one of the senior sports journalists of Hyderabad named Radhakrishna from the Indian Express, heard that I would be going to Nizamabad to cover the match between Hyderabad and Karnataka, he told me: "Take a good look at Azharuddin's game. That boy will play for India one day," he said. Those were prophetic words indeed.

As it turned out Azhar did not do anything outstanding in that match. He was then about 18 years old. He took two good catches but failed with the bat. He was caught and bowled by Roger Binny for a duck. So I did not have any opportunity to study Azhar's batting.

But in subsequent matches I did get to see the full extent of his wonderful skills. Over the next few years, I covered several more matches in which he played along with the top-notch players of Hyderabad such as Shivlal Yadav, M.V. Narasimha Rao, Arshad Ayub, Vijay Mohan Raj, Khalid Abdul Qaiyum, Shahid Akbar, Abdul Azeem, Rajesh Yadav, Kawaljeet Singh and others also took part.

Over the course of time records tumbled in a heap as he flicked, cut and drove the ball to all parts of the ground and no bowler escaped punishment.

Azhar's unique quality was that he seemed to spot the ball very early. Almost as soon as it left the bowler's hand he knew where the ball would pitch and how much it would turn or bounce. This uncanny knack gave him plenty of time to choose his shots and play according to the need of the hour.

Back then, as a person he was tongue tied and rarely spoke. When he was not on the field, it looked like he just wanted to be left alone. He used to be a quiet and skinny young man sitting in one corner. But unfortunately for him, given his shy nature, his skills as a batsman ensured that he would be mobbed by adoring fans wherever he went.

After three centuries flowed off his bat in his first three Test matches, cricket-loving fans followed him about and waited patiently in front of his house to get a glimpse of him whenever he emerged.

Sublime skills.

On one occasion I happened to meet former Ranji trophy player Khalid Abdul Qaiyum who used to play with Azhar. Khalid now lives in the USA and had come to Hyderabad to work on a project.

Along with me there were some other journalists. We talked about the past and recalled the exciting matches that we had all seen. One journalist asked Khalid who was the best fielder he had ever seen.

Without even thinking twice about it, Khalid replied that the best fielder he had ever seen was Azharuddin. The speed which Azhar covered the ground while running after a ball, the accuracy of his throws, and the lightning fast reflexes with which he snapped up even the half chances, was unmatchable and unforgettable.

The sweetly timed drives and the flashing square cuts that Azhar played cannot be forgotten after one has seen them. It would be very difficult to say for sure which was his best innings. Probably every cricket follower would have a different choice and a different opinion.

He scored 121 against England at Lord's in 1990 when India was faced with the prospect of a follow on. Azharuddin came in to bat at number five and scored his hundred off 88 balls in a display which stunned everyone including the Englishmen. Former England cricketer Vic Marks, writing a column in The Observer, called that innings "the most dazzling Test century" he had ever witnessed.

No bowler could control him.

During Azhar's playing days, no bowler knew how to control his strokes. They found it difficult to figure out his strengths and weaknesses. Azharuddin was conferred the Arjuna award in 1986 and the Padma Shri in recognition of his distinguished contribution to the field of sports in 1988. He was named by Wisden as one of the five Cricketers of the Year for the year 1991.

Appointed captain.

Azhar became the captain of the Indian team, succeeding K. Srikkanth. He led the Indian team to victory in 90 ODIs.

This was a record until it was surpassed by M.S. Dhoni. His 14 Test match wins as captain was also a record until it was broken by Sourav Ganguly.

The day he was first appointed captain of India by Raj Singh Dungarpur, I was covering a match at the Gymkhana ground in Secunderabad. Around tea time I received a phone call from my head office that since Azharuddin had been appointed captain of India, I should immediately do an interview with him and write a report which should be of 3000 words.

I hurried down from the press box and I found Azhar sitting on a chair surrounded by fans and autograph seekers. I managed to squeeze myself into a chair near him and began firing my questions. He was not an articulate person back then and he answered each question with a one word answer.

In between there would be onlookers interrupting with pats on his back and words like: "Mubarak Azhar Bhai. Please ek autograph," and so on. In between this chaos I managed to ask him about five questions before he was called away for a meeting with the selectors.

A daunting task.

So, in response to my five questions, I had got five words. These would have to be stretched out to three thousand words - it was a daunting task!

It was a tall order but I went back to my office and began working on it. I padded up his answers with facts and figures and quotes of other players about Azhar and also inserted my own analysis and interpretations. After two days of work, I managed to complete a 3000-word story.

Over more than a decade, right until his career ended with the controversial match fixing allegations, I interacted with him many times. While talking to him, one gets the impression that he is a simple man. Yet, just when you think you have understood his nature, he comes up with a reaction you do not expect from him.

My interview with Azhar.

After being elected President of the Hyderabad Cricket Association, Azhar became embroiled in a tussle with his fellow office bearers in the Hyderabad Cricket Association. In 2021, I decided to get his views on the various aspects of cricket administration in Hyderabad. He was straightforward and forthright with his answers to my questions.

In a candid and wide ranging interview which was published in Siasat.com he outlined his approach and his plans to improve cricket in Hyderabad.

I asked him what were his plans to take the game forward in Hyderabad. There had been a lot of disagreement within the HCA regarding appointment of the Ombudsman. But players and fans want a peaceful and constructive atmosphere.

"What is your vision of the future and how do you plan to resolve the conflicting issues and develop cricket?" I asked him.

He answered: "Well, what I say is that everyone must work together and follow the rules. Without cooperation, there can be no progress. All the people in the HCA are experienced hands and everyone knows their responsibilities. So everyone should come on board and work together to bring about an atmosphere where the game will progress. The game is bigger than each of us so we must focus on cricket and nothing else. At present all the talk is about many things other than cricket. We must all get back to talking and planning about the game."

My second question to him was: "There have been allegations of widespread corruption and malpractices in the selection of teams and other aspects. How are you planning to eradicate these misdeeds?"

His answer: "We will go strictly by the rules and any player or umpire or group of individuals found indulging in crooked practices will find themselves out of the picture and cooling their heels in their own houses or even in the custody of the law. All forms of corruption will be stamped out with a heavy hand, I promise you. You will see some positive changes very soon and the game will be played in a fair and square manner," he added.

"The club secretaries should realise that their players are of utmost importance. I would urge all clubs to focus on developing the careers of their players. When I was an upcoming player, I was promoted by my school, then my college which was Nizam college and my club Deccan Blues. It is because of the help I received in my young days that I could play for the Under-19 side and climb up the ladder step by step," he said.

"All players can come up only by playing for the affiliated clubs. The club officials must nurture them and promote them. That is how it should go for every young cricketer in Hyderabad. We will ensure that there is transparency and honesty in the system," explained Azhar.

Question: "A fair amount of time has passed since you took charge as President of the HCA. Why is there a delay in implementing the ideas?"

Answer: The Coronavirus issue has been a big setback. It is difficult to get any work done or conduct any cricket events because of the complexities that it has created. It is something that my predecessors never had to face. It created a completely new situation for all of us. I had taken charge and was taking stock of the situation when the Coronavirus struck," said Azhar.

"As we all know, the entire country came under a lockdown and all work came to a grinding halt. We had to abide by the new restrictive rules. Difficulties arose when holding meetings. Even now it is difficult to contact people when you need them. They are unavailable much of the time. Right now, the second wave has engulfed us all. Sometimes people Test positive. Then they have to go into quarantine. At every step there is some difficulty or the other. But I am hopeful that after a few months things will normalise and we will be able to implement the plans that we have in mind," he told me.

Question: "The young players of Hyderabad need to be encouraged. They need top class coaching and infrastructure. Only those states will progress which can unearth and develop talent. What will HCA do about this and how will Hyderabad regain its status as one of the top class teams in India?"

Answer: "Yes, my dream is to take Hyderabad to the top. We must conduct camps and tap talent from the grassroots level. I have plans that will unearth talent from an early age. Quite often I find that boys who do well in some junior level tournaments are not really that good. When I make them play in the nets and watch them, I find that some can't even connect the balls that are bowled to them. I can see that their technique is wrong. We have to separate the grain from the chaff," Azhar said.

"As for infrastructure, I agree that facilities need to be improved all over Hyderabad. Some grounds are good but some are in a pathetic state. We need to have better grounds so that young players can develop their talent and their game can flourish. Even at the Rajiv Gandhi stadium in Uppal a lot of work needs to be done before we can host a big match. We have been given the right to hold the T20 World Cup but we have to put in a lot of work before that."

Question: "Since you began your career, in what way has Hyderabad changed as far as the game of cricket is concerned? Before the Rajiv Gandhi stadium was constructed, all matches were conducted at the Lal Bahadur stadium. How do you compare the old ground with the new one?"

Answer: "The Fateh Maidan ground (Lal Bahadur stadium) was a good venue. It has a special place in my heart. There used to be so much sports activity there. I would love to see the ground restored to its previous eminence. If I have the opportunity I will make the LBS ground important again," he said.

"I have many fond memories of watching famous players there. Like Clive Lloyd, Gordon Greenidge, Andy Roberts, Keith Fletcher, Sunny Gavaskar, Karsan Ghavri, Gundappa Viswanath and many others. The Sri Lankan team used to take part in the Moin ud Dowlah tournament and we used to see players like Roy Dias, David Heyn, Tony Opatha and others," said Azhar.

"I used to sit in the stands and watch them play. My favourite player back then was Greg Chappell. And I used to love listening to the Aussie commentator Alan McGilvray. But now all that has changed after the scene shifted to the Uppal stadium. Each stadium has its own ambience and this one is different from Fateh Maidan," Azhar said.

I asked him several other questions too but those issues are no longer relevant due to the passage of time. In many cases the situation has changed and much has happened since then. But the image of Azharuddin that will always endure in one's mind is Azhar the player. The superbly gifted batsman whose wristy strokes had a magical quality about them. A perfectly bowled delivery would be sent soaring into the stands when Azhar waved his magic wand at it. Those shots were unforgettable.

Chapter 13

The Ambience At The Lal Bahadur Stadium

At the Lal Bahadur Shastri stadium where cricket matches used to be held before the Rajiv Gandhi stadium was constructed, evidence of Hyderabadi culture at work could also be seen in the stands. Hyderabad's spectators were friendly and forgiving. They loved their cricket and the players and were very knowledgeable about the game. Whenever the run scoring slowed down, they were understanding and patient.

The people of Hyderabad, in keeping with their reputation for being laid back, did not lose their temper easily. When a home team player dropped a catch in the outfield, the shouts from the stands were all aimed at encouraging him and sympathising with his bad luck. I have never seen the spectators venting their frustration or anger upon any player.

Instead, such mishaps are met with responses like "Bad luck, boss" or "Good try, brother". Not everywhere are the crowds so forgiving and sympathetic. Sledging and barracking by spectators in Australia is something that many cricketers have experienced.

But running down an already dejected player is not a done thing in Hyderabad. There's an appreciation that sportspersons on the field give their full effort, and it's usually not unpreparedness or laxness that is to blame, but the rub of the green.

The famous (or infamous depending upon one's viewpoint) England fast bowler Harold Larwood who was the main weapon of his side during the controversial Bodyline series once said: "A cricketing tour of Australia would be the most delightful experience of your life. Provided you were deaf." He was referring to the constant heckling and abuse he had faced from the spectators while bowling against Aussie batsmen.

Crowd favourites.

Then there were players who were crowd favourites. Derek Randall who used to play Test cricket for England in the 1970s and 80s was a big hit with Hyderabad's cricket fans. That was because he loved to speak to the spectators when he was fielding near the boundary line. Sometimes he would entertain them by doing cartwheels.

The tall England all rounder Tony Greig was hugely popular too because he loved Hyderabadi fans and the fans loved him back.

On one occasion England was facing a minor crisis while playing against the South zone. The spectators were eagerly looking forward to an imminent collapse. Tony Greig was batting when a ball seemed to have taken the edge of the bat and flashed into the keeper's gloves. The south zone players appealed loudly for a catch and so did 50 thousand spectators.

Without waiting for the umpire's signal, Greig tucked his bat under his arms and began to walk away. There was a deafening cheer throughout the stadium. But it was just Greig carrying out one of his pranks. He took five steps away from the crease like a soldier marching on the parade ground and then did a sudden about turn and walked right back to resume his innings. He was not out and he knew it but he was just playing a prank on the spectators.

The fans roared with laughter and were not at all disappointed that an England wicket had not fallen. They wanted more such jokes from Grieg. Players who entertained the crowds either with their game or with their antics were always loved and appreciated.

Chapter 14

Venkatapathi Raju

I first met S.L. Venkatapathi Raju when he was a 14-year-old schoolboy. I wanted to write about him for The Sportstar magazine in a section called 'Stars Of Tomorrow". As the title indicated, that section was meant for young players in different sports who were likely to become well known achievers in the future.

My choice fell on Raju because I had been following his performances and I knew he was performing well. Thereafter I had consulted a few experienced cricket coaches in Hyderabad including Rehmat Baig who also confirmed my opinion that here was a boy who could turn out to be a star of tomorrow and upon whom an article could be written.

It so happened that I was the first journalist to write a feature on him. Till today Raju remembers that the article was the first one of his illustrious career and that it helped him to be noticed by those who mattered in Hyderabad cricket.

Two nicknames.

Raju has two nicknames - Latchi and Muscles. The latter name was given to him by the burly South African all rounder Brian

Macmillan. The name Muscles was given in a sarcastic vein because Raju was a very skinny young man in those days.

When I wrote my first article about him, Raju had recently been selected skipper of Hyderabad's under-15 team for the south zone inter-state cricket tournament for the V. Pattabhiraman trophy. The tournament was first begun in 1951 to honour the services of V. Pattabhiraman, also known as Pattu, a tall and commanding personality who was once the vice president of the Tamil Nadu Cricket Association and who helped to develop cricket between India and Sri Lanka.

Raju's impressive record in the inter school and state tournaments and also the local league matches prompted the selectors to name him captain of the Hyderabad junior team. He had represented the under-15 team on several occasions before being appointed the captain.

Born in 1969, Raju first joined the Hyderabad Public School (Ramanthapur branch) where he played football and also took part in track events and long distance running. He also played cricket but it was just one of the games that he played.

Incidentally my two younger brothers also studied in the same school although both of them were several years older than Raju. When I mentioned that fact to Raju he did recall one of my brothers named Aniruddha who was a good football player.

Switching to left arm spin.

Raju began his cricket career as a right arm off spinner and a useful middle order batsman. But amazingly he was ambidextrous when it came to bowling. He could bowl just as well, and sometimes better, with his left arm. When one of his teachers by the name of

Mr Sastry noticed that he could bowl a very deceptive length and line with his left arm, he advised Raju to switch completely to bowling with his left arm.

When Raju began seriously trying out the new method, he found that he could command a better line and length than he could while bowling with his right arm. Moreover, as his success increased in cricket, he began playing cricket exclusively, leaving the other sports which he had played earlier.

So that was how Raju became well known as a left arm spinner and went on to carve out a career in international cricket with his left arm spin.

In the T.V.B. Subramaniam trophy inter school tournament in 1980-1981, he took six wickets for 18 runs in the semi-final and impressed the seniors with his performance. In another inter school tournament the same year, Raju played a key role in ensuring a victory for his school team.

Playing against Hyderabad Public School Begumpet in the final, Raju captured seven wickets for 47 runs in the first innings and five wickets for 25 runs in the second innings besides scoring a valuable 54 runs with the bat. He hit the media headlines in a big way that day and his name became famous throughout the state.

He was selected for the Schools XI in the Ghulam Ali trophy tournament that year and later also found a place in the Under 19 team for inter schools and colleges tournaments. There he captured four wickets while conceding only one run in the quarter final match against Tagore's Home High School.

He then followed up this remarkable display with a haul of four wickets for 28 runs against a strong team from Wesley Boys junior college. However, his effort could not prevent the Wesley Boys team from winning the match.

During that very first interview when he was still a teenager, Raju struck me as being a very focused youngster. He knew what he wanted and what he had to do to achieve his goal. Moreover, he had the confidence to pursue his strategy and perfect his art all by himself.

Preferred to bowl flat rather than with flight.

He told me that he referred to bowl flat rather than to give the ball more flight in the air. He would use the deception of flight only when he was sure that it would pay off. He usually concentrated on the leg and middle stumps and his objective was to turn the ball just enough to catch the edge of the bat. For left handed batsmen he would use a different strategy according to the requirements.

When he was batting, the hook and straight drives were his favourite shots. He admitted that he had a weakness for the flick off the toes although at that time he had not fully mastered this shot. His off drive too needed more practice.

He was all praise for his coaches namely Prem Kumar of the HCA and Rehmat Baig the well known expert board coach who corrected many of the errors in Raju's bowling.

Raju got his big break when he was inducted into the Indian side in 1989–1990. That was the time when he had captured 32 wickets in the domestic season. He made his Test and ODI debut in the tour of New Zealand. When sent in as a night-watchman in his first Test innings, he did much more than was expected of him. He batted for more than two hours for 31 runs while six wickets fell at the other end.

Test debut against legends.

On his Test debut Raju played against some of the legends of New Zealand cricket including Richard Hadlee and Martin Crowe. Raju snapped up three crucial wickets in that match at Christchurch including that of Martin Crowe who at that time was rated as the world's best batsman.

Later Raju also served as a national selector and he has had the opportunity to witness from close quarters, the players of both countries, their attitudes and their approach to the game.

On one occasion he provided me with a good analysis of New Zealand cricketers. He told me that the Black Caps could never be taken lightly. "New Zealand is a tough outfit and we should not take them lightly. They are capable of pulling off surprises and they have produced some very talented fast bowlers and batsmen like Kyle Jamieson. He has what it takes to cause a great deal for rival batsmen."

"His record against India is very good and besides being a wonderful bowler, he has also done well with the bat. The Kiwis always seem to play in a carefree and relaxed manner but give some very good performances," explained Raju.

No pressure on New Zealanders.

"Another advantage that New Zealanders have is that in their country they do not face pressure. Cricket is just another game for them. Their most important sport is rugby. But in India expectations are very high. We always want our team to win every tournament. This puts a lot of psychological pressure on our players. That does not happen in New Zealand," Raju explained.

"Their batsmen are very sound. Kane Wiliamson and Ross Taylor are hugely experienced players and could take the team very far. Martin Crowe once called Kane the best ever New Zealand batsman which is high praise indeed. As a captain too, Kane is a very shrewd leader. Having played in the IPL, he knows the plus points and minus points of our players and teams," said Raju.

He was part of the Indian team which toured England in 1990, but the knuckle of his left hand was broken by a delivery from the tall West Indian fast bowler Courtney Walsh in India's match against Gloucestershire. Thereafter Raju could not play in the matches.

After he had recovered, he helped India to win a one-off Test against Sri Lanka. That match was played at the Sector 16 stadium in Chandigarh and not at Mohali where the matches are usually played. But Raju did well in that game. He was picked at the last minute because the selectors felt that he would be useful on a wicket that would be very likely to give the spinners some help.

On the second day, Raju ran through the Lankan middle order with a spell of five wickets for two runs in 39 balls. He took one more wicket on the next day to finish with six wickets for 12 runs in 17.5 overs. Eventually his match figures of eight for 37 in 53 overs won him the Man of the Match award. It was the first such award that he won in his international career.

Raju represented India in two World Cups namely the 1992 edition and the 1996 edition. His last Test match was the one against Australia in Kolkata wherein he got the prized scalp of Mark Waugh. But he continued to represent Hyderabad for many years. He was in the team that entered the final of the 1999–2000 Ranji Trophy.

Later he became a commentator and now listeners can hear his well modulated voice analysing the swings of fortune of various teams as they battle it out on the cricket fields.

Chapter 15

V.V.S. Laxman

V.V.S. Laxman's batting skills ranked him among the top batsmen in the history of Indian cricket. When he was in form there were no bowlers in the world who could counter his fluent strokes. His mastery was acknowledged even by Aussie speedster Brett Lee who once said in an interview that Laxman's technique was perfect, both against pace and spin. "It was hard to get past him. He was never scared, his footwork was great and he had a lot of time to choose his shots," Lee explained.

Laxman hails from a family of doctors. His parents are doctors Shantaram and Satyabhama. Moreover, Laxman is also related to India's former President Dr. S. Radhakrishan. He began his schooling at the Little Flower High School in Hyderabad. Coming from a family where both his parents were doctors, it was but natural that Laxman also joined a medical school for his undergraduate studies.

But soon cricket took precedence over everything else. Laxman has mentioned in his autobiography that what inspired him was India's thrilling victory in the Prudential World Cup in 1983 when Kapil Dev's underrated Indian team defeated the mighty West Indians to lift the World Cup. It was a thrilling moment for many youngsters and Laxman was one of those who found it mind boggling.

The slide began when Balwinder Sandhu sent back the famed West Indian opener Gordon Greenidge with an incoming ball that Greenidge had no clue about. Laxman almost went crazy at that sight. He rushed out to the balcony of his house and found that all the children in his neighbourhood had also come out to their balconies and everyone was cheering and shouting joyfully.

The children continued to do that with the fall of every wicket as the West Indies began to collapse. Finally, when Kapil Dev received the trophy and hoisted it over his head, all of them including Laxman wanted to touch that glittering Cup and bask in the glory of a historic win for India.

Learnt the basics at St. John's Cricket Academy.

Laxman's initial days of learning the rudiments of cricket at the St. John's Academy in Marredpally in Secunderabad helped him to forge his technique and temperament under the guidance of expert coaches.

Laxman made his first-class debut when he represented Hyderabad against Punjab in the quarter-final match of the Ranji trophy in the 1992–1993 season. But he was not immediately successful. He scored a duck in the first innings and 17 in the second. The selectors were not enthused by his display and he was able to play only one match for Hyderabad in the next season, before being shelved.

But because of his performances in the under-19 series against Australia, the national selectors were willing to try him out. So he was picked in the south zone squad for the Duleep trophy in 1994-95. But again Laxman did nothing noteworthy.

However, when he was given another opportunity in the following Ranji Trophy season, Laxman notched up 532 runs from five matches at an average of 76. He scored two centuries along the way. In the semi-final of the Duleep Trophy of 1995–96 season against West Zone, Laxman scored a spectacular 121 in the second innings and shared a 199-run partnership with skipper Rahul Dravid.

A brilliant season.

He had another brilliant Ranji season the next year, as he piled 775 runs in just 11 innings at an average of 86 with three centuries and a top score of 203 not out against Karnataka. Sadly however, Hyderabad lost the match and Laxman had no further role to play in the tournament.

Then he was selected to play for Rest of India against Karnataka in the Irani Cup and was also picked in the BCCI President's XI when it played against the touring Australian team. He played only three matches in 1996-1997 Ranji season, where he scored three half-centuries, before getting picked for the Indian Test team against South Africa and then began his wonderful international career.

His technical excellence made him unbeatable and immune to the tricks and strategy that the opposing bowlers tried out on him. His timing was invariably perfect and the way he used his wrists to guide his shots reminded many of another great Hyderabadi batsman Mohammed Azharuddin. In 2002 he was deservedly named one of Wisden›s five Cricketers of The Year.

Height advantage.

His athletic physique, his height of more than six feet and his long arms gave him a wonderful reach. He could reach out to deliveries or play over a short pitched ball in a way that shorter batsmen would find difficult to do. When he began playing at the international level, England's famous opener Geoff Boycott said that Laxman was one of India's best batsmen when it came to tackling the new ball.

The number three slot seemed to suit him best. The position at which a batsman excels often depends upon his mental make up. It is the same with footballers. Different footballers have their favourite positions where they perform at their best. What applies in football also applies to batters in cricket. For Laxman it was the number three position where he felt at home.

Laxman has himself written in his autobiography that as a number three batsman, one has to be prepared to face the second ball of the innings if the opener gets out first ball. It keeps one alert and primed for action. This is the state of mind that Laxman preferred. He was always ready for action if the openers failed. He played for many years for the Hyderabad team in the number three slot.

His most famous knock - the 281 against Australia at the Eden Gardens in Kolkata in 2001 - came when he was batting at the number three position. Rahul Dravid came in at number six in that innings and scored 180. Laxman and Dravid pulled India out of the woods.

But it was extremely fatiguing and difficult for both of them because of the length of the innings and also because of the heat and humidity. Laxman needed to get a hard leg massage to get his blood circulation going in his legs and feet while Dravid had to be put on drip to replace the body fluids that he had lost through sweat on the field of play.

It is understandable that the Eden Gardens became Laxman's favourite ground. He also loved the atmosphere of the city of Kolkata where the cricket crazy fans idolised him. After their own hometown hero Sourav Ganguly, the man they admired most was the Hyderabadi Laxman.

Shunted up and down the order.

But even after that epic innings, when Laxman had proved himself at number three, the Indian selectors and the team management often shifted him up and down the order. Whenever India needed a position to be filled, Laxman would be sent in at that position. Laxman being a thorough gentleman put up with these changes and did his job as best as he could.

He was often compelled to play in almost every position, including opening. Though it was Laxman who was best suited for number three, often Rahul Dravid was given that position with Sachin Tendulkar in number four. That meant Laxman would have to come in at number five or six. It made a big difference to his career.

Whenever he played lower down in the batting order, on many occasions he remained not out. He may have been able to score more runs if he had the opportunities to complete his innings.

Fought grave injuries.

As a player he has had his injuries but overcame them each time with his customary fighting spirit. There was a serious issue before the Eden Gardens match. He was hit by a big injury - a slipped disc - but magically physio Andrew Leipus was able to help him out. The next day he was feeling better and was able to play. The credit went to the physio and Laxman's own never say die spirit.

Needless to say, Laxman always loved playing against the Aussies. The players with the baggy green caps brought out the best from Laxman. The men from down under always play their cricket hard and with a great deal of passion and aggression. This is an emotion that Laxman can understand and deal with.

Whether it is Australian Rules Football or cricket or tennis, an Aussie player gives his heart into his sport and those who have the same emotions can understand what it is all about.

Since the time he was a junior player at the under-19 level, Laxman had the experience of facing Australian rivals like Brett Lee and Andrew Symonds. Laxman made his Under-19 debut for India against Australia in 1994. He batted at number six when he scored 88 in his debut innings against a bowling attack that included Brett Lee and Jason Gillespie.

These two were then the most promising among the Australian youth brigade of fast bowlers and both of them made their debut in the same match as Laxman did. In the second game of the series, Laxman came up with an unbeaten 151 in the first innings and 77 in the second innings to help the Indian boys to register a 226-run victory.

So when Laxman began playing at the senior level in Test and ODI cricket, he was already familiar with the strengths and weaknesses of several of the Australian bowlers. It is not surprising therefore that Laxman's first Test century came against Australia in Sydney. He scored 167 off 198 deliveries with the help of 27 boundaries before he was caught behind by Adam Gilchrist off the bowling of Brett Lee.

Fast pitches helped him.

The fact that the ball came through faster on the Australian pitches helped Laxman's penchant for executing his shots. Those conditions are often helpful to batsmen who can counter the fast bowlers with fluent drives and cuts. He was also adept at adjusting his mental and physical abilities to suit the existing conditions wherever he played.

In 2005, Laxman helped India to a memorable triumph over Sri Lanka with a fine century. In June 2006, Laxman again rescued India from a difficult position against the West Indies with a hard fought century. In November 2006, he was selected in the Test team for India's tour of South Africa. In the first test in Johannesburg Laxman scored 73 in the second innings to help India achieve a historic 123 run win.

In India's home series against Pakistan in 2007, Laxman once again showed his importance to the team with a disciplined batting performance in the 1st Test by scoring 72 not out in difficult circumstances. He then followed that up with 112 in the second Test. These fine performances ensured him a place in the squad which was to tour Australia. It would be his third to that country.

But all good things must come to an end. In 2011, the runs stopped flowing from his bat with the customary ease. In eight innings he aggregated 182 runs. In 2012, less than a week before the series against New Zealand was to begin in his home town of Hyderabad, Laxman announced his retirement with immediate effect. He had decided that enough was enough and decided not to wave a last goodbye in front of his hometown fans. It was a sad day for Hyderabad cricket and for all those who admired his fluent strokes.

❖

Chapter 16

Mithali Raj

What is common between classical dance and cricket? At first thought it would seem that there is nothing that is common between the two. But if one stops for a moment to reconsider this question then one would have to acknowledge that both these disciplines, one from the broader field of art and culture and another form the realms of sport, do have some things in common.

The common things are physical fitness, agility, flexibility, dedication, discipline and the ability to achieve and maintain a high level of motivation and determination to undertake rigorous practice on a daily basis.

In the case of Mithali Raj, her early practice in dance probably helped her to increase and develop the mental and physical qualities that made her one of the world's leading players in women's cricket.

Mithali Raj was born on 3rd December 1982, in the city of Jodhpur in Rajasthan where her father Dorai Raj, an employee of the Indian Air Force, was posted then. Later the family moved to Hyderabad where Mithali started playing cricket at the age of ten. She did her intermediate schooling at Keyes High School for Girls in Hyderabad and Kasturba Gandhi Junior College for Women in Secunderabad.

Her cricket career took off when she began to play for the Air India team. Her teammates were well established players such as Purnima Rau, Anjum Chopra and Anju Jain. Later she joined the Indian Railways and that was the team she represented in domestic tournaments.

When she was employed and playing for the Railways her coach was Murthy Rayaprolu. Talking to me on one occasion he disclosed facts about Mithali that she herself has not revealed to anyone. This was when I sought his comments for an article in Siasat.com soon after Mithali announced her retirement from cricket.

The coach's comments showed the dedication that Mithali possessed. He said: "Sometime ago, she discussed with me her desire to retire from all international cricket. I felt that she could go on for at least two more years at the top level. But she was of the opinion that if she retired now, it would open a path for the youngsters who are waiting to show their talent. She is always ready to sacrifice for others. I respect her decision," said Mr. Murthy.

Her coach admired her dedication.

"I have always admired her dedication. She sacrificed all her social life and practised cricket every evening without any exceptions. Even on occasions when she arrived in Hyderabad from another city, she would turn up for practice that very day. She set an example for the other players," he said.

"Rain or sunshine, hot weather or cold, she would be present at the ground. Her preparation was very thorough. She maintained her fitness and watched over her diet. To do this continuously for 23 years is an amazing feat. Many of our male players cannot do it," said the coach.

"I was her coach from the year 2000 till 2021. I know what sacrifices she has made. As a railway employee, after she got a promotion, she was eligible to stay in an airconditioned room when we were playing on tour. But she stayed in a dormitory with the other players. She refused airconditioned accommodation and air tickets and traveled and lived with the team. She took pride in playing for Railways. How many international players will do that?" Mr. Murthy asked.

It was that drive and passion which enabled Mithali to reach the top. Before she retired, she added one more feather to her already crowded cap by becoming the world's highest scorer in ODIs. Then she overtook England's Charlotte Edwards to become the overall highest scorer. She achieved a landmark in her career by going past Edwards' tally of 10,273 runs. The English player was one of the leading figures of women's cricket throughout the world.

Once I asked the former Test cricketer M.V. Narasimha Rao to provide me with his opinion about Mithali. Bobby Rao was one of the players who saw Mithali from an early age and then followed her career as she developed into the world's best woman cricketer.

Very hard working says Bobby Rao.

"She started practicing at my academy in Marredpally. Even at that age we could see that she had tremendous motivation and determination. She was extremely hard working and never shirked any work that our coaches gave her. From her there was no laziness or excuses. She took up every task with enthusiasm and did not rest till it was completed. It was wonderful to see the little girl with so much composure and maturity," said Rao.

"In every way she has set a good example for the Hyderabad girls. I remember that she also used to be a dancer. My niece Mamatha and Mithali used to learn dancing from the same teacher," explained Bobby.

"I knew that in addition to cricket, Mithali was also attending dance classes. I admire the positive attitude that she displayed at all times even when the going was tough. She had those champion qualities in her. Success is not obtained by talent alone. There has to be the right mental quality and she had this too," said Rao.

It would be interesting to travel back in time by about three decades to take a look at how this outstanding player made her beginning. How and why did she take up the game? Who or what motivated her? Who encouraged and guided her? These are the questions that would be most likely to come up in any cricket lover's mind.

Mithali started to play the game at the age of 10 but at around the same time she was also following her second passion which was classical dance. However, after about eight years she realized that she would have to focus only on one discipline and she chose cricket.

By this time she was living in Hyderabad where she had plenty of opportunity to get worthwhile and valuable guidance from experienced coaches at the St. Johns academy as well as at the Keyes High school in Secunderabad.

Played against men.

What gave her an added edge was the fact that she often played against more experienced and older male players. As a result, the bowling she had to face at this crucial stage of her budding career was more hostile and penetrative than the level that most of the other girls had to tackle.

Perhaps this helped to lay the foundation for her technique and the confidence that she later had. And it also helped her to develop the wide range of strokes that she possessed in her armoury.

After doing exceptionally well in national and domestic tournaments, she was named among the Indian team's probables for the 1997 Women's Cricket World Cup when she was just 14 years old. But she was disappointed when she couldn't make it to the final squad.

A memorable ODI debut.

Eventually she made her ODI debut in 1999 against Ireland at the Milton Keynes ground and scored unbeaten 114 runs thus getting her international career off to a flying start. She made her Test debut in the 2001-02 season against South Africa at Lucknow. On 17 August 2002, at the age of 19, in her third Test, she broke Karen Rolton's record of the world's highest individual Test score of 209 by piling up a mammoth score of 214 against England in the second and final Test.

However, this record has since been surpassed by Kiran Baluch of Pakistan who scored 242 against West Indies in 2004. But for Mithali, an impressive string of successes followed. Although it did not come immediately, for in the 2002 World Cup, she fell ill with typhoid and her absence seriously hampered India's performances.

But on the next occasion she led India to its first World Cup final before losing to an overwhelmingly strong Australian squad. In 2006, she led the side to its first ever Test and series victory in England and wrapped up the year winning the Asia Cup - the second time in 12 months - without dropping a single game.

Her calm composure when at the crease (she was once spotted absorbed in reading a book before going in to bat) and her ability to score briskly make her a batsman who was feared by all the rival bowlers.

In addition to her ability with the bat, Mithali could roll her arm over and bowled leg-breaks sometimes. Thereby she was able to provide a variety to her team's bowling attack. Her run scoring abilities have made headlines regularly in the Indian media and a few years ago she was honoured with the prestigious Arjuna award by the Government of India.

How the lockdown affected her routine.

The only time that she felt unsure about the future was during the period of lockdown following the Coronavirus outbreak. Like all athletes the lockdown affected her practice and preparations. She was not used to being confined to her house for such a long period. As an active athlete, even in off season, she was frequently seen on the ground doing fitness training.

But during that phase of lockdown there were months that went by without visiting the sporting arena. Training at home was difficult because of the space constraint. It was important for her to be in touch with her trainer and physiotherapist because if athletes are not active physically, in terms of training or practising, plenty of adverse factors take a toll on their bodies. After the lockdown was lifted, she lost no time in getting back to her regular routine.

Shivlal Yadav's assessment.

Former Test cricketer, captain of Hyderabad, N. Shivlal Yadav who has also served the HCA and BCCI in various capacities, made an interesting point after he came to hear about the retirement of India's ace woman cricketer from all forms of international cricket.

According to Shivlal, a player like Mithali with her vast experience of having played in different situations can make a huge contribution to the future of Hyderabad cricket. Not just Hyderabad but on a broader scale, India too can benefit from her services. "She must now take the role of an advisor and mentor," said Shivlal when I asked him to comment about the future role that Mithali could play after retirement.

This is what Shivlal Yadav said:

"Her experience and her achievements are phenomenal. See what she has achieved. Surely a player of her standard will be able to guide the future of players in Hyderabad. If we handle this aspect correctly, we will be benefited by having the advice of a person of her calibre. Not just the women players but also the young boys can learn a lot from her," said Shivlal.

In 2022 a film on her life titled "Sabash Mithu" was released. It was a Hindi film based on the dramatic events of her sports career. It was directed by Srijit Mukherji and produced by Viacom18 studio. Tapsee Pannu acted as Mithali Raj and the story chronicled the ups and downs and moments of glory in Mithali's life. The film was released on 15 July 2022. It received a fairly positive review from critics but was a disaster at the box office.

Mithali Raj stepped away from the international arena after playing for 20 years. She was the first woman player to be able to do so. She has often been compared to Sachin Tendulkar. There are those who call her the Tendulkar of women's cricket but that is a term she does not like. On one occasion she rebuked a journalist: "Would you call Sachin the Mithali Raj of men's cricket?" She made her point that day and thereafter the Hyderabad media always respected her sentiments.

Chapter 17

Mohammed Siraj

One of the most exciting prospects to have emerged from Hyderabad cricket in recent times is fast bowler Mohammed Siraj - the bowler nicknamed Miyan Magic by his friends and admirers. He was born into the family of an auto driver in 1994. As a young boy his liking for cricket and his habit of playing the game for hours every day sometimes got him into trouble. His parents felt that he was not devoting enough time to studies and so he was frequently scolded. He would assure them that they need not worry about his future because one day he would become a famous player and earn a lot of money from the game that he loved passionately. Many children have similar dreams out in most cases the dreams are not realised.

However in the case of Siraj everything worked out as he had planned and predicted. As a result, both he and his country profited from the developments that followed. His fast medium pace bowling has fetched India many breakthroughs and he has shot to fame and earned money beyond the wildest imagination of his once worried parents.

Sadly, his father passed away when Siraj's career was beginning to blossom. His impressive Test debut against Australia in 2020 confirmed his ability to take wickets against very strong opposition in Test matches. According to star batsman V.V.S. Laxman, he is likely to gain more success in the coming years.

Laxman's view about Siraj.

A couple of years ago I had a chat with Laxman to sound him out about the future career of Siraj to write an article for Siasat. com. There is nobody who can speak with more authority on fast bowlers than Laxman since he had faced some of the greatest fast bowlers of his days. Bowlers like Glenn McGrath, Jason Gillespie, Allan Donald and many others - Laxman has tackled them all and so he knows what he is talking about. It stands to reason that his assessment of Siraj is bound to be very accurate.

Speaking to me, V.V.S. Laxman expressed his optimism about Siraj's future career in world cricket. "Provided he continues to work hard over the next few years, Siraj can be a big name in international cricket. He certainly has the qualities and the potential to do so," said Laxman. "Siraj is a very skilful bowler.

"For any fast bowler there are two very important requirements. Firstly, he must have the ability to swing the ball deceptively. Siraj has this ability in abundance. Secondly a fast bowler has to be able to bowl long spells. This ability too, Siraj has in him. He has tremendous stamina. He can come back for his third spell and bowl with just as much venom as he did in his first two spells," said Laxman.

What makes Siraj a dangerous bowler

"This ability to maintain his speed and bounce and movement over a long period is what makes Siraj such a dangerous bowler. There is no time for the batsmen to relax. Siraj just keeps coming back again and again and he keeps hammering away at the batsmen. That is why he picks up wickets even in his third spell. It is an important quality for any fast bowler to possess," explained Laxman.

"Now in India, we are fortunate to have a battery of good fast bowlers. I feel that all Indian skippers should use Siraj for the longer spells while giving the others short and sharp bursts. I feel that Siraj is only going to improve further. We have seen him in action in Australia where he played a very important role in our attack and he will become even better with experience," said Laxman.

"However, one of the important things that he has to be careful about are stress related injuries resulting from work overload. Fast bowlers are often hampered by injury problems. So, this is one aspect on which Siraj must focus. He must stay fit and take care to remain injury free. Then only will he be able to fulfil his potential," said Laxman.

Speaking about the effect of the IPL on the confidence and morale of the younger players like Siraj and others, Laxman agreed that the tournament had given them a chance to gain valuable experience against top class opponents and build up their belief in their own abilities.

"The IPL, or any T20 format game for that matter, makes you work hard. You have to think up new ideas for every match. You are under constant scrutiny. It is a high-pressure situation. If you can come out on top, then you can be sure you have done a great job," said Laxman.

All Hyderabadis know that Siraj has come a long way since he first got hooked to cricket while studying in class 7. Like many other kids he would bunk classes to play in cricket matches. Surely back then his parents who were worried about this kid's future could never have imagined that this game would provide Siraj with a grand lifestyle.

But what is an advantage can also be a disadvantage. The cricketer who is now at his peak, should make a conscious effort not to get carried away by the glitz and glamour associated with the game. Financially he is now well off. So, all he has to do now is keep his attention on the game. A strict fitness regimen and a controlled diet will go a long way to enhance and prolong his career. His countless fans in Hyderabad are looking forward to watching him play for many years more. They hope that the gifted fast bowler who has acquired a cult status in the twin cities will rise to the topmost rung of international cricket.

Last year Siraj astounded everyone by capturing a record eight wickets at Lord's surpassing even the great Kapil Dev. Siraj created history by chalking up his name as India's best bowler at the Lord's cricket ground. His match haul of eight wickets for 126 runs were the best by any Indian bowler on the famous ground. The previous best match haul was by Kapil Dev who had taken 8 wickets for 168 runs in 1982.

Superb bowling by Indian pacers.

Thanks to the superb bowling of Mohammed Siraj, Jasprit Bumrah, Ishant Sharma and Mohammed Shami, India romped home to a 151 run victory which had seemed impossible at one stage. According to Harsha Bhogle, this will be ranked as one of India's most memorable victories.

Coincidentally, the victory came one day after India celebrated its 75th Independence Day from British rule. Former England captain Michael Vaughan admitted that England had been crushed by the Indian team which showed great courage and determination of the highest order. Siraj captured 4 wickets for 94 runs in England's first innings and then followed it up with another 4 wickets for only 32 runs in the second innings as England collapsed like a house of cards.

It was highly refreshing to see an Indian pace quartet demolishing the England team. Earlier it was the spin quartet of Prasanna, Chandra, Venkat and Bishen Bedi. But now India has a pace attack which can do the job just as effectively.

Experts praise Siraj.

Sachin Tendulkar, Ravi Shastri and Harbhajan Singh were among those who have heaped praise on the Hyderabad speedster. Recently even Dale Steyn, himself a feared fast bowler, also said in an interview that when he saw Siraj in action he immediately knew that he would succeed in a big way because his attitude was right. It is one of the reasons that make him special, said Steyn.

To analyse the pacer's career at that stage, I spoke to former Test cricketer and Hyderabad captain Narasimha (Bobby) Rao who had coached Siraj at the Hyderabad Cricket Association's academy when Siraj was beginning his career. Bobby Rao was the Director of the Academy then.

"Siraj has come a long way since he began his career. I remember him coming to the HCA Academy when he was a raw young pacer. He had a lot of talent but it had to be fine tuned which is what we did when he was undergoing training at the HCA Academy. Now he has gained in stature and confidence and I am so glad every time I see him performing well," said Rao.

"Now he has gained pace and accuracy. He can land the ball in the right place along the right line and create difficulties for every batsman. His variations and the way he gets the ball to move is remarkable. I really admired the way he bowls to left handed batters. He knows exactly what he has to do against every batsman," said Rao.

Asked what Siraj should do for maintaining fitness, Rao said that he had worked on that issue with Siraj at the HCA Academy. "I had chalked out a plan for all the trainees and I am glad that their fitness improved a lot. I had also made up a diet plan and instructed the players about their daily diet. Now, Virat Kohli is very particular about fitness and I am sure he will keep all the players including Siraj in fit condition" Rao concluded.

After that performance at Lords, perhaps the best congratulatory message for Siraj came from former international cricketer Mohammad Kaif. He wrote on social media: "You fulfilled your Abba's dream, stood up for your team. People take a lifetime to do all this miyan. You did it in months. Keep smiling Siraj and never lose your innocence." That was Kaif's message to the bowler from Hyderabad.

In India, the rise of Mohammed Siraj has been a welcome development. He is there along with Bumrah (when fit), Shami and the other fast bowlers to take the upper hand against rival teams. Now Umran Malik is also there and he has tremendous speed.

Speed is not his only forte.

It is not just speed which is Siraj's forte. Siraj has perfect control over length, line and movement. Against left handed batsmen he is at his best.

Former England opener Geoff Boycott is among those who are highly impressed by Siraj's abilities after watching his record breaking feat of eight wickets for 126 runs at Lords. Since Boycott has faced the legendary West Indian fast bowlers like Michael Holding and Andy Roberts, he knows what he is talking about.

"I like Siraj. He is full of energy. No one should tell him to curb himself. Let him flourish in his own way. He is an asset for India although he is fairly new," said Boycott who has the distinction of having 151 first class centuries under his belt.

Former Australian player Brad Hogg says that Siraj has shown that he doesn't get distracted by taunts and racial abuse. Instead, he gathers his emotions and puts it into his bowling. He makes the ball speak for him and that is the ideal thing to do in any sport.

Ravi Shastri too has described Siraj as an exceptional talent. "He was the find of the Australian tour for shoring up the attack in the way he did. He fought through personal loss and racial remarks and channelised his emotions to confirm his place in the team," said Shastri.

Like all sports, cricket too is a battle of mind as well as body. The player who can succeed is the player who can mentally conquer his rivals. Former cricket coach of Hyderabad - the vastly experienced and respected E.B. Aibara - used to say that a bowler must be clever enough to understand the batsman's mind.

"That bowler will be consistently successful who can understand every batsman. Some batsmen are immature. They can be upset by sledging. But some are mature. Those tactics won't work against them. So what will work in one case may not work in another case. The bowler has to very quickly understand what is the batsman's weakness. Not just his technical weakness but his psychological weakness also," Aibara had told this correspondent many years ago.

Modern day professional sport is a field where a tremendous amount of work and mental toughness is required. So far Siraj has exhibited all those qualities and all he needs to do is to stay focussed and continue to learn and develop.

Chapter 18

P.R. Man Singh

P.R. Man Singh who is better known in the Hyderabad cricket circles just as "Maan," had the distinction of being the longest serving Secretary of the Hyderabad Cricket Association. He was an administrator with a vast amount of experience and knowledge about the game and its rules. But his main claim to fame is that he had been manager of the Indian team when it won the Prudential World Cup at Lord's in 1983.

25th June, 1983, is a date that will not be forgotten by any cricket lover of India. It was the day when an unfancied team from India defeated the mighty star studded West Indies to win the cricket world cup which was officially known as the Prudential Cup. The man who worked quietly behind the scenes and contributed to India's great victory was P.R. Man Singh.

Recently and quite deservedly, a film was made to mark this great moment in India's cricket history. This film was titled "83" and is based on the real life story of India's momentous achievement.

Interestingly some of the sons of the old players have acted in the film. The actor who plays the role of Sandeep Patil is his son Chirag Patil who has acted in Marathi and Hindi films.

Furthermore, the sons of the West Indian players Gordon Greenidge and Malcom Marshall have acted as their own fathers in the film. India's top all rounder Mohinder Amarnath appears as his famous father Lala Amarnath on the screen.

In the film Man Singh's role has been played by the well known actor Pankaj Tripathi. He spent a day with Man Singh in his home in Secundrabad to study his mannerisms and speech.

Background of Man Singh.

Man Singh was the only person from Hyderabad who was involved in that historic triumph. The life story of 'Maan' is itself very interesting. There is a town named Poundri in Haryana. It was there that the family was based and it was there that Man Singh's father Ramsingh Aggarwal had his early education. Man Singh's uncle Amarsingh Aggarwal was a contractor in Meerut who supplied goods to the army.

In 1930 a large contingent of the army moved from Meerut to Secunderabad and the gentleman also moved to Secunderabad so as to continue his business. He also helped his brother Ramsingh to get a job in Secunderabad with the Deccan Wine Stores which was then located in James Street.

Although he was a teetotaller, Ramsingh understood the liquor trade very well and had a keen mind for business. After a while he opened his own wine stores, one in Abids and one in Secunderabad. In 1937 he got married and his wife Laxmidevi joined him in Secunderabad. The business flourished and in time they were blessed with two children, a boy whom they named Man Singh and a girl whom they named Usha.

Before his SSC examination, the school principal added the initials P (for his native place Poundri) and Ramsingh (his father's name) to Man Singh's name and by some error the family name of Aggarwal got left out. That is why he is still known as P.R. Man Singh. Cricketers call him Maan Bhai and Ravi Shastri calls him Mannu Bhai.

Man Singh grew up to be a good cricketer but after a while got into the administrative side of the game. He became secretary of the Hyderabad Cricket Association and served for many years in that capacity. Before the 1983 World Cup the BCCI was toying with the names to be appointed as manager for two series. One against the West Indies and one for the World Cup. Finally after a lot of deliberation, Man Singh was given the responsibility of being the team manager for the Prudential World Cup.

Interview with Man Singh.

During the Prudential Cup, it was Man Singh's job to see that everything went smoothly off the field. I interviewed Man Singh about his role in the film and its connection to the real life incidents for an article which was published in Siasat.com. Talking to me, Man Singh relived the memories of those heady days and related some extremely interesting incidents.

"The idea for the film came to Balwinder Singh Sandhu who was a player in the team which won the Cup in 1983. He lives in Mumbai and he put this idea to some filmmakers whom he knew," said Man Singh.

"In 2016, I heard that a film on the 1983 World Cup was being planned. Gradually it took shape and all the players and myself were asked to sign contracts with the filmmakers. Various actors would play our parts but they needed our inputs and information," said Man Singh.

"Incidentally I know the director Kabir Khan and his family elders. His mother was my senior at Nizam College. HIs father was Rasheeduddin Khan who comes from a very highly respected family of scholars. He was also a member of the Rajya Sabha. So, I easily became friends with Kabir," Maan stated.

"The cast and crew worked very hard to bring out this film and nothing was left to chance. The story of the film is almost 100 percent accurate. Only one or two incidents have been inserted for entertainment. Otherwise, everything in the film really happened," explained Man Singh.

Talking about the actual tournament itself, Man Singh said: "It was my responsibility to ensure that there was nothing to disturb the minds of the players. They should be able to focus entirely on the game. It was my guru from Hyderabad, Mr. Ghulam Ahmed who gave me some invaluable advice about managing the team and his guidance was immensely helpful."

"My first task was to become a friend of the players. I did not want them to think that I was a spy of the BCCI in their midst. I am very grateful to the players for their cooperation and the respect they had for me. Before the trip, we all assembled in Mumbai and set off by an Air India flight. Nobody expected much from this team. The BCCI did not even arrange the usual farewell dinner. There was no conditioning camp and no media reports about our chances," said Man Singh.

Maan's father had a premonition.

"But strangely my father, Ramsingh Aggarwal, had a feeling that we would definitely win the trophy. Just a day before we set off, he instructed the staff in his office to clear a big shelf and paint it and make it look nice. "We will place the World Cup on that shelf when it comes to us," he told them. As for me, I thought that we may go up to the semi finals at the most but probably not any further," related Man Singh.

"When we reached England, things went well for us. At some grounds the facilities were very basic. But we adjusted and we fought hard. I made sure that the team was provided with three vegetarian meals everywhere," said Maan.

Syed Kirmani became a temporary vegetarian.

"One vegetarian meal was for Krishnamachari Srikkant, another for Yashpal Sharma and the third for Syed Kirmani. Kiri said that he could never be sure if the meat being served was Halal meat so he preferred to become a vegetarian for the duration of the tournament," explained Man Singh. "Where the cricket was concerned, I did not interfere. I left it to Kapil Dev, Mohinder Amarnath and the senior players to decide everything," he added.

"Then in the final we faced the West Indies again. How we won the match at Lord's is a famous story. That remarkable ball with which Balwinder Sandhu dismissed Gordon Greenidge, Kapil Dev's fantastic catch to send back Viv Richards off the bowling of Madan Lal, and the collapse of the overconfident West Indies is a story that all cricket lovers know very well," said Man Singh.

When David Frith ate his words.

"But at the end, there was one more incident that I want to reveal. David Frith, the well known journalist had written disparagingly about the Indian team. He had written that such teams should not be allowed to play in the World Cup."

"Therefore, after our victory, I wrote a strongly worded letter to him and suggested that he should now eat his own words. And I could hardly believe it, when a few days later, I saw a photo of him with a glass of wine in his hand and his mouth stuffed with the paper on which he had written his report." said Maan with a smile.

"I am told he really ate up the paper on which he had written his report. The film 83 has brought out all these interesting stories behind our great victory. I hope many people will see this remarkable film and enjoy it," said Man Singh.

The Revenge series.

Maan had more to tell me about the aftermath of that great victory. Soon after that the West Indies team arrived on a tour of India. The tour began in October 1983. They were looking at the Indian tour as a revenge series and they accomplished their task by humbling India. West Indies won the six match Test series 3-0 and the five match ODI series 5-0.

India failed to win even a single Test or an ODI match and the cricket fans who had begun worshipping their heroes just a few months earlier, now began to curse them endlessly. Man Singh told me that when he met Clive Lloyd during that tour, the burly West Indies captain told him: "Hey manager, we have come to India to......you all this time."

Despite the sorry display, India did have a few moments of glory too. Kapil Dev showed his mettle and produced his career best innings spell when he took nine wickets for 83 runs in one innings. Sunil Gavaskar scored his career best 236 not out in this series against the West Indies.

This innings of 236 runs not out took Sunil Gavaskar past the great Don Bradman's record of 29 Test centuries and Vinoo Mankad's Indian record of 231. Many players made their debut in this series. For the West Indies, Gus Logie, Roger Harper, and Richie Richardson made their debut while for India Navjot Sidhu and Raju Kulkarni made an entry into international cricket.

Man Singh also managed the Indian team for the 1987 World Cup known as the Reliance World Cup. The two host nations, namely India and Pakistan, failed to reach the final. Both the host nations were eliminated in the semi-finals. There was a decline for the West Indies too. They could not advance beyond the group stage. The winner was Australia.

The Pavilion - a cricket museum.

Man Singh is a passionate cricket lover. In his house in Secunderabad he has set up a mini cricket museum which he has named The Pavilion. It was inaugurated by Sachin Tendulkar and it contains a huge number of cricket memorabilia including photos, ties, caps, bats and balls used by famous cricketers. All the items have been painstakingly collected by Man Singh over a period of five decades. His most prized item in that collection is the World Cup medal that he won in 1983.

Man Singh began collecting all types of items connected with cricket from the time he was very young. Over the years, the number of items grew and accumulated. Then he started thinking of putting up a display for cricket lovers to see and he thought of setting up the museum in his house.

In 1950 Man Singh's cousin in Meerut who was a great fan of cricket, would bring out his radio and listen to the running commentary. That was when Man Singh also began following the commentary and got hooked to the game. Maan is in his mid-eighties now but still goes to his shop in Secunderabad which he manages daily from morning to evening. His mind is still as sharp as a knife and his knowledge about the rules of administration cannot be bettered by anyone in Hyderabad.

Chapter 19

Purnima Rau

Purnima Rau was one of the most talented women cricketers who emerged from Hyderabad in the 1990s. She made her international debut for India against West Indies in an ODI at Nottingham on July 20th, 1993. Her Test debut was made against New Zealand on February 7th, 1995.

Purnima Rau's career began to flourish when women's cricket in India was not a popular sport. Although they put up commendable performances, the women players were consigned to the shadows of the far more popular men's version of the game. It was Purnima Rau and other players like Diana Eduljee, Shantha Rangaswamy, Subhangi Kulkarni, Anju Jain and Anjum Chopra who fought to popularize their game and obtain for it the recognition that it deserved. These were the women players who were primarily responsible for revolutionising the women's cricket scenario in India. They did so after battling against heavy odds and even braving neglect and ridicule at times.

The modern day players who are far more famous and financially better off, owe a lot to the pioneers of women's cricket. Players like Mithali Raj, Jhulan Goswami, Harmanpreet Kaur, Deepti Sharma, Smriti Mandhana, Poonam Yadav, Shefali Varma,

Shikha Pandey and others have reached the top because of the foundation that was laid by their predecessors.

A shrewd tactician, Purnima Rau was perhaps one of the first women players in India to attempt to take advantage of the field restrictions in place during the first 15 overs of a limited overs game. She captained India in three Test matches and eight ODI matches in 1995. She also captained the formidable Air India team in the 1999-2000 season.

Although she was basically a middle order batter, she was also a very capable opener. She had the ability to strike the ball cleanly and her timing was almost always perfect.

As a bowler, Purnima could spot the rival batter's weaknesses quickly. This quality made her a dangerous bowler in all situations. The batters could never relax when she was on the job. On many occasions she broke a partnership or stemmed the flow of runs.

When she became a coach for the Indian women's team, she did so with a rare understanding of the players in her charge. She believed that a coach should not be the dominant figure of the team and the game. Players should be allowed to flourish and their individual characteristics and strengths should be allowed to blossom. Purnima is still considered to be a pioneer in devising strategy and tactics in women's cricket in Hyderabad.

As a captain and coach, Purnima Rau left an indelible mark on the sport with her leadership and cricketing prowess. Rau's captaincy stint came when there was a period of transition and growth for women's cricket in India. She had that spark of leadership which came in handy when the team needed it.

No player will be willing to play under a leader who lacks self confidence and courage. These are qualities that Purnima had in abundance. In short, she was the kind of captain who was willing to go the extra mile and lead from the front. Basically, that means that when the going got tough, she never hesitated to do the rough jobs which carried a great risk of failure. If the requirement was to adapt to a change in batting order on a difficult wicket, or opting to bowl the crucial end overs, she was not the person to back down.

Moreover, she had marvellous self control. This is an essential quality in all sports but especially in cricket. One has to battle that inner demon inside one's brain which is screaming out to hit the ball when the requirement is a steady, long and patient innings. Being able to overcome those impulses and playing for your team is what Purnima Rau was good at doing. In the process she often sacrificed considerable amounts of her personal goals. Former England captain Mike Brearley who was known as one of the best captains in the game, has emphasised in his book "On Cricket", that this quality is an essential one for every cricket captain.

Self control also means not reacting negatively to a poor umpiring decision. Also not getting provoked by harsh comments and sledging by rival players. She always set an example for others to follow. It was not just on the field of play that her commitment was clearly visible. Even when a match was not in progress, she led the way for the others by turning up punctually every day for practice, never shirking her duty to her team and coach.

When she was a captain, her planning was very meticulous. She never left anything to chance. In cricket, all good captains have had a clear plan for every situation. Captains are keen students of the game. A man like M.L. Jaisimha was a perfect example of a person who watched and studied the rival players very closely.

Purnima was like that too. She could sense the strengths and weaknesses of the opposition and made her plans accordingly. Even when she was a coach, she used her team's resources in an optimal way to gain maximum benefit for India. She knew the strong points of her own bowlers and what they could do under different circumstances.

Her strategic acumen and dedication to the game helped in nurturing a competitive team. Under her leadership, the team saw notable successes, including a series win against New Zealand. Purnima Rau's commitment to promoting women's cricket paved the way for future generations, inspiring young players to pursue the sport professionally.

Nowadays she lives on her farm in Mulugu where she does organic farming, harvests paddy, tomatoes, corn and fruits and also keeps a host of animals. Looking back at her chequered career she has no regrets. In an interview to the Times of India she said: "I enjoy watching our girls in action on the television and I also read newspaper articles about our present-day players. I am very proud of them and wish them all the best."

Now she is happy to be living and working on her farm. She told the interviewer: "When I was a young girl, I never thought that one day I would become the captain or the coach of the Indian team. Yet life took me to those levels. Now in this village I can see a lot of energetic young boys and girls. Maybe I will teach them a little about sport and perhaps from among them a good player may emerge.

Despite facing challenges typical of her era, including limited resources and recognition, Purnima Rau's resilience and passion for the game set her apart. Post-retirement, she continued to contribute to cricket as a coach and mentor, sharing her valuable insights with aspiring players. Purnima Rau remains a celebrated figure in Indian women's cricket, leaving a legacy that echoes the growth and evolution of women's cricket in the country.

Chapter 20

Habib Khan

Hyderabad has produced many good spin bowlers, especially off spin bowlers. But when it comes to fast bowling, the names are very few. Now we have a Mohammed Siraj who plays regularly in the Indian team and does well on many occasions. In the past, there were some very good fast medium pacers who could move the ball either way and pose difficult questions for the batsmen with their seam movement.

Names like D. Govindaraj, Syed Abid Ali, P. Jyotiprasad, Rajesh Yadav, Abdul Bari Wahab, K. Sainath and Narenderpal Singh are the ones who come readily to one's mind when talking about this category. They were hard working, had stamina and used to give Hyderabad the breakthroughs when the need arose.

Unmatchable in speed.

But for sheer pace and hostile bounce there were few bowlers who could match the towering Habib Khan. His tremendous height (he was about six feet six inches tall) and his burly physique made him look like a West Indian fast bowler born in Hyderabad. Indeed, he was no less intimidating than Wesley Hall or Charlie Giffith, the duo from Barbados, who were then the most feared bowlers in the world.

I have heard from M.L. Jaisimha that on many occasions batsmen were terrified of facing him. Another person who told me about the speed of Habib Khan was badminton coach S.M. Arif. The soft spoken badminton coach who guided the careers of many top Indian shuttlers such as Saina Nehwal, Gutta Jwala, Manoj Kumar and many others, was a cricket player and an opening batsman when he was young.

Arif sahab told me once that he had faced Habib Khan on matting wickets and he could hardly see the ball after it left the tall bowler's hands. Most batsmen would play by guesswork when Habib Khan was bowling with the new ball.

Habib was terrifying, says Arif.

"The ball used to come in a flash. Delivered from that great height, it often kicked up terrifyingly. And you must remember that back then we had no helmets or good quality protective gear. It was very difficult to face him," said Arif. Why the Indian selectors did not give him a try was a mystery. especially since India did not have genuinely quick bowlers back then.

Habib Khan had the pace and the ability to extract bounce from the pitch which could have rattled the best international batsmen. But despite being ignored at the national level, Habib Khan never showed any disappointment. He was truly like a gentle giant who was ferocious only when he was bowling on the cricket field. When not bowling, he was very gentle mannered, jovial and affable in nature.

In first class cricket he represented Hyderabad, Railways and Services by turns. He played 40 first class matches between 1956 and 1971 and picked up 114 wickets at an average of

23.28 per wicket. His best bowling performance was eight for 51. Later he took up coaching and did a good job there too.

When he passed away Hyderabad lost one of its famous cricket personalities. In his heyday, the towering Habib Khan was reckoned to be the fastest bowler in India. When I met him in the 1980s, he was no longer a player but some of his fans used to refer to him as the Joel Garner of Hyderabad.

One can imagine the plight of S.M. Arif. Since the badminton coach was an opening batsman, one can visualize that coping with the new ball in the hands of the fearsome Habib Khan must have been a daunting prospect.

A gentle giant with phenomenal strength.

Habib Khan was also known for his phenomenal strength. Umpire Swaminathan told this writer once that if Habib Khan gripped a bat with one hand and if you tried to wrench it out of his grasp with both your hands, using your full strength, you would never be able to pull it out of his grasp. Such was the strength of his grip.

But at the same time the huge fast bowler always had a bright smile on his face. He was always ready to exchange a joke or a few friendly words with everybody he encountered on the streets. Moreover, he was a down to earth and humble human being.

When interacting with him, you never got the impression that he was a reputed fast bowler. He did not get the rewards that he deserved in his game but he took the ups and downs of life in his stride and did not put on any airs.

P.R. Man Singh who was the Secretary of the Hyderabad Cricket Association for many years and had managed the Indian teams on some occasions, has written in a book:

"Even today, Mohammed Nissar and Amar Singh are talked about as the greatest fast bowlers to have played for India before the advent of Kapil Dev. During the 1950s and 1960s anyone with a bit of pace could have played for India, such was the dearth of fast bowlers in the country."

Man Singh adds: "One may recall that India's number two wicket-keeper Budhi Kunderan once opened the bowling for India in a Test match. Once M.L. Jaisimha opened the bowling wearing tennis shoes. The whole concept of opening the bowling for India had become a joke. It was during this period that Habib Khan of Hyderabad came into the scene. It is unfortunate that despite such a shortage of fast bowlers, he did not play for India in Tests."

Habib Khan belonged to a family of cricketers. His father was Ibrahim Khan who was also a good fast bowler who played for Hyderabad in the Ranji trophy with great success. Ibrahim Khan who was affectionately referred to as Bade Khan sahab was a very intelligent bowler who could spot and utilise the rival batter's weaknesses. In this respect he was even superior to Habib Khan, say the old timers.

Habib Khan showed promise in his early years and went on to play for Hyderabad juniors and then made his Ranji trophy debut against Madras. After Retirement he offered his services to Hyderabad cricket in various roles, but is most fondly remembered as a popular cricket coach. He passed away on 10th January in 2021 mourned by thousands of cricket fans and people who knew him and loved him.

Chapter 21

Kawaljeet Singh

One of my favourite off spinners of Hyderabad is my friend Kawaljeet Singh. He had a lovely action and delivered the ball with a beautiful loop. There was beauty in his bowling and one could watch him bowl for hours without getting bored of it. His superb flight often deceived many batsmen into committing errors. But Kawaljeet was also a very unlucky bowler. Very often catches would be dropped off his bowling. Being the fighter that he was, he took it all in his stride and soldiered on like a true sportsman.

Kawal's close friends also know that he is an excellent singer and can sing Hindi film songs very beautifully. His rendition of soulful ghazals can charm the listeners. During his student days he used to take part in several cultural programmes and kept the audience mesmerised with his songs. That is yet one more talent that the tall slim Kawal has.

Kawal used to come to my office from time to time - just for a chat with me and my colleagues - and we would go over to a nearby eatery for a cup of tea and Osmania biscuits that Hyderabad is famous for. He constructed a beautiful house for himself and his family and still lives there with his attractive looking pet dogs which are very well trained and obedient.

An unlucky player.

He was unlucky not to have ever been considered for the Indian Test or ODI teams but he did play for the Indian A team against Holland. His case is yet one more of those examples where we see players of great merit who should have been picked up by the Indian selectors but for unknown reasons were never considered to play for the Indian senior team.

Many experts of cricket including famous former players and experienced cricket writers in the media have often praised Kawal's ability to make the ball talk. His teammates say that from close in positions, they could hear the ball spinning like a top when he bowled one of his viciously turning deliveries.

He was praised by all analysts of the game as a genuine spinner of the ball and an excellent prospect. So why he was not given an opportunity to display his potential at the highest level remains a mystery to this day. He was one of the unluckiest cricketers of Hyderabad along with players like Govindaraj and Jayantilal.

Kawaljeet made his first-class debut for Hyderabad in the 1980 season of the Ranji trophy but he had to struggle in the first few years of his career because Hyderabad already had senior spin bowlers such as Shivlal Yadav and Arshad Ayub. However, his talent did enable him to give a good account of himself and he caught the media›s attention in several important matches.

Genuine reason to feel disappointed.

It is not difficult to imagine how disappointed Kawal feels at not having got a chance to don the India colours for Test and ODI matches. He took about 150 wickets in three seasons of the Ranji trophy in the mid-1990s. He was the leading wicket taker in India during that period. He never lost his love for the game and he never lost his confidence and fighting spirit.

Selected for Indian A team.

Eventually in the 1994–95 season he got a big opportunity to prove himself when he was selected for the South Zone, India A and the Board President's XI. He took 47 wickets at an average of 21.31. He followed up his good work in the 1998–99 season, when he snapped up 51 wickets at an average of 23.58.

He was one of the five cricketers to be named as Indian Cricketer of the Year in 1998. In the Ranji season of 1999-2000, Kawaljeet who was by then a veteran of 40 plus years, took 62 wickets. It was a fantastic performance indeed. Only the great Bishan Singh Bedi had more wickets in a year when he scalped 64 victims in 1974-1975.

Kawal made his final first-class appearance in 2001 in which he took nine wickets and thereafter he announced his retirement from the team.

An excellent coach.

After retirement, Kawaljeet took up coaching. He worked as the bowling coach of Hyderabad and then the IPL team of Deccan Chargers signed him as the assistant coach in the first season. The Deccan Chargers management bowed out of the event and the Hyderabad team is now known as Sunrisers Hyderabad under a new management. Kawal also worked as the Hyderabad Under-19 coach and was the director of Hyderabad Cricket Academy for a period.

Later Nagaland offered him the job of coaching its state team and he has been doing that job diligently ever since. Thanks to Kawal's guidance Nagaland has improved its standard considerably.

The Hyderabad franchise in the IPL, which is now owned by the Sun Group of Chennai, was founded in 2012 after the Deccan Chargers (sometimes also called Chargers by Hyderabad fans) were terminated by the IPL council. Kawal was one of the coaches for Deccan Chargers.

The Sunrisers team is currently being coached by West Indies batting legend Brian Lara. The captain is Aiden Markram of South Africa and its home ground of the Rajiv Gandhi International Cricket Stadium which has a full capacity of 55,000 spectators.

Chapter 22

Khalid Abdul Qaiyum

Khalid had returned to Hyderabad for an extended stay to set up a cricket coaching centre named K & S Residential Academy at CBR ground in Gollur near Shamshabad along with another former Ranji trophy player Salamath Ali Khan.

Before leaving for the USA in 1990, Khalid had already trained several youngsters at the All Saint's High School premises who later played in the Ranji trophy. The new academy will have all the latest facilities and the enterprising duo of Khalid and Salamath hope to produce more top level cricketers.

Khalid belonged to the Golden period.

Khalid belonged to the golden period of Hyderabad cricket of the 1980s. He made his debut in 1976 in the Ranji trophy. He was a sound middle order batsman and a reliable bowler. His best moment was when he won the Ranji trophy as a member of the Hyderabad team in the 1986-1987 season.

When Khalid was at his best, he was the sheet anchor of the Hyderabad batting line up. There were many attractive stroke players in the side but that also meant that sometimes Hyderabad would lose a few quick wickets without too many runs on the board.

That was when the side needed someone with a steady mind and a sound technique to hold the innings together.

That is the role Khalid was fully prepared for. He was the right man for the job. With admirable focus and discipline, he could stop the fall of wickets and also compile runs at a steady but not galloping pace. Every team needs a player like Khalid in the middle order and Hyderabad was lucky to have his services for 14 long years.

Khalid ended up playing 67 first class matches in which he scored 3368 runs at an average of 40.57. His highest was a superbly gritty knock of 203. Whenever he was handed the ball, he had the ability to break a well settled partnership. In first class cricket he took 27 wickets at an average of 39.77 per wicket. His best was three wickets which he scalped for only ten runs.

Khalid was a left hander both in batting and in bowling. According to some scientific theories, left handed people are more artistic than right handers. Some famous people like the sculptor Michelangelo, artist and inventor Leonardo da Vinci, actors Tom Cruise, Robert de Niro and Julia Roberts are left- handed. In cricket there have been some legendary batsmen who were left handed such as Sir Gary Sobers, Brian Lara, Mathew Hayden, Sourav Ganguly and many others. So Khalid is in great company.

Most cherished knock.

His most cherished knock was the century that he scored for Hyderabad against the Rest of India team in the Irani Trophy in the same year. That was the season, when under the leadership of Hyderabad's most successful captain M. V. Narasimha (Bobby) Rao, Hyderabad won the Ranji as well as Irani trophy tournaments.

In 1990 Khalid left his home town and settled in Atlanta in the USA where he worked in the IT sector. There he also coached about 100 boys who were interested in cricket. Mostly these boys were from Indian, Pakistani, Bangladeshi, Australian and English backgrounds. So as a coach Khalid has had a huge amount of experience.

But the way things are being done in Hyderabad has left him disappointed. "This is not the Hyderabad that I used to know in my student life. People were caring and social life was easy going. There was a sense of pride in being a Hyderabadi. We were different and there was a feeling of harmony with nature.

Life in Hyderabad used to be leisurely.

"Life in Hyderabad was not a rat race. We had time to sit and chat endlessly in Irani hotels over a cup of tea. But now many of those famous old cafes have been demolished. The old cinema halls have gone too. They have been replaced by posh shopping malls. Life has become very fast paced. Nowadays the people of Hyderabad don't spend as much time with friends like we used to do when I was young and permanently residing in this city," said Khalid.

Chapter 23

Hyderabad, the Home of Talent. Part One

NOEL DAVID

There have been some players from Hyderabad who played for India for a brief period but had enormous talent. One such player was my friend Noel David. I have covered several of his matches and what struck me most about his game is that he is willing to back up his inborn talent with a lot of hard work. He played four ODI matches for India in 1997.

He attended the All Saints High School which has produced some famous players like Syed Abid Ali, Mohammed Azharuddin and Venkatapathi Raju. Back then his forte was running on the track. He was a very good 100 metre and 200 metre track athlete. Later when he began to play cricket this sprinting ability was immediately apparent because he could cover the ground like lightning in the outfield.

In fielding nobody could match him. Sunil Gavaskar once said that Noel was the greatest ever fielder in the Indian cricket team. So too did the Caribbean commentator Tony Cozier. Gavaskar even compared Noel David with the legendary Jonty Rhodes.

On one occasion when he ran out Kapil Dev the famous all rounder sportingly applauded his superb fielding.

Noel used to enjoy showing his ability in fielding. For him, fielding was the most enjoyable aspect of cricket and he always loved it. And he loved to hear people say that he was India's best fielder.

The man who helped him to hone his fielding skills was the reputed coach Sampath Kumar. It was Sampath whose training and guidelines helped Noel to become one of the finest fielders in the land. Unfortunately, this excellent coach who helped many players of Hyderabad passed away early.

Noel David was a bowling all-rounder - a dependable off-break bowler and a reliable man with the bat. But his strength was his fielding with which he saved dozens of runs in every match. Noel scored a double-century in just his second game as part of Hyderabad's record 944.

That record was one of the greatest moments of his career. None of the Hyderabad batters had realized that they were heading for a record. But it turned out to be a glorious day for Hyderabad cricket. Two double hundreds came from Noel and Vivek Jaisimha and one triple hundred from M.V. Sridhar.

Noel followed it up with the then quickest hundred in the Ranji One Day game. He scored a century in 74 balls. This was a record which was later broken by Sachin Tendulkar who scored his century in 71 balls.

Noel David was sent to the West Indies during the 1997 series in order to replace Javagal Srinath who was on the injured list. Once Noel got the opportunity to show his mettle in the ODI matches people sat up and took notice. Not only was his fielding at a fantastic level, he also showed the ability to take wickets. In his debut match he took three wickets for 21 runs.

Noel left for the USA in 1999 when he knew that he had no chance to get back to the Hyderabad side. He played and coached in the USA till his contract had ended. Thereafter he returned to Hyderabad to try and make a return to the Hyderabad team at least for limited overs matches.

But he could not gain the nod of the selectors. So, once again he went abroad to seek greener pastures. He got an opportunity to go to Dubai to work as a coach and he accepted that opening.

Noel still carries some great memories. When he was junior, he had never dreamt that he would one day play alongside the legendary Sachin Tendulkar or that he would become a good friend of the Master Blaster. Noel also got to meet players like Brian Lara, Arjuna Ranatunga, Carl Hooper and many others who were all great players of spin.

Bowling to these wonderful batsmen was an unforgettable experience for Noel. He also met some of his idols in spin bowling such as Muttiah Muralitharan and Saqlain Mushtaq during the Asia Cup.

PRAGYAN OJHA

Pragyan Ojha showed his class as an attacking left arm spinner and left-handed tail end batter for his side Hyderabad. Interestingly, he was one of the very few players who have taken more wickets than the runs they have scored in Test cricket.

Ojha was born in Odisha and he began showing a great interest in cricket when he was a schoolboy and started training at the Sahid Sporting Club for a summer camp in Bhubaneswar. His game developed further while he was studying at the DAV Public School in Chandrasekharpur.

Three years later, his family moved to Hyderabad and he resumed his studies at the Bhavan's Sri Ramakrishna Vidyalaya in Sainikpuri. At this time he also found a very able coach in T. Vijaya Paul. The coach had been a good first class cricketer and played 34 matches for Hyderabad in the Ranji trophy.

Vijaya Paul had been a very good player himself and played from 1974 to 1883. He was a solid middle order batsman who could hold one end firm and also score at a rapid pace if required. In the Hyderabad league he used to represent Andhra Bank. After retiring from the game as a player Paul continued to be associated with the game as a coach and his vast experience was useful to Ojha.

Paul who became a very sought after coach in the twin cities, known for his systematic and disciplined coaching methods, trained both Ojha and Ambati Rayudu. **Paul taught Ojha the basic principles of spin bowling, when to flight, what length to bowl to which batsman, how to develop different varieties and how to probe a batsman's weaknesses.**

Ojha prospered under Paul's guidance and made his debut in first class cricket in 2004. He represented the Indian under-19 team too. In the 2006–2007 Ranji Trophy season Ojha finished with a creditable 29 wickets at a noteworthy average of 19.89 in just six games.

Ojha represented Hyderabad in domestic cricket tournaments from 2004 till 2015 and then played for the Cricket Association of Bengal as a guest player for two seasons. When the IPL tournament got underway, Ojha was picked up by Deccan Chargers and then Mumbai Indians.

His wonderful rate of success in the domestic cricket matches fetched him a place in the Indian squad for the Bangladesh tour and Asia Cup in 2008. He played his first ODI match against Bangladesh and took two wickets for 43 runs.

In 2009 Ojha made his Test debut for India in the second Test against Sri Lanka in Kanpur. Again he achieved moderate success by taking two wickets for 37 runs in one innings and two for 36 in the second innings. But he contributed to India's win over Bangladesh.

On his T20 debut he got off to a great start. Playing against Bangladesh on 6th June 2009, he took four wickets for 21 runs in four overs. He was awarded the Man of the Match title for his outstanding performance which tilted the match in India's favour.

Thereafter Ojha performed exceedingly well in the following editions of IPL. Among those who lavished praise on him were Adam Gilchrist and Sachin Tendulkar. In the third edition of the IPL, Ojha was awarded the Purple Cap for picking up the most wickets in the tournament. On three occasions he has been a member of IPL winning teams, once for Deccan Chargers and twice for Mumbai Indians.

In August, 2011 he signed a contract to play for Surrey for the final few weeks of the season. His 24 wickets in four games helped Surrey to gain a promotion to Division One of the LV County Championship. During the first Test of the West Indies Tour of India, he engineered a rout by taking six wickets for 72 runs in the first innings.

In an interview in 2008 Ojha credited Venkatapathi Raju with being his inspiring figure. He took motivation from Raju's feats and decided to emulate his idol.

On 21st February 2020, he announced his retirement from all forms of cricket. He had a noteworthy career to look at. He played 48 international matches including 24 Tests, 18 ODIs and 6 T20 internationals. In his last game for India which was a Test match against the West Indies, Ojha took 5 for 40 in the first innings and five for 49 in the second innings to finish off with 10 wickets in the match while conceding 89 runs. Fittingly he was named the Man of the Match.

AMBATI RAYUDU

Even when he was a beginner in cricket, Rayudu was a player of immense talent. For India he played 61 limited overs matches for the national team as a reliable middle-order batsmen. Sometimes he also showed his skill as a wicket keeper as well as an off spin bowler.

His father Sambasiva Rao was the one who inspired Rayudu to take up cricket seriously and devote his life to it. His father got him admitted to coaching camps under good coaches and saw to it that Rayudu's talent would get a chance to blossom.

In 1992 Rayudu's father took him to the cricket academy that was being run by former Hyderabad first class cricketer Vijaya Paul and there Rayudu's career flourished. According to Vijaya Paul, Rayudu's father used to ferry him around the twin cities from school to coaching camp to matches on his two-wheeler. The father used to stand at the side of the ground and watch his son playing and practicing every day.

Rayudu began his career by playing for the Hyderabad youth teams in the late 1990s. He played for the Under-16 and Under-19 levels and got a place in the India Under-15 side for the ACC Under-15 Trophy. There he finished as the leading run-scorer of the tournament and bagged the Man of the Match award in the final against Pakistan.

Some steady scoring at age group levels saw him getting promoted to the senior team of Hyderabad in 2002. He made his first class debut for Hyderabad in January of that year at the age of 16 at the season's Ranji trophy tournament. It was a notable achievement indeed for a boy so young. Rayudu appeared in all matches for Hyderabad in the 2002-2003 season of the Ranji trophy which saw him at his peak.

While playing only his third Ranji game, Rayudu scored 210 and 159 not out against Andhra in the same match which made him a contender for an India cap. With that knock he also became the youngest player in the history of Ranji Trophy to score a double century and a century in the same match.

In 2003, Rayudu got more experience as a member of the India A team during its West Indies and England tours. He averaged 87 on the England tour following which experts opined that he is "sure to play for India in the near future".

In 2007 when the unofficial ICL cricket tournament was organised Rayudu joined the bandwagon. The BCCI issued a stern warning that participating players would be banned from the BCCI's domestic season but that did not prevent several of India's leading stars from getting involved in the ICL.

In 2009, the BCCI granted amnesty to 79 Indian players in the ICL, including Rayudu, allowing them to return to Indian domestic cricket. Rayudu returned to play for Hyderabad. But when Hyderabad was relegated to the Plate division, Rayudu switched his allegiance to Baroda.

Rayudu finished as Baroda's leading run-getter with 566 runs in nine matches including an unbeaten double hundred. In the 2011-2012 Ranji season, he averaged 48.75 with two centuries. He was then recalled to the India A squad on its New Zealand tour and scored 105 and 26 not out against New Zealand A.

In December 2012, the newly formed selection panel, chaired by former hard hitting batter Sandeep Patil selected Rayudu as the replacement player for the injured Manoj Tiwary for the forthcoming T20 series against England. But unfortunately, Rayudu was not included in the playing eleven for the matches.

In 2013 Rayudu was selected in a second string Indian squad for the tour of Zimbabwe. He made his international debut in the first ODI of the series, on 24th July 2013, and played a crucial role in India's victory. He became the 12th Indian batsman to score a half-century on ODI debut. In domestic cricket Rayudu has represented Hyderabad, Andhra, Baroda and Vidarbha while in the IPL he has been picked up by Mumbai Indians and Chennai Super Kings.

HANUMA VIHARI

Test cricketer Hanuma Vihari, born in Kakinada, can be classified mainly as a player from Andhra but he has also represented Hyderabad and Sunrisers Hyderabad team in the IPL. In August 2018, Vihari was selected to join the Indian Test team for two Tests against England. He made his Test debut in September 2018, in the fifth Test match and scored his maiden half-century (56 off 124 balls) in the first innings. In that match, he dismissed England's highest ever Test run scorer Alistair Cook.

In December 2018, Vihari was called up for the series against Australia where too, he gave a good display. India won the series 2-1. Later against the West Indies, Vihari scored 93 runs off 128 balls in the 2nd innings of the 1st Test match. It was a very crucial innings for India. In the second Test match against the West Indies, Vihari scored his maiden Test century.

In 2019, he was selected for India's three match Test series against South Africa in India and played only in the 1st Test and this was his first ever international match in India. In February 2020, he was called for India's Test series against New Zealand in New Zealand and scored a half century in the first innings of the second Test.

He overcame the Australian attack in the 2020–2021 series between India and Australia in the third Test at Sydney with an unbeaten 23. He played 161 balls and ensured that India was able to draw the march. While batting in the 4th innings and last day of the match, Vihari suffered a hamstring injury but bravely carried on and saved the match for India. Given his talent, he still has many years of cricket left in him.

N.T. TILAK VARMA

In recent times, one of the most exciting prospects to have emerged from Hyderabad is the dashing run getter Tilak Varma. Born on 8th November, 2022, he rose rapidly in the ranks of Hyderabad cricket under the guidance of an able coach named Salam Bayas.

Bayas took him under his wing and trained him at the Legala Cricket Academy in Lingampally. The coach used to ferry Tilak to his academy and back home on his scooter, a journey of more than 40 km each way, until the Varma family relocated themselves closer to the academy.

Tilak made his first class debut for Hyderabad in the 2018-2019 Ranji trophy season. In the tournament, he scored 215 runs in seven matches at a strike rate of 147.26. He made his T20 debut for Hyderabad in the Mushtaq Ali trophy in the 2018-2019 season. In 2019, he was named in India's squad for the Under 19 World Cup of 2020.

Tilak has done well in the IPL. In 2022 he was bought by Mumbai Indians. The base price was Rs. 20 lakh but he was bought for Rs. 1.7 crore. In the second match of the league, he scored 61 off 33 balls against Rajasthan Royals.

In April 2023, he scored an 84 off 46 balls against RCB Bangalore in the first match of the 2023 IPL. In the playoff match against Gujarat Titans he scored 43 runs off just 14 balls.

In July 2023, he got his maiden call-up for the Indian cricket team for its T20 series against the West Indies. In his T20I debut on 3 August 2023, in the first match of the series, he top-scored for India with 39 off just 22 deliveries and he managed to take 2 catches in the same match. Later he made his first half century in T20 internationals for India.

Chapter 24

Hyderabad, The Home of Talent. Part Two

Hyderabad has produced several wonderfully talented cricketers who have made a mark for themselves in domestic cricket as well as international cricket.

ABDUL AZEEM

In the 1980s, Hyderabad cricket was blessed to have a galaxy of exciting stroke makers in its batting line up. Led by M.V. Narasimha Rao, Hyderabad won the Ranji trophy and the Irani Trophy in the 1986-1987 season. Foremost among the Hyderabad batters was the hard hitting Abdul Azeem whose shots could send the ball like a bullet to the boundary line.

There was a saying among all teams in those days. They used to say: "Azeem miya ka hath set ho gaya, to Hyderabad ki jeet pakki." The dashing opening batsman passed away on 18th April 2023 and left his admirers in sorrow. He had been suffering from a kidney ailment since 2021 and finally lost the battle at the age of 62.

In the dressing room he was a quiet person. He preferred to find a corner chair where he could remain unobserved. He spoke when someone else spoke to him. Otherwise, he stayed absolutely silent. That was his personality. But put a bat in his hands and he transformed into a rampaging run scorer who forced all rival bowlers to duck for cover. The audacity of his shots was astonishing and he packed immense power behind every hit.

He was the first player from the south zone and the seventh Indian batsman to score a triple century in the Ranji trophy championship (versus Tamil Nadu). In a 15-year career for the Hyderabad team he scored 4644 runs in first class cricket. He was unlucky never to have been considered for the Indian team. Had he been born several years later and taken part in the IPL, he would have been a great success.

Azeem hailed from a family of cricket players. His brother Abdul Jabbar carved out a very successful career in domestic cricket. While Jabbar represented Tamil Nadu, Azeem rose to the top while playing for his home state of Hyderabad.

He was a batsman who was never afraid to play his shots and cared little for the reputation of the bowler who was bowling to him even if it was Kapil Dev or Manoj Prabhakar.

That devil-may-care bravery was possessed by very few batsmen in India. Yet he was always humble. Aiming for big name and fame was not in his mental make up. He told journalist Sudheer Mahavadi once: "I always played because of my passion for the game. I never had dreams of making it big or becoming famous, Cricket meri shauq thi. Aur kuch nahin."

India's batting maestro G.R. Vishwanath once described Azeem thus: "He was an aggressive batsman and a class entertainer who enjoyed the game himself and made the spectators enjoy it too."

Later Azeem became a coach and helped Mohammed Siraj to reach the level he has reached now. Azeem was also a selector for the junior team.

These days what is needed are a few good men like Abdul Azeem. He was an excellent batter and an upright sportsman. Hyderabad has lost an asset who will always be remembered by his numerous fans.

M.V. SRIDHAR

M.V. Sridhar was one of the most consistent batsmen ever produced by Hyderabad. He became the state's leading scorer in the Ranji trophy with a combination of a sound defence and equally sound temperament. His batting style was always unruffled and calm. But he never allowed the bowlers to dominate him.

He played in 97 first class matches and scored 6701 runs at an average of 48. 91. This was really an extremely good average and his top score was 366 against Andhra. This happened when Hyderabad piled up a record total of 944 for six declared. Vivek Jaisimha and Noel David both scored double centuries to give him a stand.

A prolific right-hand batsman, Sridhar had 21 first-class centuries in a career that lasted from 1988 to 1999-2000. Sridhar was one of three Hyderabad batsmen to record a first-class triple-century. The others were VVS Laxman and Abdul Azeem. His knock of 366 against Andhra in 1994 is the third-highest individual score in the Ranji Trophy, behind Bhausaheb Nimbalkar's innings of 443 not out and Sanjay Manjrekar's knock of 377.

Later Sridhar became secretary of the Hyderabad Cricket Association as well as a General Manager (Operations) in the BCCI. He was a qualified doctor and to many friends he was known only as Doc. But eventually as it turned out he failed to take care of his own health. He passed away due to a sudden and massive heart attack at the age of 51, a few days before his daughter was scheduled to get married. The news left Hyderabad's numerous cricket fans and all his friends in deep shock.

SAAD BIN JUNG.

Saad Bin Jung was the nephew of Tiger Pataudi and played for Hyderabad and south zone. After playing inter-schools cricket in the Coch Behar trophy tournament, Saad was selected to play his first-class debut match for India Under-22s against the touring West Indies team in 1978.

Opening the batting, he scored an impressive 58 against the top level West Indies fast bowlers. A few days later, also against the West Indians, he made 113 for the south zone team. Thereafter he was selected for an Indian Board President's XI against the West Indians later in the season, and also against the Pakistan team. However, that match was washed out.

In the Ranji trophy season of 1979-1980 he scored an unbeaten 136 against Tamilnadu. The following season he was unable to play all the matches due to illness. After playing for Haryana in the 1983-1984 season, Saad decided to devote his energies to nature conservation and retired from cricket although he was only in his early 20s then. He and his wife now run a resort in the forests of Karnataka.

SHAHID AKBAR

Another fine player who passed away early was Shahid Akbar. He was truly a great player gifted with extraordinary natural talent. He could play shots on a difficult wicket against top class bowling that would leave his own teammates and the spectators awestruck. As a fielder there was no one better than him at sprinting after the ball in the outfield. He was a very fast runner and it was a thrilling sight to see him covering the ground.

He used to visit my office frequently since he lived nearby. After retirement he was keen to receive the pension that the BCCI had just then brought out for former players. There was some discrepancy in the BCCI records about the number of matches he had played and he was seeking to rectify the mistake by providing documentary proof of his career record.

Shahid died of multiple organ failure at the age of 54. When he began his cricket career everyone had expected that a man with so much talent would surely play for India one day. But finally, that did not happen. He ended his career with just 31 first-class matches, and a highest score of 97.

SULTAN SALEEM and NAGESH HAMMAND

When I became a journalist, I heard a lot about two exciting players namely Sultan Saleem and Nagesh Hammand whose exploits were on everyone's lips back then. But I never covered their matches because they had stopped playing when I became a sports writer.

I have heard that Nagesh was a very sound batsman and a great fielder in any position. As a batsman he had hammered all opposition in the Rohinton Baria trophy while representing Osmania University. He also led Hyderabad juniors in the south inter association tournaments for the P. Ramachandra Rao trophy.

Sultan Saleem, according to my seniors, was a player who should have been given the opportunity to play for India. His journey began in a dazzling manner but for some reason he was unable to keep up the momentum in the later stages of his career.

While still a schoolboy he scored a triple century and a double century which led many knowledgeable observers to predict a bright future for the young lad from All Saints High school. After doing well for the south zone schools team he was selected in the Indian schools team that was to tour Ceylon (now Sri Lanka) in 1962. Unfortunately, the tour had to be called off because an epidemic had broken out in the island nation.

As a student of Osmania University Sultan Saleem played an important role in guiding Osmania University to victory in the inter university Rohinton Baria trophy tournament.

JUNIOR STARS

Other Hyderabad players who represented India's junior and schools teams included Zahid Ali Khan, Sultan Saleem, Khader Hussaini, Syed Iftekharuddin, Mazhar Ali Baig, D. Inder Raj, P. Jyothiprasad, Abdul Aziz Sayeed Asif, M.A. Iqbal, Mohammed Mushtaq, Gour Mohan Raj, T. Pawan Kumar, Ananta Vatsalya, Masood Ahmed, Abbas Ali Khan, Akram Quadri, Arjun Yadav, Ambati Rayudu, Aaron Paul, Abhinav Kumar, Mohammed Ghouse, T. Suman, D.B. Ravi Teja and Conrad Fruvall whose father Norbert Fruvall had been selected in the Indian football team for the 1948 Olympic Games. In the 1940s, Norbert Fruvall was the captain and the coach of the famous Hyderabad City Police football team which was then among the best football teams in India. He also captained Hyderabad in its first appearance in the Santosh trophy national championship. His son Conrad was a batsman who played for Indian Schools in 1973 and represented the Hyderabad Cricket Association's team in the Moin ud Dowlah

Gold Cup tournament. Hyderabad players who played for the India A team include Kawaljeet Singh, Vanka Pratap and Shivaji Yadav while S.A. Hadi represented UAE in the qualifying rounds of the ICC World Cup.

We cannot forget the coaches who guided and helped these players to realize their potential. Few coaches ever got the recognition that they deserved. But in this respect too, Hyderabad was lucky to have had the services of excellent coaches.

The list of coaches is a long one but to name just a few of the most reputed coaches, there were A.R. Bhupathi, E.B. Aibara, M.R. Baig, Sampath Kumar and Vijaya Paul. Many years ago, I also used to see the two brothers Waseemul Haq and Kaleemul Haq coaching little children and girls daily at the Lal Bahadur stadium.

Among all of them, I knew Sampath Kumar, the Haq brothers, Aibara sahab, Baig sahab and Vijaya Paul very well. Bhupathi, Aibara and Baig were immensely knowledgeable men and the players whom they guided benefitted monumentally from their experience and instructions. I often had interesting discussions with all of them. I had also covered many matches in which Paul was playing before he became a coach so I knew him very well and his methods enabled many budding youths to blossom.

❖

Chapter 25

Pacers and Spinners

Hyderabad has been fortunate to have had the services of some excellent bowlers both in the seam as well as spin departments. Although it must be admitted that the spinners achieved more success and fame than the pacers. The pacers included Habib Khan, Ibrahim Khan, Govindaraj, Abid Ali, P. Jyothiprasad, Abdul Bari Wahab (who could also bowl spin), C. Sainath (who terrified many batsmen when he was in form), Rajesh Yadav and Narender Pal Singh (both of them being very destructive seam bowlers).

But it is the spinners who are more often talked about. Starting with Ghulam Ahmed, the list includes Mahendra Kumar, V. Ramnarayan, Naushir Mehta, Mumtaz Hussain, Shivlal Yadav, Arshad Ayub, Kawaljeet Singh, Venkatapathi Raju, Pragyan Ojha and several others.

P. JYOTHIPRASAD

P. Jyothiprasad was a hard working, strongly built right arm medium pacer and also a useful batsman. He began as an off spinner then tried out leg spin, before taking up swing and seam bowling in which he became very successful. Jyothi guided the career of fast bowler Mohamed Siraj before the latter made an entry into the Indian team.

It was Jyothi who perfected the newcomer's action and saw to it that Siraj did not give in to the temptation to bend his elbow and chuck rather than bowl the ball. This was when Jyothi was the chairman of the selection committee in Hyderabad. The veteran recalls that when he saw Siraj bowling for the first time, he was amazed that after many years a Hyderabadi bowler had arrived on the scene who could bowl so fast.

ABDUL BARI WAHAB

Abdul Bari Wahab was an excellent cricketer in all respects. He could bowl left arm medium pace or spin and was also a hard hitting batsman lower down in the order. When Sainath and Wahab opened the bowling for Hyderabad, it was a formidable new ball pair and rival teams had to face a double edged weapon.

He made his first class debut under the captaincy of M.L. Jaisimha. After he stopped playing cricket, Wahab became a coach and gained success as coach of the women's teams. Even at the age of 60 he was still an enthusiastic participant in coaching schemes.

K. SAINATH

K. Sainath was an excellent seam bowler who had a good turn of speed. On a matting wicket he could be ferocious. In first class cricket he represented Railways in the 1977-78 season and then played for Hyderabad from 1978-79 to 1982-83. His best performance in first class cricket was seven wickets for 30 runs while with the bat his top score was 48 not out.

RAJESH YADAV

Rajesh Yadav, younger brother of Shivlal Yadav, was at his best in the mid 1980s. He was a tall and strongly built medium pacer who could extract lift from even slow wickets and he also got some movement off the pitch.

In the role of a right-arm medium pacer Rajesh Yadav played in 60 first class matches. His career lasted 10 seasons, starting from 1984-1985, during which he represented Hyderabad, South Zone and Wills XI. When he was only 19 years old, he made his first-class debut in 1984 against Andhra and picked up four wickets for 65 runs and seven wickets for 64 runs to get off to a brilliant start.

In the 1986-1987 season he was a member of the Hyderabad team that won the Ranji trophy. It was Hyderabad's second triumph in the championship. In the final against a strong Delhi batting line up, Rajesh took five wickets for .114 runs in 33 overs. He was instrumental in denying Delhi the crucial first innings lead which finally decided which team will lift the trophy. "It was an unforgettable experience to defeat the star studded Delhi outfit. It was a very big moment in my cricket career," Rajesh told me later.

Rajesh played for Wills XI in the Wills Trophy later that season and was named in the probables for the 1987 Cricket World Cup. Yadav did not eventually make it into the list of players who represented India in the World Cup. But he continued to have a good first class career which came to an end in 1993. He took 159 wickets at an average of 30.20, including seven five wicket hauls in an innings and two performances of ten wickets in a match.

Rajesh became a cricket coach after retirement as a player. He worked as the head coach of Hyderabad and as a coach at the HCA satellite academy where he trained young fast bowlers. Yadav also served as match referee and selector for HCA.

N.P. SINGH

Narender Pal Singh often known as N.P. Singh or just "NP" was another superb seam bowler who engineered many collapses in teams which played against Hyderabad. He represented Hyderabad for 14 seasons and then worked as a selector.

Such was his mastery over the new ball that he could fox the best batsmen with late outswingers and in cutters. He did not bowl at a fast pace but he was often unplayable because of the late movement. The batsman would play along the right line and when the ball took the outer edge or went through the bat-pad gap, the hapless batsman would have no idea about how it happened.

NP made his first-class debut for Hyderabad when he was only 20 years old in the Ranji season of 1993-1994. In all, he played in 101 first-class matches and took 319 wickets at an average less than 27. He was one of the top four wicket-takers of the 1998-1999 season of the Ranji trophy.

MAHENDRA KUMAR

Mahendra Kumar was a leg spinner who was among the best in India. Those who saw him in action (I was not among those fortunate ones) told me that they had never seen anyone better than Kumar, not even Chandra. When Kumar bowled a googly, the best of batsmen could not spot the wrong one. He was born in Vijayawada but represented both Hyderabad and

Andhra in the course of his career. He also played for VST and Indian Universities.

He ended up with 191 first class wickets with a best performance of eight wickets for 45 runs and later he became a coach. It was when he was a coach that I first got to know him. He was always genial and jovial and was never seen without a smile on his face.

V. RAMNARAYAN

Off spinner V. Ramnarayan was from Tamil Nadu but moved his base to Hyderabad in search of greener pastures in his job and in cricket. In his book titled "Third Man", Ramnarayan has described how he joined the State Bank of India as a Probationary Officer, was posted at Anakapalle and then transferred to Hyderabad because the bank team in Hyderabad needed a cricketer.

He received help and support from Nagesh Hammand, Sultan Saleem and rubbed shoulders with established players like D. Govindaraj, P. Krishnamurthy and other stalwarts. After he took eight for 75 in the final of the Moin ud Dowlah Gold Cup tournament he was picked in the Hyderabad Ranji team.

He made his debut for Hyderabad against Kerala and took six wickets for 33 runs in the first innings. Later, in the first innings of the match against Andhra, he took six for 41. In the quarter-final against mighty Bombay (now Mumbai) he took seven for 68 in the first innings, although Bombay won the match and went on to win the championship.

But Ramnarayan had made a huge impact. With 28 wickets at an average of 17.32, the season of 1975-1976 was his most successful season. He continued to play for Hyderabad in the Ranji Trophy until 1979-80. He also played for the South Zone in the

Duleep trophy. In 1980-81 when, in his last first-class match, he took four wickets for 144 runs off 51 overs. In his first class career he played 25 matches and took 96 wickets with a best performance of seven for 68.

After leaving the game as a player he continued to write articles and books and showed that he was just as good at writing as he was at bowling. His articles on cricket are widely read and enjoyed by a huge readership all over India.

NAUSHIR MEHTA

Naushir Mehta was a wonderful off spin bowler with great potential. Being tall and athletic in physique, he started off as a fast bowler before he switched to bowling right-arm off spin where he found greater success. His father S.R. Mehta was also a very good player and represented Hyderabad in the Ranji trophy in the 1930s and 1940s..

Naushir represented Hyderabad at the first-class level for ten seasons starting from 1967. Naushir and Mumtaz Hussain formed a deadly double spin attack for Hyderabad in the early 1970s. Naushir took 29 wickets in the 1970-71 season of the Ranji trophy and 34 wickets in the next season including five wicket hauls on four occasions.

In the same season, he played for Rest of India against an Indian XI and took the wickets of India's Test captain Ajit Wadekar, Test opener Ashok Mankad and leading all rounder Syed Abid Ali. In his first class career Naushir played 57 matches, took 178 wickets with a best performance of six wickets for only 16 runs.

Naushir's father S.R. Mehta popularly known as Soli was born in Bombay in 1914. Later he moved to Hyderabad and worked in the police department as a fingerprint expert. But apart from his profession, his love was cricket and he was a very talented off spinner.

He represented Hyderabad in the Ranji trophy for ten years from 1936 to 1946. He was a member of the Hyderabad team that won the Ranji trophy in 1938 under the captaincy of Mohammed Hussain. Later Soli became the secretary of the Hyderabad Cricket Association in 1943. He held the post till 1952 and passed away in 1998.

MUMTAZ HUSSAIN

Mumtaz Hussain first caught the eye when he was a university level player. He could bowl different kinds of deliveries including the orthodox left armer, the chinaman, the finger spun delivery that came into the batsman and so on. And he mixed it with a bewildering panache that foxed all the batsmen.

Even his own wicket keeper would fail to read him and he would have to work out a system of signals to indicate to the keeper what he was going to bowl.

Mumtaz made a big impact with a 48 wicket haul for the Osmania University team that won the Rohinton Baria Trophy for the first time in the 1966-67 season. Among his victims in the final against Bombay University was a 17-year-old Sunil Gavaskar who was left stranded on the track and stumped when he failed to read a googly by Mumtaz.

In his book Sunny Days Gavaskar has written that Osmania University with its balanced attack used to bundle out the other sides. He writes that the hero of Osmania University's win that year was left arm spinner Mumtaz Hussain who could mix his Chinaman bowling with his orthodox spin in such a way that nobody could understand what the ball would do.

Gavaskar tried to play a psychological trick on Mumtaz by telling his batting partner: "Don't worry. I have got him sorted out." Mumtaz just smiled and kept pegging away. Suddenly he came up with a well flighted ball that Gavaskar thought could be hit. He stepped out of his crease and found himself nowhere near the pitch of the ball as it dipped suddenly. Gavaskar was stumped when yards out of the crease.

But later when Mumtaz was playing in the Ranji trophy he was less successful for reasons unknown. Maybe batsmen began to figure him out. Mumtaz was also a hard hitting batsman and a good fielder. He was a key member of the illustrious Hyderabad team that was led by M.L. Jaisimha. Other famous names in the side included players of the calibre of Tiger Pataudi, Abbas Ali Baig, Abid Ali, Govindaraj and others. Mumtaz took 173 wickets in a ten year long Ranji trophy career.

Had the famous spin quartet of Bedi, Prasanna, Venkat and Chandra not been ruling the Test scene back then, bowlers like V. Ramnarayan, Naushir Mehta and Mumtaz Hussain could have walked into the Indian team. Unfortunately in those days there was a glut of spinners in India and the Hyderabad spinners never got the opportunities that they deserved.

——◆◆——

Chapter 26

The Commentators

I first began listening to cricket commentary when I was about eleven years old. In 1966-1967 the West Indies team was touring India led by Gary Sobers and I began listening to the running commentary on the radio (we had no TV back then) of every match of that series. I remember some of the names of the commentators included Balu Alaganan (who led Madras in the Ranji trophy), Anant Setalvad and Pearson Surita.

But John Arlott and Alan McGilvray were my favourites. John Arlott was a part of the BBC's Test Match Special team of commentators and he had such an attractive method of explaining the game that he made cricket more fascinating.

Alan McGilvray played several first-class seasons for New South Wales in Australia in the mid-1930s before becoming the doyen of Australian cricket commentators. He became identified as the voice of Australian cricket through his ABC radio broadcasts.

I loved listening to Richie Benaud, Tony Grieg and Henry Blofeld too. Every sport has its own legendary voices that are very closely connected to the game. Cricket, like every other, has its own pantheon of commentators who will be remembered as the voices behind the game.

HARSHA BHOGLE

Many years after I had listened to my first cricket commentary on the radio, Hyderabad's Harsha Bhogle created a niche for himself in the field of commentary. I used to see Harsha at Osmania University several times when I was a student myself. But I did not know him well.

Harsha was a good cricketer himself and had studied at the Hyderabad Public School where his teammates became top level players of those days. Harsha represented Osmania University in the All India Rohinton Baria inter university cricket championship.

He started his commentary career with the All India Radio when he was still a teenager. He had a natural gift for describing the game to listeners and knew what should be said and what need not be said. Much of the proceedings are visible on the screen to the television viewers so a television commentator does not have to give a ball-by-ball description like the radio commentators used to do earlier.

Harsha's wit was brilliant. His one liners were enough to compensate viewers for a boring day's play.

Harsha used to write a column titled Out of The Box in which he shared some of his deep insights and understanding of the nuances of cricket with his readers. In one article he had addressed the question of burnout which plagues many players these days because of the huge load of international cricket that is being played nowadays.

He wrote that the money and the glitz and glamour hide the fact that cricketers are forced to work very hard to keep the system going. The question of how much cricket a player should play is a matter that should be sorted out between those who run the game and those who play it, Harsha has written. If there can be no meaningful debate and no meeting point can be reached then there is trouble ahead.

In his column Harsha had written about his viewpoints on many issues such as match fixing, sledging, ball tampering and many other aspects of the game from the vantage point of being an experienced commentator and a former player himself.

Explaining his role as a commentator Harsha once told an audience: "I remain the teller of the story. Not the story itself". With his gift of humour and quick repartee, he made cricket more exciting and interesting.

CHARU SHARMA

A television personality I used to know well was Charu Sharma. He lived and worked in Hyderabad for a few years and I used to meet Charu often at different sports meets. We sports journalists of Hyderabad once played a cricket match against the VST (Vazir Sultan Tobacco) team where Charu was on the opposing team. He was a lively medium pace bowler and a steady batsman.

Later he moved away from Hyderabad and I lost contact with him. The last occasion when I met him was when I was covering the Commonwealth Games in New Delhi in 2010 and he too was covering the same event for a television channel or was involved in the conduct of the Games in some way. Now I don't recall exactly what role he was playing then.

Charu Sharma served as the stand-in auctioneer during the 2022 Indian Premier League's auction after Hugh Edmeades, the original auctioneer collapsed due to a sudden attack of ill health.

Charu conducted the auction after lunch on the first day, and continued till the last session on the next day, until felt fit enough to Edmeades return to the show.

Other friends I know who work in the field of commentary are C. Venkatesh, Sudheer Mahavadi, A. Joseph Antony and a few others. It is always a pleasure to discuss the various nuances of the game with them from time to time.

ESSAYS ON LIFE FROM THE IN-BETWEEN

SANDWICHED

BETH BULLARD

ISBN: 9798840350690

For my parents,

Charles and Margaret,

who taught me that the true meaning of family

extends far beyond its biological roots.

Contents

Acknowledgements

There are those in my life I have come to consider family. Individuals who have chosen to invest their time and energy cultivating our connection, and the resultant beauty of this intentional commitment is an eternal bond that extends far beyond heredities.

The gratitude I have for these souls knows no bounds. Their steadfast and unconditional love bolsters me in times of uncertainty and cradles me when I fall. The friendship we share has enriched my perspective, produced an infinite catalog of memories and brought prosperity to my life.

To my family, whether friend or genetic, celestial or earthly, you are the foundation from which I leap and the wind beneath my wings.

The Shift

Just exactly how do you think you're going to do it? I asked myself while gazing into the bathroom mirror. The dumbfounded reflection looking back at me confirmed my lack of a plausible answer. I found myself drawn into examining the face before me. That of a woman who by society's standards would be considered middle-aged. The glow of her youth had been dimmed by experience and a suggestion of maturity was sprinkled about her face. Eyes once bright appeared dampened by the weight of responsibility, sorrow, and change.

On the surface, one might think her weary and defeated, but underneath that exterior lay a tenacious soul determined to drop-kick life in the derriere. That girl opted for a cheeky reply. *I'm not sure, but either way it's comin', so buckle up!*

It was life. An unexpected life. In the blink of an eye, a tragic accident claimed my husband declaring me a widow. I'd become a single mother of two teenagers ripe with the angst and anguish that accompanies the age. My son, Jackson, started college in the fall, and my daughter, Kate, high school.

Both awkward freshmen, unsure, insecure and intimidated by everything.

Neither one of them was a risk-taker. Far from it. They required time, clarification and encouragement before braving new situations. When they were younger, I considered their style a gift, as I never worried about them doing impulsive, crazy kid stuff. However, at this age, their approach appeared to be more of a detriment.

The kids weren't the only ones adjusting to new situations. After thirty years on the job, I exited the hamster wheel, electing to take what I considered a self-induced sabbatical. I'd become a stay-at-home mom with two kids who needed me around but didn't want me there. That, coupled with an absent social life, made for a lonely existence. During the first year, I frequently struggled to find my footing, and my sense of purpose often escaped me. I stumbled down a rabbit hole or two but over time discovered a rhythm that suited my new existence.

The dogs, on the other hand, were thrilled with my constant presence as it meant they were no longer resigned to their kennels on weekdays. They became my persistent companions and oftentimes unwelcome distractors, believing that most of my day should be dedicated to the care and keeping of their needs. I attempted to school them otherwise with little success.

Living on four acres with an animal count of three dogs, four cats, thirteen chickens and two horses, suggested there wasn't a lack of things that needed doing. My blank calendar seemed to fill overnight, and I promptly learned I would never be bored. Like many who find themselves free from the nine to five, I began to wonder how I ever did it all. Single mom,

CEO, daughter, friend, caretaker of animals, custodian of the land, and the list goes on.

My role of consultant and caregiver for aging parents shifted upwards on the priority list. They required my support to navigate the health and ability changes that come naturally to octogenarians. At eighty, my mother's health was relatively stable, but my father, now eighty-four, was another story. He'd been diagnosed with prostate cancer a few years earlier, suffered a small stroke the past spring, and sadly, his cancer had metastasized. I'd been able to manage things remotely, but it would only be a matter of time before I'd need to up my game around their care. Fifteen hundred miles lay between us. Remaining flexible and travel-ready became a necessity for my life.

Oh, and if that wasn't enough for my proverbial plate, there was the matter of myself. It was time to get to know the woman in the mirror. She needed to abandon her relentless companion of three years—grief—and begin to navigate the expected and oftentimes unexpected changes presented to us in the in-between: the moment in time where life stops giving and starts taking away.

So much of my existence up until now had been focused on growth. Expanding family, cultivating careers, and building the physical and financial footprint to realize those goals and dreams. Over the years, homes and cars swelled, and career advancement was a must to accommodate the family as well as realize professional aspirations. Creating a life for yourself and those you love is the ultimate development project.

In what seemed like a simple flip of a switch, I found myself facing The Shift. An often unwelcome season in life when matters that previously gave us purpose begin to fade into memory. Traditions once considered sacred become passé, and the magic and wonder of innocence evaporates. Children, now older, no longer hunt for Easter eggs or write letters to Santa Claus. Thoughts of friends, freedom, and moving on dance in their heads.

Shifters begin to reflect on life thus far, identifying priorities and bidding farewell to those things that no longer serve us. Career paths are reevaluated, and leisure pursuits adjusted for physical change. The notion of downsizing and a soon-to-be empty nest swirl in our heads.

I'd become a card-carrying member of the Sandwiched Generation. A group, that at the time of my reflection, was over nine million strong in the United States alone and growing. Each of us struggling to balance the demands of caring for our multigenerational families while simultaneously trying not to lose ourselves amid feelings of depression, guilt and isolation.

I likened my pursuit of life balance to Dorothy's quest in the *Wizard of Oz*. The key to her desire was thought to lie at the end of the yellow brick road—a golden path filled with pitfalls and pleasantries, and she alone must decide which is which. The twisted lane that lay before me felt very similar, and like Dorothy, I encountered beings who supported and furthered my journey as well as creatures who sidetracked my endeavors, but in the end the answers we both sought were within us all along. We simply needed to listen to our hearts and believe in ourselves to realize our desires. A task that sounds so effortless yet many struggle to achieve it in a lifetime.

I believe we all have yellow brick road moments throughout our lives and that path often reveals itself during instances of change or when we need to be reminded of our self-sufficiency. Shortly after being widowed, I found myself in a much different place than I ever expected, planned, or dreamed. I threw myself into work, caring for my children and anything else that would allow me to evade the pain that was emanating from my heart. I knew the road was there but, much like the Lion, needed a catalyst to summon the courage to take those first steps. I don't recall when that happened or what exactly triggered my initial step, just that one day I glanced over my shoulder to discover a road not only before me, but behind me as well. I'd begun to move on.

This epiphany simultaneously excited and frightened me. I became concerned and began to question my path, but with the help of a few fateful companions, I found my footing in the present, focusing on the current month, week, day, and sometimes even the hour. Immersing myself in the moment, savoring every step. I made it a point to remind myself of this action often and am thankful for the incredible memories I've harvested for it.

The past warrants reflection, consideration and respect, but the present is where the magic is made, and if you can do that, the future will be of little consequence as you'll be right where you're supposed to be. A concept that makes perfect sense, but I struggle with it, as I have a tendency to future trip. On that point, I'd say I'm a work in progress.

As I made my way along the golden road, I encountered barriers and distractions aimed at delaying or detouring my progress. Some were strategically placed by creatures I'd stumbled upon or the universe in general, and others came from within. Regardless of the source, the scuffles yielded tools or tidbits I could tuck away in my bag of tricks for future confrontations. I examined how to recognize and side-step doubt and negative self-talk and learned to say "no" to distractions that no longer served me. I became mindful and selective about those who surrounded me, welcoming travelers who brought growth and light to my journey and bidding farewell to companions whose path no longer aligned with mine. When I made mistakes, I studied the missteps, and each time I did, found my load a little lighter and my stride slightly longer.

Outnumbered

Greg, get your ass down here and help me! was my recurrent thought when it came to our children. How dare he leave me to shepherd these two alone, and although I knew it wasn't his choice, I couldn't help but feel I'd gotten the short end of the stick.

Parenting teens can be an unforgiving, relentless affair, and the idea of going through it without my partner in crime was frightening. Gone was our good cop/bad cop tactic and the muscle behind my mandates. I'd lost my heavy, my back was exposed and I was outnumbered. A circumstance I hoped they would never employ to their advantage. I was on a solo mission bound for the asteroid field of adolescence and there was no turning back.

Remaining positive, nimble, and just plain being there was my flight plan for the journey of twists and turns before me. Maneuvers that proved to be relatively successful, but my hull sustained damages that required venting sessions with fellow parents, counseling and a few girl getaways to mend.

My efforts in "being there" were generally accepted by Jackson throughout his teens. He'd listen politely, consider my suggestions and acted on those he deemed logically necessary. Basically, he humored me.

Kate, however, was another story. She considered our time together novel but only as long as it suited her agenda and had no reservations telling me when I crossed the proverbial line. If I talked too much during the morning carpool, I'd receive an eye roll or a searing glance demanding my silence. If I asked too many questions or led the conversation in any way, I'd hear, "Stop CEOing me Mom." But most of the time she'd just say, "Yeah, I'm done talking now," which was code for I don't want to share with you, please go away. I quickly learned that "being there," although necessary, was a thankless solitary assignment.

Brain function in teens expands but doesn't mature until they are well into their twenties. Concrete thinking, lack of insight and inability to appreciate the big picture made communicating a point challenging, and at times impossible. I'd frustratingly stare into dumbfounded faces unable to comprehend or appreciate my position, but from their vantage point, I was without a doubt the daft one. "You don't get it," "You won't understand," and, "You don't know anything," were frequent comments regarding my mental capacity. "It's a miracle I make it out of the house every day," I'd offer in reply.

Kate's egocentric thinking gave rise to insecurity, judgment and peer pressure. Jackson managed to sidestep this teen pitfall due to a keen sense of self and an old soul, but as girls tend to do, Kate landed right in the middle of the enormous sinkhole. She insisted on mirroring the fashion trends of her peers, spent hours on her makeup and hair, and missed the bus countless times her freshman year because of it. I'd explain to her that every time she does that, it makes me late for work, which is unacceptable. My comment was ignored as the thought meant nothing to her.

Puberty launches the physical progression from child to adult, and if unprepared, can bring unwelcome irreversible change, which often gives rise to body image issues and further anxiety. Few of us make it out of our teens unscathed and given that belief, I made sure to talk with both kids about what to expect, when and why. They didn't always appreciate my candor but learned to live with it.

We talked about sex, relationships, and bodily functions while driving from here to there. Car rides offered us unin-terrupted time, and me, a captive audience. We covered a lot of ground during our jaunts around town. I was the initial instigator of our chats, however, over time that shifted to a more fluid exchange, but the one thing that didn't change was how I concluded any sex conversation: "If you think you're mature enough and ready to engage in sex, then you need to demonstrate that by taking the appropriate measures to protect yourself and your partner."

Jackson's facial hair and acne seemed to appear overnight. Thankfully, Greg lived long enough to teach him to shave, and later, a hairdresser friend gave him a full-on male grooming tutorial. Jackson's acne was unrelenting, so after exhausting lesser methods, we elected to navigate the Accutane process. It's complicated, detailed and extensive for boys, but even more so for girls as the drug is known to cause significant birth defects.

The process required a monthly oath of chastity or birth control declaration in the I-Pledge medication portal and a trip to the lab for blood draws. A urine sample was required of girls for pregnancy testing, and some physicians even insisted on oral birth control before beginning the regimen. Jackson endured the process with few side effects and Kate would fare even better years later. I, however, was exhausted by it. Monitoring if and when they took their medication and ensuring the necessary follow up appointments and I-Pledge portal submissions were completed within the prescribed window of time felt like a full-time job.

My mother believed it necessary to offer her assistance when it came to Kate's development. "How's Kate, has she started her period yet?" Mom asked for the umpteenth time.

"No, but she's educated and prepared for when it arrives," I indicated.

We revisited this exchange regularly for over a year. Mom harbored a bit of post-traumatic stress around menstruation, and for good reason. She'd come of age in the 1950s, an era when virginity was valued above practicality or comfort. Tampons, although available, were discouraged for fear they'd sully a young lady before marriage. This misconception resulted in only one appropriate option for unmarried women: awkward belts with bulky pads. I can't imagine how difficult it must have been to wear white in those days.

My mother was trying to look out for her youngest grand-child, her sole biological granddaughter. "You know, she's the only one I have from scratch," she'd say. As a gender reveal, I decorated the nursery in soft pastels, placed a canopy over the crib and had my friend, Lori, paint fairies on the walls. I can still picture the surprise and delight on my mother's face when she learned her daughter was going to have a girl. I also recall the shock and horror on Greg's face when he heard the news.

"I thought I only had to worry about my boys, but now I have to worry about all the boys," he'd say trying to process the fact he was going to have a daughter.

Knowing the special place Kate held in my mother's heart, I understood how important it was for her to shield her granddaughter from the menstruation humiliation she'd endured decades before. I'd acknowledge her concerns and afterward explain to her how our society's ideals have shifted over time. "Mom, menstruation is more mainstream today. The girls in the carpool talk openly about it, and the boys tolerate the conversation."

"Well, that's good," she said with skepticism.

Clearly, we're not done here, I thought.

Two months later, Kate woke to find she'd crossed the menstrual milestone. "My life's over," she said to me.

"Nope, it's just gonna be different," I replied. I pictured what the next forty years had in store for her but said no more.

It was a benign matter from there. She felt comfortable with the mechanics but was crampy and nauseated, so I called her out of school for the day. *Surely this milestone deserves a day off,* I thought. By the time I got home from work, she'd watched YouTube tutorials on the subject, downloaded a period app and was good to go. Kate evaded the bullet of shame that had struck so many before her, and my mother couldn't have been happier to hear it.

My foray into adolescent male self-discovery was aided by those who'd ventured before me. One of the benefits of working in a female-dominated industry is that inevitably at least one coworker had traveled the road you just discovered yourself on. For this particular issue, it was Tess.

Tess and her husband had two boys who frequently colored outside the lines. She'd often shared stories of her recent predicaments with the rest of us. "Welp, last night I found out my oldest spent four thousand dollars on porn," she said while taking her seat at lunch. "I confiscated every electronic in the house, lined them up in the garage and asked him to choose the one I was going to smash first." The table was stunned silent.

"Did you call your credit card company?" I asked after my initial shock faded.

"Yep, working on it," she offered.

In the past year, we'd heard stories about school trouble, fistfights, speeding tickets, acne and sprouting body hair, but we reached a climax with this ditty. Pun intended.

"Oh, and I finally found my missing sofa pillow under his bed. Can you believe it? My expensive designer pillow reduced to a masturbation receptacle. It's ruined!"

The table burst out in laughter.

Later that week I inquired about how things were going, and Tess gave me a follow-up report. "We got the charges reversed but we're not telling him. He's working off the cost of the pillow and the porn." She also asked her husband to have a conversation with both boys about the rules of engagement. Jackson was a toddler at the time, but I tucked away the nuggets Tess offered knowing someday we'd be there. What I didn't know was, by that someday, our we would be reduced to a me.

I leaned on my medical training as a platform for discussion with the kids around bodily functions, and my talk with Jackson was no exception. He'd made a few references that felt like an olive branch, so I went there. We talked openly about nocturnal emissions, masturbation, and the need for a dedicated receptacle.

"Your dad would've wanted you to have this," I said while handing him the pink towel he'd reserved for such activity.

"Was this Dad's?" Jackson asked while staring at the neatly folded bath towel in his hands.

I smiled, nodded in affirmation then said, "From here on out it's your responsibility. Wash it regularly, and that goes for the rest of your laundry as well." As I left his room, I sensed Greg hysterically laughing beside me. I smiled, shook my head and said, "Shoulda been you."

I bought Jackson a mega pack of condoms from Costco for his eighteenth birthday. He'd voiced concern about this lack of knowledge and desire to be confident in their use if the situation ever arose. I wrote, "Luck favors the prepared," on the gift tag.

Kate, being almost four years his junior, wasn't interested in exploring her sexuality yet, but I made a promise to myself that when the day came, I'd treat her no differently than her brother. The centuries-old sexual double standard that judges women differently than men for the same behavior wouldn't be welcome in our home.

A pivotal milestone for teenage independence is a driver's license, and while it's an unnerving notion for parents, it's a rite of passage that's necessary for our freedom. I'd schlepped kids to school, appointments and social events for years, and lately spent most of my weekend nights dozing on the couch waiting for their pick me up from work texts. The thought of liberation from this relentless chore eased my anxiety about unleashing them onto the road.

We made it a year before the first traffic incident call came in. Jackson led with, "Mom, I need to tell you something." I could hear the panic in his voice, and I immediately blurted out, "Are you okay?"

"Yeah, but I got a speeding ticket." My heart sunk for him, and I began to see dollar signs. He was snagged in a well-known speed trap and was cited for traveling fifty-two in a forty mile per hour zone. A blunder that cost him a hundred and thirty-five dollars. His next came six months later and was far worse.

Kate called in a panic, screaming, "We've been in an accident!"

I'd asked Jackson to pick up Kate and a friend on the last day of school. He graciously agreed, took the girls for ice cream, and on the way to drop off the friend, made a left-hand turn on what he said was a yellow light, but the car traveling straight proved otherwise. I immediately dropped what I was doing and headed to the intersection. Thankfully, no one was physically hurt, but the trauma of the experience would take both girls and Jackson some time to recover from. The insurance company totaled the car, raised our rates through the roof, and Jackson and I were headed to traffic court.

"Well, think of it this way, you just proved the accuracy of teen male driving statistics," I offered as we left the courthouse.

"Yep, I certainly have," he despairingly confirmed.

Kate received her license right before the Governor closed schools and restaurants due to the pandemic. I felt utterly jilted. I'd done my time behind the wheel and this moment was supposed to be my release from imprisonment, but instead our cars sat idle and both kids became unemployed online students.

I'm not sure what else is in store for us during this precarious time in life, but what I do know is that my children are preparing to leave the nest and it's time for me to step aside to let them falter so they can eventually learn to fly. Their attempts, accomplishments, and most importantly, mistakes will define their futures. I couldn't help but think that adolescence is nature's way of preparing parents to let go.

Sandwiched

Chicken School

It began as many things do. A friend of a friend asks you for a favor, and the next thing you know you're headed down a road you're not prepared to travel. This particular foray began a year before Greg's death during one of my morning strolls with my former neighbor and bestie, Nora.

"Hey, I recall you saying you might want to try your hand at chickens," she said as we rounded the first corner of our three-mile trot.

"Yeah, maybe," was my abrupt response.

Greg and I had talked about wanting to try our hand at chickens, but it hadn't gone further than that. We'd only lived at the farm for a few years and there were more important things ahead of chickens on the punch list.

"I've got this friend who's moving and needs to rehome her five hens. You interested?"

"I don't know … maybe. Let me run it by Greg," I said before picking up the pace.

That evening on my way home from work, I stopped at the local feed store to replenish our dog food bin. As I pulled into a parking spot, an adorable red and white barn-shaped chicken house with a sale sign on it caught my eye. Spring is chicken season, and with fall rapidly approaching, the feed store was clearing their stock of hen supplies. I took this chance encounter as a sign I might want to consider the hen acquisition a little more seriously. Besides, the coop was forty percent off, and those who know me well, know I'm all about a bargain. When checking out, I inquired about the coop and took pictures of it to show Greg after dinner.

"Nora told me about a gal who needs to rehome her hens due to a move. Any chance you're open to becoming chicken farmers?" I asked Greg after clearing our plates. He didn't provide an answer, so I continued. "I discovered this cute hen house at Poudre Feed today." I handed him my phone so he could see the pictures I'd taken of it earlier. "Oh, and bonus, it's on sale!"

"Guess now's as good a time as any. I'm pretty sure I have all the fencing we need behind the shop," he offered before slipping out the backdoor and heading that way. He took an inventory of our supplies while I arranged for a visit with the hens and their current owner.

"The ladies are very special to me, and I want to make sure they go to a good home," she said while escorting us to the chicken yard. The elaborate setup indicated the girls were indeed a pampered flock. As for their owner, she was a walking encyclopedia of chicken knowledge. I followed behind her, taking extensive notes as she instructed us on the how-tos of chicken farming, making sure to ask detailed questions to signify my capable and willing adopter status. Greg wandered off a few lessons in to evaluate the coop with her husband. At the end of our almost two-hour visit, it was determined the girls would be ushered into our care the following Friday evening.

Lesson one: Transitions.

Chicken's sleep from dusk to dawn, and their strong homing instinct drives them to return to the same place to roost at night. Transferring the birds after dusk is typically easier on both human and hen. Their sleepy nature makes them effortless to handle and waking up in their new digs aids in the hens' adjustment.

Our ladies endured the transition with little angst. A few hens roosted outside the coop the first two nights but once I moved them into the nesting boxes a couple of times, they got the memo.

In the following weeks, I spent my free time reading all about chickens in books, magazines and on the internet. Our flock of five, made up of an Americana, two Buff Orpingtons, a Rhode Island Red, and a bantam Campine, had settled quite nicely into their new surroundings and were happily laying eggs daily.

"What are we going to name them?" Jackson asked one evening while watching the hens roam the back acre.

"Not sure," I answered. "You know … technically they're not pets. They're livestock we raise for eggs. Might be best not to get too attached."

"Yeah, I get it, but either way we need to know who we're talking about," he suggested.

"Okay then. Got any ideas?"

After a bit of discussion, we elected to go with solid ladies' names. Ones that had transcended generations and had an air of maturity to them. The Americana became Bea, and the Buff Orpingtons were now identified as Harriet and Martha. We dubbed the Rhode Island Red, Olivia, as she had a genteel quality befitting of the name. The smaller Campine gained her moniker from her behavior. Roberta was a lively, curious gal who pecked at everything including our legs. She was always up in your business, which we found annoying, alarming and at times, painful. Her name came from a past coworker who had displayed a similar demeanor.

Lesson two: Flock dynamics, a.k.a., The Pecking Order.

In support of attaining and maintaining order amongst the flock, an alpha is determined. She sets the tone and is the first to the food, nesting boxes and roost. The rest of the hens vie for their ranking in the group, and said rankings shift as birds age, die, or when new hens are introduced. Chickens can be ruthless to one another as this process of dominance plays out, and for that reason it's best to only bring in multiples when adding to the flock, and often easier if the newbies are younger.

In the spring, I added two blue Cochins I bought from a local farmer. The prior winter brought our first flock loss and I wanted to shift the milieu. Martha, the lowest in the pecking order, either fell ill or became the object of the other's boredom or stress. Jackson discovered the large hole in her neck at the base of the skull when feeding them. Greg presumed she'd been pecked to the point of no return and gallantly put her out of her misery—an action Jackson was party to and recalls in detail to this day. That night I hugged my little man and listened to his tale, and after I acknowledged him. "Caring for livestock is not for the faint of heart. When we welcome these animals on our farm, we make a promise to see them through life and to do what's in their best interest. I'm proud of you." Jackson grew up tenfold that day.

The Cochin breed was brought to our country from Asia in the eighteen hundreds. They're a large breed known for their hardiness and fluffy, thick feathers that span from head to, literally, toe. Our two girls were a blueish-slate color and appeared to be inseparable, which is the reason we nicknamed them, The Blues.

The Blues tended to be a bit daft and had a fondness for the road. Not a good combination for longevity. About a year or so later, these traits resulted in our Blues becoming Blue. Jackson discovered the aftermath of the collision and called to tell me of our loss. "Must have been a semi," he reported. He followed with, "I scraped her up with a shovel and put her in the dumpster." I thanked Jackson for his efforts and for respecting another of the farm's golden rules: he who discovers the problem deals with it.

Lesson three: Chicks.

One can acquire a clutch of chicks in a variety of ways, but buyer beware, or more precisely, be aware of what you're choosing from. Every spring, local feed and farm stores carry what I call, troughs of adorableness. Hundreds of fuzzy hatchlings chirping away, calling to you to take them home. Store chicks are typically pulled as a straight run, meaning they've not been sexed or sorted, and for those of us who raise chickens for egg production, straight runs are a no-go. At times, the stores will carry clutches advertised as strictly pullets, which is the term for a young hen. I threw caution to the wind a year ago and purchased four pullets from my local Tractor Supply store. I ended up with three pullets, one cockerel and an I told you so moment.

Given that I like to diversify my flock for colorful egg production and truly want nothing to do with cockerels, I usually order my chicks from established hatcheries or buy older pullets from local breeders. I've also taken in a couple of hand-me-down hens from people getting out of the business.

My largest flock expansion came shortly after Greg passed away in 2015. I needed something other than grief and loss to set my mind to, and the thought of a dozen or so baby chicks entering our lives sounded like a wonderful place to start. I bought a used shed from a pumpkin farm, hired a guy to move it to my land, called in a few handyman favors and coordinated a brunch to accompany the coop raising. I learned long ago it's best to ply your volunteers with food and drink after they'd labored on your behalf. In addition to being a gesture of goodwill, it helps them to forget about any frustrations they encountered during their efforts.

We placed the shed adjacent to the smaller hen house and expanded the yard enclosure. My highly skilled DIY friends ran electricity to the coop and installed heat. In the matter of one Saturday morning, the old shed was converted into a palatial chicken palace and not a moment too soon, as my young girls were outgrowing their nursery. Our little garage, better known as the nursery, had housed these little beauties for the past eight weeks, and in that time, they'd transformed from darling balls of fluff into fully feathered young ladies ready to join society.

A few months earlier, I'd agreed to share an order of chicks from a hatchery in Iowa. At the time, their minimum order was twenty and I only wanted a dozen. The USPS ships day-old chicks with a guaranteed two to three-day delivery. After placing our order, I lined a large dog crate with cardboard and shavings, gathered the needed food, hung a heat lamp and waited for the call. Two days later I picked up our new editions at the local post office. Thankfully all survived the journey.

I moved the established flock into their new digs and fenced off a small area around the old coop to use it as a dormitory for my young recruits. This is a must, as it's best to have young and old get to know each other through a barrier prior to combining the flock. I did this for about a week or so before I slipped the pullets into the big house after dusk and opened up the yard. Over the coming days, and thankfully without bloodshed, a new pecking order was determined.

Lesson four: Predators.

Sadly, chickens are sitting ducks for a host of natural predators, and over the years we've seen our fair share of skirmishes. Each encounter offers an opportunity to examine exactly how an intruder made it past your security measures and where to sharpen your defenses.

Roberta was our first casualty in the predator war, and entirely our fault. Well, not mine but Greg's. He agreed to but forgot to lock the hen house, which essentially meant he rolled out the red carpet for raccoons and coyotes to dine at their leisure.

If you recall, Roberta was a bit of a pain in the ass and the alpha of her flock. She took one for the team that night, but it appeared she didn't go down without a fight. To my shock and horror, feathers were everywhere and not a chicken to be found. My initial thought was the entire flock was erased, but thankfully in walking the property, I discovered the rest of them huddled together in a mass behind a garden loveseat. They were leaderless and traumatized, and I was livid with my spouse. "I guess we won't get our legs pecked at anymore," was all he cared to offer.

With the addition of the chicken Taj Mahal, I heightened security measures by tightening perimeters and securing entrances. Or so I thought. After extensive examination of the crime scene, investigators determined that a stealth raccoon scaled my defensives, disabled the lock on the hatch door and wedged it open. The blood-stained walls inside the coop were thought to be the result of a slashing at the neck, but again no victim was found on the scene. That piece of the puzzle came two weeks later when a stiff wind blew the dead carcass off the shop roof and back into the chicken yard.

How awful it must have been for the other hens to watch their flock-mate die at the hands of a known serial killer, I thought.

World War III erupted when a pack of huskies moved into the farm to the south of us. They were said to be highly trained sled dogs. Except for one, Buddy. His owner told me of his rough birth, resulting in brain damage, and his tendency to scale fences. He promised me he had a plan to secure him, but alas, Buddy had other ideas.

"Mom, a dog is running around our property and it's driving our dogs nuts," Jackson reported.

"Okay, don't let our dogs out and see if you can scare him off."

Our conversation was interrupted by a call from my neighbor. "Hey hon, there's a dog in your chicken run and the girls are going crazy. I'm headed over."

I rushed home.

It was a massacre. Bodies of the dead and severely wounded were scattered everywhere. We combed the scene for survivors, treated the wounded and remitted the dead to their final resting place. Thirteen of our twenty-one unsuspecting hens met their end that day, and so did my egg business. I was beyond furious.

I immediately drove to the husky farm. The owner listened quietly as I told him of the annihilation, spoke of the loss of income and the fact that he was going to pay for every lost life that day and then some. He handed me four hundred dollars on the spot, and that's the last we ever saw of Buddy.

Lesson five: Veterinary medicine.

I've come to appreciate the fact that being a livestock owner also means you've agreed to be an honorary veterinarian and fortunately, my medical background in humans aided my skill development.

During the battle of Buddy, I was able to nurse one hen back to health. He'd bit her in the back, resulting in a gaping hole where the poor girl's feathers and skin used to be. Upon examination I found her body to be intact, meaning the wound was gnarly but superficial. I treated the opening, wrapped her well with a cohesive bandage and hoped for the best. Within a month the skin healed together and feathers returned to the area. For self-sacrifice in the line of duty, we awarded her The Purple Egg.

Bea, one of our original ladies, took up permanent residence in a roosting box. In the mornings I'd pick her up and place her in the yard only to find her back in the box on my next visit, and when I attempted to remove the eggs from underneath her, she squawked in disapproval. A quick Google search suggested I had a broody hen on my hands. Bea's maternal instinct was in overdrive, making her bound and determined to hatch some chicks!

I learned that reducing body temperature can break broodiness, and placing a bag of frozen vegetables under their body or putting the bird in a wire-bottomed cage with no bedding were options. A third option would be to allow her to hatch a clutch of chicks. *But where might I acquire fertilized eggs? I* wondered. eBay, was my answer. I found an egg supplier in Puerto Rico who sold Americana fertilized eggs. Not that it mattered to Bea, but it felt right to me to match her breed. I ordered seven of them.

The eggs arrived individually bubble wrapped amid a nest of padding. We placed the six eggs that survived the trip under Bea and waited. It takes twenty-one days to hatch an egg. We marked the time on a central calendar, checked on our girl regularly, and like clockwork, on day twenty-one the tapping began. We listened in amazement as their little beaks knocked away at the shells that had been their home. Hours later, we spotted a tiny head and then another, and another after that. We ended up with four precious chicks and more importantly, a hen who was no longer broody.

Veterinary follow-up note: Of the four chicks, three ended up being cockerels. Not an ideal outcome for egg farming. The three boys were rehomed for breeding purposes, and the sole pullet has integrated well into her flock. It's this clinician's assessment that a bag of frozen peas is an efficient and effective intervention for broodiness, and from now on will be the preferred course of treatment should the issue arise again.

I've come to believe you can learn to do just about anything via YouTube. I received my training in home maintenance and repair by following the guidance offered by others. Therefore, it came as no surprise to me that my career as a veterinary surgeon would be launched from the same platform.

One of my girls took to limping about and her foot appeared disfigured. Diagnosis, a case of bumblefoot was afoot. The medical term for this condition is *plantar pododermatitis*, and if left untreated the infection has been known to spread to other areas, and in serious cases can be fatal. My girl was suffering and there was no other option, I had to intervene on her behalf.

I watched several videos studying surgical techniques, post-op care and prevention measures for the flock. I stopped by my local veterinary supply store to obtain the proper medical equipment and transformed the kitchen into a surgical theater.

Jackson was tapped to be my surgical assistant as he had an affinity for the girls, and truth be told, he drew the short straw. He wrapped our girl in a towel and exposed the injured foot. I cleaned and prepped the area, then with scalpel in hand, began the task of excising the infection.

Once the surgery was complete, we treated her foot with topical medications and bandages and changed them per protocol. I'm happy to report that the surgery was a smashing success, and after a few weeks of convalescence, our girl was as good as new.

In completing our post-op notes, we noted that the patient remained rather stoic during the procedure, which made the experience easier for all. A trip back to the internet suggested her behavior had nothing to do with my skill as a surgeon and everything to do with the fact that chickens assume a calm demeanor in the face of pain as a self-defense or preservation mechanism.

Upon discovering this finding, we instituted distraction measures for all future surgeries. Going forward, we'd play a video Jackson recorded of the girls when they were a clutch. He felt the injured hen would enjoy hearing the sounds of her flock during moments of distress or pain.

Given the nature of our patient population, we've yet to receive any satisfaction surveys to determine the accuracy of his hypothesis, but we persevere on their behalf nonetheless.

Lesson six: Eggs.

Eggs come in a variety of magnificent shell colors, which are determined by the breed of the bird. It's felt that a hen's ear color is an indicator of egg color, but I've never given it much mind. I focus on selecting a variety of breeds best for my area of the world and have never been disappointed.

The multi-color eggs I harvest look great in a bowl and negate our need to dye eggs at Easter, but truth be told, shell color is simply window dressing, and the eggs inside are all the same. One can see a difference in the yolk color of my flock to that of a commercial egg, and that's due to diet and accommodations. Free ranged birds tend to have richer and darker yolks.

Every afternoon, I trod out to the coop with a wire basket in tow to collect the day's eggs. The number I gather is impacted by a host of factors such as light, age of the hen, and molting season, which occurs when the days begin to grow shorter. I recall one November, the molt seemed to go on forever, and even I was forced to purchase eggs from the store.

Hens typically lay during the daylight hours and enjoy using the same nesting box. This works well for gathering but oftentimes a clumsy hen will damage one of her sister's freshly laid eggs. If this happens, I throw the remains into the yard and watch the melee ensue. Fun fact, hens are big fans of eggs, shells, and all.

My kids are fans of twin eggs. We'll get one once in a while, and it's a battle to see who gets to fry it up for breakfast. Twins are almost twice the size of regular eggs and have two yolks. I feel for any hen who passes a twin, it can't be comfortable.

When my newcomers begin laying, it takes their bodies a bit of time to find its groove. We enjoy gathering their tiny eggs, and at times will discover an egg with only a membrane. These eggs are called oops or fart eggs and often slip out without their knowledge. I had the pleasure of watching an oops and the hilarious behavior of the hen afterward. She was shocked, startled and confused. A priceless moment for this crazy chicken lady.

Girl Getaway

"I've got a brilliant idea," Kathleen declared, settling into the loveseat opposite the roaring fire. *One that will either cost a lot of money or end in disaster*, I wondered. Her comment elicited both intrigue and skepticism, a learned response on my part. We'd become country neighbors about three years ago, and in that time I'd either met emergency services at their home or transported family members, notably Kathleen, to the hospital more times than one would expect in a lifetime.

It began with horse-related catastrophes and farm calamities then steamrolled from there. A broken nose or hand, a ruptured spleen, and a pulled shoulder or two were all compliments of horse handling mishaps. I would typically receive the emergent call to capture the roaming herd or clean up a catastrophe when they were sprinting to the hospital. Falls up or down stairs, through or in holes, and sometimes even on the flat ground, resulted in twisted bruised body parts in need of mending. Car accidents, sports injuries, and a few hypothetical cardiac events round out the array of misfortunes seeming to follow their bright ideas.

Last summer, Kathleen called the fire department to get one of her barn cats out of a tree. He'd been up there awhile, and the daily temperatures were in the high nineties. "I was worried he'd get dehydrated," she said when I arrived on the scene. We watched the rookie firefighter suit up and scale the forty-foot ladder to rescue the feline, and I thought to myself, *I didn't know they still did such things.*

As he descended with the cat in tow, Kathleen asked the crew chief, "Do we need to pay you for this service?"

"Nope, we consider such calls training missions," the captain replied with a smile.

If emergency services had a frequent flyer program, Kathleen's entire family would qualify for elite status.

I poured a glass of wine then snuggled into the antique chair next to the woodstove. Kathleen's husband, Phil, knew I didn't have a fireplace, and during cooler months made sure we ladies always had a crackling blaze for our fireside chats. Occasionally he'd sneak in a color packet, and we'd gaze at the brilliant rainbow of flames before us. "So … about this grand idea … should I be scared?" I asked.

Kathleen smiled, took a sip of wine to further my anticipation then said, "You know I've been wanting to visit Lea and Manon and I think … we should go this summer."

"We? What about the family?" I inquired.

"Someday, but for now, one ticket to France is more doable than four, and you need a change of scenery more than they do."

"You're right there. I could definitely use some time away." Kathleen knew I'd be facing a milestone in the summer: the year mark of Greg's death, and while the subject never came up in conversation, the need for levity was mutually understood. We spent the rest of the evening tossing around possible dates, messaging France, and dreaming about our girl getaway.

In a few short months our daydream became a reality. "To us," I stated as I lifted my mimosa in the air. "To France," Kathleen added as she touched her glass to mine. It's tradition to honor any girl getaway with a toast prior to boarding the flight, and we weren't about to break the custom.

Our adventure began in the French Alps. Manon, the first of two exchange students Kathleen hosted years before, picked us up from the airport in Geneva, and after a detour to town for ratatouille and a walk around the lake, we headed to the Venice of the Alps: Annecy. The town is known for its cobblestone streets, winding canals, perialpine lake, and perched on a hilltop keeping watch over the quaint city, the medieval Château d'Annecy. Once home to the Counts of Geneva, the Château is now a museum housing artifacts from the region. I was amazed how the toilets, or privies as they were called, were carved into the exterior walls and quite private. Marvels of efficiency at the time as the waste conveniently fell into the river or moat below.

Over the coming days, we explored the colorful streets of the alpine city and traveled the entirety of the lake, gawking at the stately estates that lined its shores. Manon's vacation home was situated on a hillside overlooking the lake. She'd spent many a weekend and holiday in Annecy with family and friends. We met her father and his wife for coffee in town and befriended several of the shop owners they knew. The Sommelier was a favorite. Since French wines are named for the region they come from, not grape variety, it was important for him to understand what we preferred before suggesting a bottle. We talked and tasted our way from Bordeaux to Champagne and walked away with several bottles to enjoy over dinner.

Manon went to the *boulangerie* daily for fresh bread and pastries, and together we selected several varieties of cheese and *saucisson* for our nightly charcuterie from the *traiteur*. At the end of each day, we'd position the glass coffee table in front of the picture window to take in the sunset as we picnicked and chatted.

Manon, now a young woman, shared stories of her life and travels since her summers in Colorado. Kathleen caught her up on the happenings of the family, and I recounted the tragic tale of my past year. Whenever emotional moments surfaced, they would graciously listen to whatever came out of my mouth, and after it did, we let it go, returning to casual conversation about our daily adventures and plans for the coming day.

During our time in Annecy, Manon suggested a day trip to Lyon, a vibrant city less than two hours away by car. She'd moved there a few years earlier and was eager to share the city with us.

Lyon is said to be the gastronomical capital of France, and on that point it certainly didn't disappoint, but what I enjoyed the big city for was its small-town charm. The pace of life was relaxed, the people were friendly and accommodating and the cities delightful boutiques resulted in multiple purchases. We explored Old Lyon, braved a suspended footbridge over the river, and marveled at the panoramic views from the basilica atop Fourvième Hill. On our way down, Manon excitedly whipped the car into an open spot and said, "I've found it! I've finally found it."

"I don't think this is a real parking spot. Plus, your car's facing the wrong way," Kathleen pointed out.

"*Je m'en fous,*" Manon replied.

"What's that mean?" I asked.

"I don't care," she explained.

"That's it! Our new tag line for the trip …*Je m'en fous!*" I declared.

The "it" Manon was excited about was the Théâtre Antique de Lyon, an ancient roman theater carved into the Fourvième hillside. We hiked around the two-thousand-year-old amphitheater marveling at its size and unspoiled condition. "It's the French version of Red Rocks," I said to Kathleen.

"Yeah, looks like it. Too bad there's no concert tonight," she replied.

I sat in the back of the car staring out the window at the French countryside thinking about all we'd done and seen in such a short time. I became ever so grateful to our hostess for making our time effortless and to my friend for suggesting we travel to France. *Saying yes to this trip … best decision ever*, I thought to myself as we made our way back to Annecy.

Ever heard of easyJet? I hadn't until we boarded a plane to the French Riviera the following day.

"I'm ready for some beach lounging and the ocean," Kathleen said as she boarded the plane.

"It's a sea," Manon called out from behind me, and I giggled.

The low-cost airline operates in more than thirty countries and has over a thousand routes. Our flight cost a whopping twenty-six euros: less than the cab fare we were about to pay into Nice.

We took up residence in a flat along the pebbled shores of the Promenade des Anglais for some relaxation in the sun, and coincidentally the European Football Championships. Unbeknownst to us, we'd planned our trip smack dab in the middle of football mayhem. France was host to the fifty-one-match extravaganza deemed Euro 2016, and Nice was one of the ten cities and stadiums chosen for the event.

Footballs—a.k.a. soccer balls for my American readers—hung from everything imaginable, and the city's historic plaza was converted into a giant jumbotron viewing area. Fans sporting the colors of their chosen teams blanketed the city, as did countless police officers with really big guns. They'd block off the entire promenade whenever a team was on the move, and during our second night we were a party to a bomb threat, which after an exhaustive search was thankfully given the all clear. Once the day's match had been decided, the local pubs became the star attraction. Rivaling hordes singing the praises of the day spilled out of doorways and patios and onto the streets. They'd lift their pints high and chant in unison declaring allegiance to country and team. The police kept an eye on the crowd, which never engaged in the slightest scuffle. I found the energy of it all intoxicating.

The next morning we ascended a long, winding staircase on the eastern edge of town to a hilltop park complete with medieval ruins, a waterfall, and spectacular views of the city, the port and surrounding hills. "Look at how blue the ocean is," Kathleen remarked.

"It's a sea," Manon clarified.

"Well, it looks like an ocean to me," Kathleen replied with a cheeky grin.

We explored the many vistas Castle Hill Park offered, taking pictures and contemplating which of the colorful houses and large yachts we'd choose. Manon discovered the free elevator that served the hilltop park. "Wished I'd known about that before we climbed all those stairs," Kathleen offered. She'd fallen through an unrepaired hole on their flatbed trailer a few weeks before our departure, severely bruising her leg. The injury made walking long distances and climbing stairs both difficult and painful. She and Manon chose to ride the small dark rickety elevator down, but I elected to take the winding, cobblestone path and made it to the bottom at about the same time.

We discovered the Cours Saleya flower and food markets and shopped them daily before heading to the beach for a VIP lounge chair and table service at one of the seaside restaurants. "They have pop and ice!" Kathleen pointed out with glee. It had been hit or miss on the soda front since we'd left the States, and ice wasn't regularly served with beverages. She'd become homesick for both and was elated whenever we came upon either. That evening we retired to the flat's patio for our signature charcuterie picnic, which now included a stunning sunset over the sea.

The next morning, we hopped a train to the ultimate playground of the rich and famous: Monaco. We walked the rolling twisted streets, soaking in the architecture, cleanliness, wealth and class that surrounded us. Tucked away in a residential area, we discovered a hidden gem, a splendid terraced restaurant overlooking the vast marina with an amazing lunch menu. After, the three of us ventured through the Monte Carlo Casino and climbed to the Prince's Palace. Our timing was impeccable to catch the changing of the guard, and the views from the once fortress were stunning.

"I can't believe the number of yachts in the marina," Kathleen said. "I wonder who owns them?"

"Rich people own them, and chances are their friends and family mostly use them," I suggested.

"*Oui*, I think so," Manon concurred, then suggested, "Shall we go to Cannes?"

"Monaco was only a twenty-minute train ride from Nice. How long is the trip to Cannes?" I asked.

"Just over an hour," Manon answered after glancing at the train schedule. "We can have cocktails on the beach."

"If it's suitable for an international film festival and movie stars, I think it warrants a look," I offered.

"It has sandy beaches, not rocks like Nice, so I'm in," Kathleen seconded. A few days ago, she'd tumbled on the rocks and lost her flip flops. Manon and I had to dig them out of the rubble before the sea swept both of them away. Never a dull moment traveling with this gal.

We spent our short time in Cannes enjoying Kathleen's number one pastime: people watching. It was fun to make up glamorous stories about those we saw aboard the yachts or sunning and sipping champagne on the beach. My favorite, though, was a group of elderly men playing bocci ball on the public beach. Their camaraderie was palpable, and the joy on their faces infectious. *It's the simple things*, I said to myself as I watched them banter and play.

Kathleen bought a painting from a local artist on the beach, and after, we strolled the red carpet, traveled down the walk of fame, and had cocktails with a friend of Manon's before taking the train back to Nice.

Sadly, we had come to the end of our time at the sea and with Manon. "Out of the three, I'd pick Monaco. How about you?" I asked my traveling companions during our final patio picnic.

"Cannes was my favorite," Kathleen announced.

"I'd choose Nice to be my home," Manon offered.

"Great, we'll be a short train from each other. Honestly, I'm more of a mountain girl. Annecy would be my real choice," I clarified. We spent the rest of the night chatting about our adventures and squeezing new purchases into our already full suitcases. Manon was headed back to Lyon and to work, and we were destined for the City of Light.

A four-day pilots' strike coinciding with Euro 2016, forced airlines to reschedule or cancel numerous flights. Manon's flight left on time, but we were delayed for over two hours and arrived at Charles de Gaulle airport late in the evening.

Lea, the second of Kathleen's ranch stay exchange students, and her mother, Florence, were waiting for us inside the terminal. Lea had fashioned a sign similar to the one Kathleen's children made for her the year before, welcoming us to Paris.

"Shall we get your bags?" Florence asked.

"We only have these," Kathleen said while pointing at our carry-on bags. Florence was astonished that we'd managed with so few bags. A thought she'd revisit several times during our stay.

It was close to midnight by the time we arrived at their home. Lea showed us to our room, and we promptly retired for the night. I woke first, and after shimmying off the top bunk, began to have a look at our new accommodations. Lea's younger brother, Benjamin, graciously gave up his spacious room at the top of the stairs for the length of our stay. I walked over to the window cranked open the shade and was astonished at what I saw before me.

"Kathleen, you up?" I whispered.

"Yep," she replied.

"I feel like I've woken up in a Jane Austin novel."

"What?"

"Come here, you have to see this," I demanded. Kathleen reluctantly joined me at the window. The centuries-old home was surrounded by gardens, and a small stable was tucked in the trees. The grounds were enclosed by a stone wall, and an iron gate framed the entry. A few minutes later, the gate opened, and Lea entered on a bicycle with a basket full of bread and pastries.

"Looks like breakfast just arrived," I announced. We pulled ourselves together and made our way to the dining room. Florence and Lea were waiting with coffee, juice, and decadent delights from the local *boulangerie*. "Today, we are going to Versailles," Florence stated.

"My mother's arranged for us to have lunch in the gardens of Versailles before touring the palace," Lea added.

"Sounds wonderful," Kathleen replied and I concurred. We left shortly after breakfast.

The massive golden marvel of art and history attracts equally massive amounts of tourists to its gates, and that day was no exception. Buses, cars and extensive lines of visitors waiting to gain entry were everywhere. Florence, however, thought nothing of it. She marched confidently past the thousands in line and through the entry. The gate attendant, annoyed by her actions, grumbled a bit and pointed to the line but let us through regardless.

"Maybe it's because of our lunch reservations," I said to Kathleen.

"No, my mother just doesn't do lines," Lea clarified.

The next day we learned that Lea didn't have much patience for them either. The stealth she employed navigating us through the streets of Paris was phenomenal. Our tour began at the Louvre where we chose to take the obligatory selfie in front of the crowd gathered at the Mona Lisa, as they appeared more impressive than the painting. Our Eiffel Tower photo included a giant football, compliments of Euro 2016. Oh, and for those who are curious, Portugal won the tournament for the first time, shutting out France in overtime.

We stopped at a sidewalk café near the Notre Dame for galettes before touring the cathedral. While inside, I lit a candle for Greg and paused for reflection. He and I had talked about traveling to Paris together but never got the chance. Lighting the candle made me feel as if he was with me. I sat for a time in silence, bought a souvenir ornament to commemorate the experience then caught up with Kathleen.

I found her at the front entrance. "Whatcha looking at?"

"The entry doors. They're enormous and the iron work is beautiful. I'd love to have a door with a similar design made for my future wine room." She started taking pictures of the doors from every angle. I wandered off to photograph the gargoyles that sat atop the magnificent cathedral. It's said they keep demons and evil forces away, which may be true, but what they also do is serve as rain spouts from the roof directing water away from the side walls and foundation. *I wonder if I should add a few to my gutter system*, I thought. I'm delighted we were able to take in this beauty before she caught fire in 2019.

A few Métro hops later, we arrived at the Arc de Triomphe. Unfortunately, Kathleen picked up an unwelcomed admirer on the metro. We did our best to be firm but kind in expressing our desire to be left alone, however, Prince Charming, as we came to call him, persisted. I wondered if he might be a pickpocket waiting for the right time to strike, but Lea wasn't about to let that happen. We finally lost him by stopping into a Maserati dealership on the Champs-Élysées. Lea explained our predicament to the salesman, and he took care of the rest. We strolled through a few shops on the famous avenue then stopped at a café to rest, refuel and people watch.

"I was impressed by the musicians in the Métro," Kathleen offered.

"I'm amazed by how much we've done," I replied.

"Yeah, Lea, you're a master. It would have taken us days to see what you showed us in one," Kathleen added. Lea smiled with pride.

An hour later, Florence met us on the banks of the Seine for a sunset dinner cruise. "The perfect cap to our ultimate tourist day. Thank you," I said to her, and as the boat moved along, the three of us relived the day with Florence while soaking in the architectural wonder of the City of Love.

Kathleen and I spent the next day exploring the magical community of Maisons-Laffitte. Built in the 1600s, Château de Maisons, a historical monument and classic example of French baroque architecture, is the touchstone of the Paris suburb tucked between the banks of the Seine and the Forest of Saint-Germain-en-Laye. The former royal hunting grounds have evolved into a charming equestrian community that's home to around seven thousand horses, thirty stables, and a park that spans the township.

Châteaus and mansions lined the vast interconnected acres of green we traversed. Some appeared to have been converted into multi-family residences and schools while others remained frozen in time. Although we tried to pick a favorite, we couldn't and felt if given the chance, we'd live anywhere in this district. After touring the historical château and its grounds, we joined Lea at the stables to meet her new horse, Colorado, and watch her riding lesson. "Great name," Kathleen told her.

"*Oui*, I think so," she replied before directing us towards the arena.

Kathleen studied the lesson, comparing riding and jumping techniques Lea was being taught to those she'd learned years ago. I was distracted by the circular stone wall surrounding the arena and found myself speculating its purpose centuries ago.

That evening Florence made dinner, and Antoine, her partner, joined us. We'd seen little of him thus far and were pleased he chose to attend. His strong yet quiet demeanor was evident the minute he entered the room. He didn't bother with the usual pleasantries and launched into the weighty subject of politics right off the bat. I glanced at Kathleen for confirmation it was okay to engage, she nodded back in affirmation, then banter ensued.

Antoine's strong command of the English language made our exchange hearty and robust. He'd pose the topic or question, and we volleyed back with comprehensive, intelligent answers. At times, it felt as if he was trying to throw us off our game, but we didn't falter. He asked about Native American culture, of which Kathleen offered tremendous insight. The organization she worked for partnered with tribal leaders and elders to capture and recognize the historical significance and connection the Northern Arapaho tribe had to our local river corridor. I glanced over at Lea and Florence, and they appeared a bit shell-shocked and bewildered. When dinner was over, Antoine stood, thanked us for the conversation and retired to his study. It was then we learned that he's typically not a conversationalist.

"I hope we didn't do anything wrong," I said to Kathleen after we'd retired for the night.

"I think he enjoyed it," Kathleen speculated.

"I hope so, I know I sure did."

For our final day, we chose to continue our explorations of Maisons-Laffitte. We walked the gardens then to town to peruse the covered markets, *pâtisserie*, boutiques, and lunched at a local bistro. That evening, Florence, along with Lea and Benjamin, took us to the city for our final night in Paris. Florence drove through several districts pointing out places of interest and took us to dinner at her favorite local back-alley brassiere. I found the lights of the Moulin Rouge an unexpected treat, and the Eiffel Tower at night spectacular. We talked of our adventures together, laughed, and raised a glass to friendships, old and new.

Florence confirmed what we initially suspected with Manon: navigating traffic in France requires confidence and oftentimes, aggression. She wove in and out of tight spaces, through roundabouts, and dodged cars like a Grand Prix driver. Artfully zigzagging through the city's districts, passing by classic landmarks on an illumination tour.

"Glad we had help navigating that craziness," Kathleen said as she took her seat on the plane.

"Yeah, not sure we would have located or chosen the right escalator to get to our gate without them. Felt a bit like the moving stairs at Hogwarts," I replied.

Our time in Paris was sublime, and our tour guides even more so. For me, the depth and meaning of our excursion expanded as I journeyed through grief toward healing, and I pictured myself returning to France for a week, a month or maybe even longer. I began to appreciate the excitement and opportunity an unexpected future held. Once my children were on a path of their own, I'd have the ability to turn on a dime and go in whatever direction my soul desired. *Life could be whatever I imagine it to be*, I thought, and the freedom and autonomy of that idea excited me.

56

Horse Stories

My foray into the equine world began ten years ago when my daughter asked if she could watch a friend's lesson. That simple act opened the door to a realm I'd long forgotten.

As a young child, I spent many memorable summers on my grandparent's farm. My cousins and I built forts in the hayloft, cuddled barn kittens, skipped rocks on the pond and played hide'n'seek in the acres of vineyards they farmed. My Grandpa Rex purchased a Shetland stallion to train and show in pleasure driving and imported two pregnant Galiceños from Mexico. One of the mares gave birth to a mule he named, Andy. I'm told he was so proud of Andy that during his son's wedding, he went around with a photo of him asking guests if they wanted to see a picture of his daughters-in-law's ass.

Grandpa Rex became quite the horse enthusiast and spent his later years breeding and training Arabians and Tennessee Walkers. Those horses were the ones we grandchildren remember. We'd ride in the arena, through the vineyards, and later, stop under the cherry trees to reach up and grab a snack. It felt as if we had free reign to do as our hearts desired on the farm, and thinking about it now, it's a miracle we came out unscathed. My mother was not so lucky.

"My horse acted up and my father wasn't happy with him, so he grabbed the reins and disciplined the horse with me still on him!" The shock and trauma of the ordeal was apparent in her face and vocal tone. "The horse reared up several times, and it scared me to death. I ran to my room and decided that was it. No more horses for me." She explained that her father later tried to apologize, but she wouldn't accept it. She chose to spend the rest of the day in her room instead and never mounted a horse again.

After Grandpa died, my Uncle Bob took Pretty Girl, the Arabian, to his farm in Indiana. The remaining horses were either sold or given away, and from then on, our horse experiences were limited to reading books, playing with figurines and pretending to ride. Grandma would throw a children's saddle over her large laundry hamper, and I rode it for hours.

When it seemed apparent Kate's riding bug was here to stay, we bought Jacaranda: a chestnut Holsteiner who needed to retire from heavy work but was perfect for a beginner rider. We boarded Jac at Kathleen's barn, and our girls took lessons, practiced jumping in the arena, and joined our local Pony Club. Being more of a novice, I looked to Kathleen to school me on all things horses. The girls were young and petite, so she appreciated having an extra pair of hands even if those hands required coaching.

We came to loath Pony Club and quit after a year. Too many rules, expenses and expectations took the joy out of riding. We opted for relaxed fun and private lessons at the barn, and the girls couldn't have been happier. Moms too.

Jac and Kate spent several years together before Jac succumbed to horse lung disease. I remember every detail of the day we said goodbye—the whinny she greeted me with when I arrived, and the happiness expressed as I led her to the pasture one last time. Jac was suffering and we needed to fulfill the most important promise you make to any animal in your care: the promise to do what they need you to when they need it. I stayed by Jac's side as she peacefully passed on.

Kate's next ride was a gray thoroughbred that had been rescued from the kill buyer. I'll never forget going to the pens to complete the brand inspection. It was heartbreaking to see all the horses destined for a not-so-pleasant end.

"You can't save them all," Kathleen said to me as we waited.

"Yeah, I know," I sadly agreed.

We'll never know how or why he ended up in a kill pen, but what we did come to know is that his bloodlines were that of champion. Race horses are required to have a lip tattoo for identification purposes, and when I entered his number into the jockey club registry, I learned more about his past. His racing name was Seiko Express, and he'd had twenty-three starts and three wins. Secretariat and Bold Ruler, among a host of other well-known thoroughbreds, were part of his bloodlines, and because of those things we named him Legend.

After his short racing career, it appears he was trained for show jumping and eventing. Mia, the girl who rescued him from the kill buyer, felt he was definitely someone's event horse as he knew all the cues and was comfortable on the cross-country course. Legend would become Kate's last ride. As she grew older her interests changed, and when she turned sixteen, she traded her horse for a car, and Legend found his forever home with a girl named Rose, who could show and ride him at the advanced level he was destined for.

After my husband's unexpected passing, Kathleen encouraged me to expand my horse adventures. She saw them as a healthy distraction and a path toward healing. A week after the funeral, she called. "I'm picking you up in ten. We're going to Laramie."

I buckled my seat belt then inquired, "Why Laramie?"

"A horse, of course. A black and white Paint."

Two hours later, we were co-owners of a beautiful black and white Paint we named DaVinci. The plan was to give him some training then sell him, but Kathleen opted to buy me out and keep him for herself when the time arrived. A decision that came back to haunt her as he bucked her off a few times, with the last resulting in compression fractures, a spinal hematoma and a prolonged hospital stay. I watched as she fell forward and off to the side, landing in a not-so-good way. I popped off my horse, put both horses away, drove her car down to the arena and then on to the emergency room. DaVinci went to a trainer who determined he wasn't a safe ride for anyone. Still, his ground manners were impeccable, so Kathleen rehomed him to a therapeutic program that does only groundwork with their clients.

Our joint venture with breeding was disastrous and astronomically expensive. Like boats, horses are money pits, and breeding is a gamble where the house, or should I say the veterinarian, always wins. Kathleen sold her Holsteiner foals for ten thousand or more each, but one pregnant mare in, I realized the blind eye she turned to the fees incurred in the making. In breeding, everyone gets their piece of the pie up front, and the risk, rests solely on the mares and their owner. Stud fees, collection fees, vet fees, shipping fees, ultrasound fees, more vet fees, supplies, and supplements. It's a rich man's sport.

Most breeders have at least fifty percent of the sale price invested before birth and a hundred percent of the risk. The mare may not take, or prematurely abort the foal, and the birthing process for both mare and foal is wrought with the possibility of peril. We had three foals from our shared mare, and two died within three months from freak and tragic accidents. The third went on to be sold but not before the mare experienced severe colic after the birth requiring ICU care, and the foal put her leg through a gate, lashing it open further, racking up way more dollar signs than her purchase price could ever hope to cover. I tapped out after that. I didn't have the heart or the pocketbook for it. We sold the mare to another breeder along with her subsequent breeding, which means we practically gave her away, and after, I vowed to own only geldings.

By this point, my horse story collection was stacking up nicely. I'd been a barn apprentice for several years, which resulted in my veterinary skills expanding to include large animals. I had learned more than I ever imagined about horse behavior and anatomy and once again, my medical background came in handy.

Horses are solid but fragile beings, and a few of their systems aren't ideally designed. The number one killer of adult horses is colic, a digestive dilemma brought on by many factors. Knowing your horse's typical behavior is crucial for identifying changes, which are often indicators of distress.

Horses require regular checkups, seasonal shots and wormers, dental care, and a trusted farrier needs to be your best friend. There's a saying among we crazy horse people: "No feet, no horse." A horse's hooves require regular attention, and injuries to the lower leg and hoof can be life-altering for the horse, and at times fatal. Just like we humans, lack of exercise, stress, overeating and diets rich in sugar and starch can increase a horse's susceptibly to metabolic disorders, which can result in *laminitis*, a crippling condition that if caught early is treatable, but the risk of recurrence remains. Horses have a V-shaped structure on the bottom of their hooves called a frog. It's a shock absorber and a vital part of the horse's circulatory system, pumping the blood back up the leg. Keeping the frog healthy and free from bacteria is necessary and vital.

You can and should read about horses, but the only way to truly understand these beautiful creatures is to engage with them thoughtfully. Study their tendencies, appreciate herd dynamics, watch and listen.

When I arrive at the barn, the rest of the world fades away, and it needs to. Horses are prey animals who rely on their flight response to evade predators. They're perceptive and often notice things we humans don't appreciate. They'll sense your body language, tone and attitude, so it's essential to be aware of how you're showing up. Humans are predators, and as such we need to respect and remain mindful of this difference when interacting with horses. Curb your natural tendencies, relax and observe. Horses will tell you how they're feeling, and you'll learn what they need. The bond between horse and human requires trust and understanding, which takes time and a commitment to build.

We may technically be brighter, but horses are bigger and stronger. Know when to get out of the way. I made this mistake once. I thought I could stop a twelve-hundred-pound animal from running through a gate. I held the gate and he pushed through it, knocking me to the ground. I got my bell rung but managed to recover quickly, and more importantly, I learned never to do that again.

Horses live fully in the present, and their needs are simple: food, water and shelter from predators. They don't overthink things or hold grudges, and accept you as you are. Oh, if we humans could learn to exhibit more of those behaviors.

"I'm thinking about adding a man to my life," I said to Kathleen as we lounged on her patio after a day of horse-related activities.

"The two-legged or four-legged variety?" she inquired.

"Four-legged," I clarified.

"Great, let's start looking for your man," she said, pulling up potentials on her phone.

I don't recall how long it took me to find my guy, just that the moment I saw him I knew he was the one. The ad described him as a "been there done that beginner-friendly horse." I read it repeatedly in disbelief, then crafted an email to his owner and waited for a reply. I knew not to get my hopes up as frequently horses aren't as they're described, or he may already have been sold. I sent the ad to Kathleen and asked her to come with me to see him if it works out. Tom called a few days later.

He'd purchased the horse from an auction in South Dakota when the gelding was two and because of that fact they named him Dakota. Tom explained that number 417 wasn't the horse they went there for, but when he followed his girls up and down the fence line and loved on them, despite his skinny, sad condition, they knew he was the one. "He had a look in his eye that was unmistakably special," he said.

Dakota ate for three months straight, and when he was ready, they trained him in both English and Western riding styles. His girls rode him in shows, around town and in the mountains, but they are all grown now, and it's time for Dakota to find his next person. *Me!* I thought to myself. We talked for close to an hour, but Tom never offered to show me the horse. I sensed his struggle with the decision to sell him, so I didn't push yet.

Three conversations later, I took control, and three days later, Tom, one of his daughters and Dakota arrived at the barn. It was unusual for him to come to us, but Tom insisted on checking out Kathleen's facility. The horse was everything he promised and more, and when the riding trial was completed, I explained to Tom that my husband died three years ago in South Dakota, so it felt fitting the bay quarter horse gelding that jumped off the sale post and into my heart came from there. "It's a full-circle kind of feeling," I offered.

It was decided that Dakota would stay with me on trial for a month, but I knew he wasn't going anywhere. We took our time getting to know each other, and later I took lessons along with the girls. They jumped and cantered while Dakota and I walked and eventually trotted about.

I was way too tense, overthought everything and flopped about the saddle sending all the wrong cues. Dakota was tolerant but didn't hesitate to take advantage of my novice status to be lazy.

"You smile the whole time you're riding," Kathleen said as I rounded a corner.

"Really?" I made it a point to tune into my face. Yep, she was right.

Being with Dakota offered me a time and a place to relax and let go. Sometimes I rode, other times we'd go on walks, or I'd bath him. I came to appreciate that time spent together out of the saddle was just as or more critical for our bond. Dakota knows when my car enters the drive, and he greets me with a whinny when I call him in from the pasture or walk in the barn. He's found his forever home, and I have my final horse.

I look forward to growing old together.

Sandwiched

Breathing Lessons

I got into the car questioning my decision: wondering why I'd said yes to being Kathleen's plus one. I should've known better when her husband passed on attending. *Probably no food*, I thought. *Phil would've said yes if there was going to be a good spread.*

Kathleen put me on her shortlist for events like these. She knew I was a socially seasoned veteran of the benefit scene and that I polished up well, had excellent small talk skills and knew how to work a room.

"Ok, just what did I agree to?" I asked her.

"It's the opening reception for the *H2O Today* exhibition at the Greeley History Museum," she explained. "We partnered with the city to bring the exhibition to town. Oh, and Dan, the museum's manager, is on my board."

"Got it," I replied.

Kathleen was the executive director of the Poudre Heritage Alliance, the managing entity for the Cache La Poudre River National Heritage Area; one of the fifty-five congressionally designated National Heritage Areas that exist in our country. The development of western water law and the evolution of complex water delivery systems happened along the Cache, therefore an exhibition dedicated to water was definitely in their wheelhouse.

"Is there gonna be food there?" I asked.

"They're having it catered. We should have both food and drink tonight," she answered.

"So why didn't Phil want to attend?"

"Truth be told, the kids have a lot of homework and he needs to make sure it gets done, but I told him you needed a girls' night out," she explained.

On the drive over, Kathleen schooled me on who would be at the reception. We reviewed the list of people she wanted to make sure she touched base with and those she'd rather avoid. My job was to facilitate and, at times, divert conversation in an effort to keep her moving through the crowd.

When we pulled up to the museum, I was immediately struck by the building's exterior. The architecture was quite different than the structures surrounding it. An exquisite, black iron canopy covered the entrance, and ornate coach lights flanked the doorway. High above the canopy, the words "Greeley Tribune" were inscribed on the building. No doubt a nod to its previous owner and purpose.

Upon entry, you were immediately required to either ascend or descend a pair of terrazzo staircases. We took the set to the upper level, which led to the museum galleries, gift shop and offices. I later learned the others guided you down to the archives and artifact storage areas.

The reception was in full bloom. People were milling about taking in the exhibits while others were enjoying refreshments and conversation. Kathleen made quick work of surveying the room, developed a plan of attack, and I followed her lead as we launched into the crowd. I met city leaders, museum employees and historical society folks and fell easily into conversation with most. One of the city's attorneys got a bit forward with his questions, and it began to feel as if he was screening me for potential dating material. *No thank you*, I thought. Dan, the host of the event, sensed my unease and quickly shifted the conversation and me away from him. I was grateful.

Midway through the mingle, Dan hushed the crowd to give the proverbial host address. You know the one. It starts with, "Thank you for coming." Then you weave in, "This wouldn't have been possible without your support," and concludes with, "Enjoy your evening." His khaki blazer with matching pants seemed of another era, and the hiking shirt he'd thrown on under it suggested he wasn't much for gussying up.

Dan's eloquence became apparent when he began talking about the museum. His tone was prideful yet humble and paired well with the expressive nature of his words. It was then you met the historian within. One that understood and respected the efforts of those who had come before. I was charmed and curious. *This is someone I'd like to know more about*, I thought.

The exhibition was part of The Smithsonian's traveling collection. Its objective was to explore the diversity and beauty of our global water supply while examining current water challenges and the innovative solution's transpiring around the world. *I get why Kathleen gave them the grant*, I told to myself.

The displays were a mix of visual, audio, and interactive stations that explored the crucial role water plays in industry, agriculture and at home. They also delved into the impact of population growth and climate change. I learned that our world is seventy-one percent surface water, yet less than three percent is drinkable, 1.2 percent to be exact. I suddenly felt thirsty.

After taking in the exhibition, I refreshed my glass, grabbed Kathleen and hit the gift shop to see if there was anything we couldn't live without. Dan caught up with us and asked if we wanted a behind-the-scenes tour of the museum. I jumped at the chance. I was eager to know more about the building, and of course a bit more about him.

The Beaux-Arts style building is known for its ornate but orderly extravagance. The French-inspired design was popular in the US from the 1880s through the 1930s. The barons of the industrial revolution were quite fond of the style as it represented the affluence of their time.

Dan escorted me through the small galleries and archives. I saw the original snakeskin dress from the famed Rattlesnake Kate and the Hazel E. Johnson Research Center, which is home to a treasure trove of documents and photographs from the area's past. The artifact rooms contained countless drawers and storage bins, filled with implements of earlier days: objects that were once family heirlooms and now obsolete implements of times gone by.

"Families call us all the time wanting to donate their antiques, but we simply don't have any room," he explained. "We need to move many of these pieces on."

"I could help with that," I said. "I'm all about cleaning out and clutter removal."

"Yeah well, I'm a historian, it's harder for me to let things go," he replied.

On the ride home, Kathleen and I reviewed the events of the evening. We both enjoyed the exhibition, made a few new business connections and felt the food was just okay.

"Not dynamic enough," she said.

"Yeah, too pedestrian," I replied, and laughter ensued.

"We're a hoot," I said. "But seriously, it could've been better."

Kathleen changed the subject. "What'd you think about Dan?"

"He's interesting," was my initial reply. "I like his energy and passion for what he does."

"I thought you two should meet," she said.

"Was this a deliberate set-up?" I asked.

"Nope, just a creative opportunity," she replied with a smile.

Once home I couldn't help myself. I Facebook bombed and Googled Dan. I learned he had a degree in American History from Penn State and previously worked for a National Heritage Area in Pennsylvania. He'd volunteered several times for HistoriCorps, preserving historic structures in the remote Colorado mountains. His Facebook posts told me he was an avid outdoorsman, an accomplished blacksmith, photographer, and an elegant writer. A renaissance man of sorts. I was intrigued.

Over the next month or so, I connected with Dan purely through Facebook. I'd comment on his photography, and he'd graciously reply. We talked about light, angles, and composition—the art of photography.

"I notice you and Dan are pretty chatty on Facebook. What's up?" Kathleen asked.

"Not much," I replied. "Just being friendly."

"It's nice to have male friends. They offer a different perspective," she suggested.

"Yeah, I know. I'm just not sure I'm ready to take that step."

"To have friends and an actual social life? That's not a step. That's called living."

Kathleen was right. It'd been over two years since Greg's passing, and I was still merely existing. I did everything I had to do to maintain life, but not much more. Work, kids, home, and repeat. It was past time to create a little me time.

With that revelation, I texted Dan asking if I could tag along on his next photo adventure. "Of course," was his answer. "Saturday, Rocky Mountain National Park, pick you up at six." I replied with a thumbs-up emoji and my address.

Done, I thought.

That morning I paced around the house asking myself, *What have you done?* I was excited and equally nervous. I truly knew nothing of this man. *I hope we can find something to talk about*, I said to myself. *Don't be silly*, I countered. *You can talk to a brick wall.*

I couldn't shake the feeling that when I stepped out the door my life would be forever changed. I didn't know why, only that there'd be no going back. Dan's car pulled in a few minutes later. I took a deep breath, gathered my gear and walked out the door.

We used the ride up to get to know each other. I told him about my recent loss rather quickly. Best to get that out of the way early as the subject tended to dampen conversation, I believed. He handled it with compassion. From there, we took turns filling in the backstory of our lives.

Dan's marriage ended after his two sons were grown. In truth, it ended much earlier, but like many they "stayed for the kids." He reminisced about growing up in western Pennsylvania, talked proudly of his two sons and seemed to have countless stories about his adventures as a young man in the Marines. His platoon was deployed to faraway lands, and he experienced things many will never know, and some of it for good reason. Dan spoke of his time in the service as if it were yesterday. I noticed moments where he'd pause in reflection before continuing the tale and couldn't help but feel there were dark sides to those days that haunted him still. *Once a Marine always a Marine*, I said to myself.

It was mid-October, and the fall colors were at their peak. No doubt the reason for our early departure time. Dan frequented the park and knew which trails were best for today. I didn't care. I was just happy to be along for the ride.

We were no more than a few feet down the trail when Dan turned to me and said, "Today's all about you. You're going to be the one taking the shots." And with that, he handed me the camera.

In that simple act, Dan unleashed a part of me that had been forgotten and buried by grief. I let go and let in the warmth and beauty that surrounded me. It was as if I was witnessing mother nature for the first time. My eye was drawn in every direction, and I discovered delight in capturing her stories. I'd found a way to breathe again, and it felt incredible.

Dan offered cues along the way. "Don't forget to look up or behind you," he'd say. He was having fun watching me, studying what my eye was lured to versus his. Big vistas and grand landscapes spoke to him while I seemed to be drawn to the little things: a puddle of leaves, small flowers or berries, and knots in trees. "I've been up this trail countless times and it never occurred to me to take those shots," he said with amazement.

That day was the start of a creative kinship. An inspiring and supportive friendship where there were no rules or expectations, just freedom. We'd hike local trails and paths capturing and soaking in the beauty of the seasons. Sometimes we'd tell each other stories or talk about the complexities of life, and other times we'd walk in silence.

"Hiking with you is like listening to a four-hour TED Talk," he'd say.

"Thanks for just listening," I'd reply with smile.

In between hikes, we'd get together for coffee or lunch to review shots, offer support with whatever was causing us angst and plan our next adventure. He'd often leave the camera with me knowing I'd make good use of it during times when he couldn't. For a time, it became my steady companion. I'd spot something out of the corner of my eye and have to pull over to take a few shots. Everyone received personalized photo calendars for Christmas that year.

In the spring, Kathleen suggested we use one of the gallery spaces at her benefit, The Poudre Pour, to show our work. We jumped at the chance. It made sense to support the river as it gave so many gifts to us. We studied the gallery space, layout possibilities, and each spent hours combing through photos trying to select just the right ones for the show. Being a closet designer, I took the lead on print sizes, display formats, etc. Dan gladly stepped out of my way, assuming construction duties as they were in his wheelhouse.

For several shots we ordered metal prints and adhered them to old barnwood backings we crafted and hung the pieces with either chains or rustic cording. Others we printed on large canvases, and the rest we framed in a variety of styles. When it came to naming the pieces, Kathleen stepped in to help. We had a blast making up silly names over a few too many glasses of wine. *No, Really the Rock was Already There* was one of our favorites. Dan and I called the show, *Where the Pavement Ends: A Photographic Journey Along the Cache la Poudre River and Beyond* and donated all the proceeds from sales to the Heritage Area. Our reward came from the doing.

On paper, Dan and I couldn't be more different. He gained peace and perspective from being in solitude with nature and frequently spent weeks living in the wilderness. His dream was to buy land in the mountains and with his own hands build a homestead to live in and share with his sons. I preferred a pillow-top mattress and room service to camping as well as being close to amenities and people. I wasn't sure what my dreams were yet, but I knew they weren't anything like Dan's.

Over the summer and following fall we'd get together to hike, take pictures or have coffee. A couple of our images were accepted onto a local show all about water, and I ended up taking second place with a piece I called *The Looking Glass*. It was a snapshot into an irrigation culvert that mirrored back an image of the river. I treated Dan to dinner with the prize money.

Later that fall, I asked Dan to teach me how to use my shotgun. I'd recently had a close call with a coyote and wanted to be better prepared to defend my flock. He took me and my son to the grasslands for target practice and later cataloged the guns and ammo in our massive safe.

"You have enough ammunition for a small uprising," he declared.

"Sounds about right. Greg liked to be prepared," I said. I later sold him some of it along with all the reloading equipment.

There was a moment where we explored the depth of our relationship, wondering if there might be more in store for us. It didn't go very far. We shared a love of photography and deep respect for each other, but our souls were destined in different directions.

In the spring, Dan called to tell me he'd worked out a way to retire early and he'd bought ten acres on a tree-lined ridge in the Colorado mountains. He was going to start building his homestead in June. It warmed my heart to know he was following his dreams.

"This is the Dan I love," I said. "You are right where you're supposed to be."

I hoped one day I'd be able to do the same. To discover what my heart truly desired. But for now, I was happy in knowing I could breathe again. And for that, I will be forever grateful my friend.

The Social Experiment

When you mix a couple of girlfriends with a few too many bottles of wine, crazy notions disguised as good ideas often surface, and worse, are acted upon. Nora suggested the girls from "the hood" gather on her patio for a bit of wine and conversation. A harmless evening, or so I thought.

Nora made the suggestion during one of our early morning runs. She and I had established the absurd ritual years earlier. We vowed to meet every Monday and Friday around five-thirty in the morning to run a three-mile loop. At the time, we both had small children and full-time jobs. The only thing that was going to be disrupted at that hour of the morning was sleep, a notion we'd learned to live without.

We set parameters around the elements; if temperatures fell below fifteen degrees or strong winds were present, we were an automatic "no go," and we agreed to text each other the night prior when ice or snow could potentially alter our path. In all other instances, we were expected to be on the corner ready to go at five-thirty.

At the time, my family had a lab-mix, Bree, and when we adopted her, the rescue told us it was short for Breeze and stood for the fact she could run like the wind. *Thank God one of us is a real runner*, I thought.

Bree was smart and all-in when it came to our morning ritual. She wasn't about to miss one. Each run morning, like clockwork, her cold nose kissed my face fifteen minutes before we were to be on the corner. I'd roll out of bed, throw on my running clothes and head out the door.

"I don't know how you do that," Nora said. "Don't you need more time to wake up?"

"That's what the first mile's for," I replied. "Besides, if I'm half asleep the run's over before I know it."

Nora took a more genteel approach. Waking an hour before to enjoy the peace and quiet of sleeping children and several cups of coffee. I'm reminded of the many times we started down the road, pacing ourselves to the slushing sound of coffee churning in her belly.

"What's that noise?" I'd ask. "Is that coming from your stomach?"

"I must have had a bit too much," she'd say with a smile, then promise, "I'll drink less next time."

Sure, I thought to myself, knowing what a tall order that pledge was. A memory of her franticly calling me to see if we had regular coffee flashed through my mind. She'd accidentally bought decaf and withdrawal was setting in. I smiled and chuckled at the thought of it all.

As the kids gained independence and our morning routines lightened, we shifted to the more reasonable time of six-fifteen. We also smartened up and raised the temperature cut-off to twenty-five degrees. Frozen fingers and toes had become old. Years later, when I moved out of the neighborhood, we stopped the practice for a few months but soon realized how much we missed our mornings together and crafted a plan to resume our runs. I'd drive to her on Mondays, and she would come my way on Fridays.

You see, it was never really about the running. It was about friendship and connection. Each one helping the other navigate the changing seasons of our lives. We set goals on Mondays and reviewed our successes and setbacks on Fridays. Each offering the other acceptance and support, and when needed, a reality check. We worked through bad bosses, annoying coworkers, family woes and our own self-doubts.

After my husband's unexpected death in 2015, our runs became vital for me. In the blink of an eye, I'd become a single parent. I felt outnumbered and alone. Our morning jaunts were moments in time where my thoughts were accepted without question, and I was loved through the pain. For me, uninterrupted adult time was a precious commodity. One I genuinely cherished.

I talked and Nora listened. She never judged or offered answers, she just gave me a place to let it all out; to think about what was before me, consider my options, and choose a path forward.

Most days we ran, others we technically jogged, and on a few occasions we were just happy to move in a forward direction. Neighborhood friends would join us from time to time, offering their current distresses and an added point of view. Our good friend, Jamie, quickly became a regular. Being that she was a college professor, she brought a fresh perspective and more importantly, interesting tales and conundrums from the academic world.

Jamie, a more seasoned athlete, convinced us to run in a few local races. "Think of them as goals," she'd say. "Something to work towards. Plus, if we do the really small ones, there's a better chance we'll win something in our age categories," she explained. "The competition tends to shrink in the advanced-age groups."

She was right. I now possessed a pair of black knit gloves adorned with pigs and the race name, The Bacon Strip. The race was absolutely horrible as it was mostly an uphill course, the roads were covered in thick sandy dirt and there was no shade in sight. It's only redeeming quality was once you crossed the finish-line, you could have all the bacon you cared to eat. I took second in the fifty to fifty-five age group and ate my fill of bacon to celebrate.

Over time I discovered I was capable of more, while Nora realized she was happy bringing up the rear. Jamie and I never let her fall too far behind. When the distance between us felt uneasy, we'd loop back assuming her pace for a while, which was better suited for conversation, and we had the problems of the world to solve in just over three miles. We talked, we laughed, we listened. We saved a lot of money on therapy.

"Let's invite the gang over for a drink and snacks. We could each bring a bottle of wine and an appetizer to share." She finished with her go-to, "It'll be fun!"

"Sure thing," I said. "It just so happens that my social calendar's wide open." Of course, it was. I'd been spending most of my time trying to figure out how to handle all that life had dumped on my plate. Somedays were smooth sailing and others not so much. Either way, there was little time left for anything else.

"I'm game," Jamie added.

It was decided. Nora would send out an email and whoever could make it would gather on her patio at 6 p.m. sharp. Well, more like -ish. We were a mix of stay-at-home moms, retired individuals, and working folk. You got there when you did and that was fine by all.

The evening was a mix of catch-up and new conversation. We learned who had been where and done what, updates on kids and plans for the future. If someone had a struggle, most likely another had dealt with it before and offered ideas for resolution. As the night progressed, some took their leave while others refilled their glasses and settled in. The conversation quickly turned to relationships or more properly, men. I happened to be the only single gal left at the gathering, thus I quickly became the hot topic.

"Beth, it's been over two years. You need to have some fun too you know," Nora offered.

"Yeah, come on Beth, we married gals need to have some fun through you," Kim suggested. She began reminiscing about her past, listing all the single things I could do now. An image of me as their pawn on the chessboard of life flashed through my mind.

It took about a year for me to shift my mindset from married to widowed. The IRS offers a two-year tax break to the newly widowed, after that you're technically equivalent to single in their eyes. I'd been in every relationship category you typically see on an application. I didn't perceive it as an accomplishment, merely a fact and wondered if two years was also the timetable for officially starting over at single.

I felt committed to my marriage vows for quite some time after Greg passed. It's not something you just turn off or tuck away with the sympathy cards. I wore my wedding ring until I felt like taking it off and later had the set redesigned into two cocktail rings. One flashy and fun, the other symbolic. Three platinum bands woven together with tiny chocolate and white diamonds tucked among them. I still remember the day I picked them up from the jeweler. It was as if a long, lost family member had come home. I cried.

For all intents and purposes, I had fulfilled the "until death do you part" commitment. I just didn't imagine I'd only be forty-nine-years-old when it happened.

"I realize I need to move forward at some point, but I'm not sure now's the right time," I said.

"Is there ever a right time?" Nora questioned.

"No time like the present," Kim declared and started pulling up dating apps on her phone.

"Doesn't hurt to look," Jamie offered in an effort to ease my mind.

I could feel their excitement and delight brewing. All eyes were fixed on me, eagerly waiting for a response. I looked at the faces before me and quickly realized the train had already left the station, and with that I surrendered, agreeing to engage in their folly.

"Okay, we can just look," I said while refilling our glasses.

With those words, the whirlwind commenced. Photos

were being selected and uploaded by some while others bombarded me with questions about my likes, dislikes, preferences and parameters. I fired back with ayes, a lot of nays, and a few maybes. After that, we were onto my favorites of just about anything: places, hobbies, quotes, movies, books, food, etc.

With my profile built, I could now discover just who else might be out there.

A thought that completely horrified me.

The last time I was on a first date was over two decades ago. I suddenly felt like a fish out of water and my mind began to spiral. *Would anyone be attracted or interested in me now? You're no spring chicken and getting older by the minute.* Panic set in and I fell further down the rabbit hole. *Greg and I grew old together. Our bodies aged together. Who would want this body now?* I thought. I was an eighties' child. An exercise-crazed decade full of unrealistic media expectations. A time when one could never be too tall, too thin or too tan. The negative body images that haunted me in my youth resurfaced and I felt completely inadequate. *Are my teeth white enough? Is my skin tan and smooth enough? What if I'm too short, too curvy or worse, too fat!* I began to regret every bad food choice I'd ever made.

Just breath, I thought to myself while backing away from the proverbial ledge. *You don't need to do anything you are not ready for. You are an accomplished, capable, independent woman. Stay open. Who knows, you might discover a new friendship.*

We spent the next hour mainly swiping left and occasionally, to the right. Quickly eliminating anyone who took their profile photo in a car or worse, in the bathroom mirror.

"A picture says a thousand words," Nora offered.

"And not in a good way," Kim replied.

"Why are there so many pictures of men holding fish?" Jamie asked.

"Nothing says, 'Hey, I'm a great guy,' better than a dying fish," I answered.

"I hope they threw them back," Nora added.

The administrator in me quickly took over. "I'm amazed at the number of men who lack insight or effort. Don't they know this is a marketing game?"

There were countless pictures of men on motorcycles, bikes or tops of mountains. Many shared photos of kids and pets. I found the ones where the ex-girlfriend or wife was cut out or shaded quite sad, but not as bad as the dirty, disheveled sparse homes in many backgrounds. "I guess the ex-wife got everything in the divorce," I concluded.

I began to feel bad for the poor, pathetic souls before me. Then the realization that I was one of them sunk in. I felt sick to my stomach. *Is this all there is for me now?* I thought. I dug deep in an effort to embrace my unwelcomed situation. *Chin-up, sister. There'll be nice guys out there, people not so different from you*, my inner cheerleader offered.

At the end of the evening, I agreed to keep the girls informed if any of our swipe rights reached out. I was further instructed that if I got to the point of meeting a man in person, I would coordinate with them so they could have my back. "You never know, Beth. Safety first," Kim stated.

The following day was like most of my Saturdays. The gym, grocery store, followed by house cleaning, shuttling kids from here to there and caring for the animals. In the evening, I planned to go crazy by washing my hair and watching television. Nights were hardest for me. I missed the adult connection time Greg and I shared. We'd make a meal and plan to watch a movie but often ended up just talking for hours. Sharing our highs and lows from the week and hopes for the future.

I settled on the couch with a bowl of popcorn and a plan to binge-watch historical fiction on Netflix. A favorite pastime of mine. I don't recall what possessed me to check my phone, but I did. I had ignored my new dating app all day but now felt compelled to check my swipe rights. I purposefully buried the app on my phone as I didn't want the kids to know anything about it. *Best to keep those two worlds separate*, I declared to myself.

In opening the app, I immediately felt insecure. *What if nobody likes me?* I thought. A vision of me as a small girl not getting picked for a team on the playground flashed through my mind. *You're being ridiculous*, I told to myself.

A few men had liked my profile, but no news from my swipe rights. *Best to expand my search*, I thought. The competitor in me took over. It was as if I was up for a promotion or a new job. I became determined to show people how wonderful I was and to discover the other wonderful people like me on this app.

I changed search filters many times to cast a wider net. I began by searching for other widowers, but later decided best not to go there as one of us in the mix was enough. I set the age parameters to be within five years of mine. Height, hair color—or lack thereof—were all flexible points for me. I said no thank you and best of luck to those who had reached out and were not a fit. I swiped away for hours. Reading about the faces I saw and making up possible stories for how and why they came to be where they were.

I contemplated what kind of man I wanted in my life now. Fabricating a list of traits: emotional intelligence, self-aware, independent, equally professionally accomplished, financially fit, physically healthy, and up for friendship and fun. I wasn't looking to start over. I was determined to keep my little trio just as it was. This was all about having a bit of adult companionship.

In the days and weeks to come, I discovered there were very few men that met my criteria on this app, or most likely any other. Men like that were happily married. Just like I used to be. *This is hopeless*, I thought.

I erased the app only to come back to it a few days later for failure was not an option. Besides, how hard can this really be? I convinced myself to expand the search criteria and consider alternatives. I wasn't looking for love. To be honest, I wasn't capable of it. My heart was sealed behind a brick wall and the probability of exhuming it was unknown. This was more of a social experiment.

After a week of statistical study and analysis, I decided it was time to conduct some field research. I agreed to meet a man for coffee. His profile picture appeared put together and he seemed well read, though rather benign. *It's a place to start*, I thought. We met on a Friday at four. I arrived five minutes early, ordered my coffee, took a seat and waited for my subject to arrive. Ten minutes passed and then fifteen. *Not looking good for this guy*, I said to myself. I considered leaving but elected to see the experiment through. In truth, I had nothing better to do. Five minutes later he finally showed. His clothes were disheveled, and he looked a bit out of sorts.

"I'm sorry to be late. I got caught up at work," he said.

"Why don't you get a coffee. After we can talk," I replied.

I watched as he procured his beverage, knowing all the while that this was not going to be a fruitful venture. I had learned that it takes about seven minutes to know which direction an interview is going to go. You'd either discover common ground on which to build a dialogue or you were going to ask cursory questions out of kindness before ending the interaction. We were going to be doing the latter.

His regional sales position in reality was more of a floor sales position for a carpet dealer. He'd been divorced for two years, most likely because of his absent personality and lack of ambition, both of which he demonstrated quite nicely in our time together. When my coffee was empty, I thanked him for meeting me, wished him well and left. Test one complete.

I learned many things from my dating site research with the most notable being, not everyone is honest or well-intended. There were quite a few deceitful trolls praying on the innocent. Scammers with false profiles and farfetched stories eager to lure hopeful hearts into opening their wallets. My widow status rendered me prime bait for the taking. It usually started with, I have a friend who is also a widow and wants to meet you. From there they'd try to draw you in with a sad story and once hooked ask you for money. I often wondered what desperation led them down this path and what delusions they employed to make harming others okay. I also wondered what they might accomplish if their energies were channeled for a good cause rather than crime. I frequently replied with that exact sentiment.

I realized that on-line dating is simply on-line shopping. Not for clothes, books or home décor, but companionship. The sites neatly package and present complex human beings for others to peruse at their leisure. If you're interested, you can click on the item to learn more but the one thing that's missing is a review section. Product reviews and ratings from past purchasers might save time and potential heartache for future customers. *Maybe Amazon should get in on this*, I thought. It all began to feel very wrong.

I did come across one nice man, Loveland. He met most of my criteria, appeared normal, and had a bright smile. I agreed to dinner and as per the girlfriend code, called Nora to tell her of my plan. She arranged to pop by our location as if by coincidence to check on me.

Our dinner together was fine. Nothing more. Just fine. Loveland was a good guy. He took pride in his work, had a caring family and many friends. We simply had no connection. How could we? He certainly showed up, but I on the other hand wasn't capable or ready for any of it. He sensed that and graciously backed away.

"How's the dating scene going?" Kim asked.

"It's not," I replied while settling into a booth at The Crown Pub.

"I think you need some inspiration. Give me your phone, let's take a look at who's out there," she directed. I complied.

Kim made her way through the list of men who had indicated an interest in me.

"I seem to be doing well in the late fifties to early sixties demographic," I reported. "Not sure what I think about that. Oh, and I get a lot of likes on my Supergirl costume photo, for whatever that means."

"Men always go for women younger than they need," she said. "They say they do it to feel young, but in reality, they're looking for someone to take care of them as they get old," she added.

"Not thinking I want to sign on for that," I offered. "I agreed to it when I married Greg, but the thought of doing it with someone else doesn't appeal to me."

"So, no big commitments, just fun, and with that in mind, how about this guy?" she replied. "He's nine years older than you, but his profile reads articulate, outgoing, likes to dance, and appears a bit nerdy. Just like you."

"Oh, but he's from Boulder," I said hesitantly. "Not sure what oddities that presents. Boulder tends to be its own cosmic universe."

"Let's respond to his text. It's time for you to have some fun!" she proclaimed.

The next week I met Boulder for lunch at the Bonefish Grill. It was close to work, and I had a limited amount of time. *Better that way*, I felt. I arrived my usual five minutes early and watched as he crossed the parking lot. He wore a suit and tie. *Points for making an effort with wardrobe and looks like his profile pic. Refreshing*, I thought.

We settled into a booth and began to get to know each other. We talked about our dating site experiences and laughed at the silliness of it all. We discussed past relationships, work, family, and more importantly, The Marvel Universe. We discovered common interests in the arts and entertainment world. He loved live theater, science fiction, fantasy, as well as historical romance movies and dancing. *How can this be?* I thought. *I've found a kindred spirit.*

What was to be an hour lunch turned into two. Boulder and I fell into conversation with ease, and he seemed genuinely interested in learning about me. I wasn't sure what I thought or felt about our initial meeting but at the end of our date, I walked away with a spring in my step and the desire to know more.

A Fellowship
of the Ring

I met Boulder outside the Rialto Café, a Denver staple for theatergoers. The restaurant was located close to the venue, served tasty food, validated parking, and the staff always made sure you had plenty of time to make curtain.

As we approached our table, I noticed a single rose had been placed at my seat. *How sweet. Smart man*, I thought. Boulder graciously took my coat then guided me towards the rose. His actions spoke to a mastery of the art of wooing a woman and the smile on his face told me he adored playing the role of a consummate gentleman. I found it refreshing and played along with ease.

We ordered off the three-course theater menu, and after a taste test, agreed to go with their higher-end house white, Angeline. I glanced across the table wondering, *Just who is this man sitting across from me?* And thinking, *It's time to get down to business.* I began my interrogations with, "So tell me about your work. Just what is it you do?"

"Oh, we're going to go there?" he said, as if I'd asked a rather vanilla dating question. I immediately felt naïve and wondered if I had committed a dating don't. It could've easily been the case as my last first date was over two decades ago. A fact that rendered me beyond rusty and quite frankly, uneasy. He indulged me anyway. I listened as he explained how he came to be in the financial services industry.

In the telling of his tale, I noticed a dramatic flair about his nature. An effeminate quality. I wondered if he truly was looking for just friendship as my profile had suggested.

If so, I'm good with that, I thought. *Gay friends are fabulous! A must-have perspective for everyone.*

By the time the entrée course arrived, I'd learned about his family, young life and current interests. His mother, an avid bowler, religiously lugged him to her leagues and practice sessions most of his young life. As a result, he now loathed the sport. *Who could blame him?* I thought.

Boulder was a big fan of strategy games and performance art. He talked fondly about his extensive experience creating and running live-action role-play events and haunted houses. He enjoyed fashioning characters, acting and had an extensive costume closet. *That may answer the dramatic flair question.*

In the course of our conversations, I gleaned that Boulder wasn't one for being alone. I recall most of his stories started with "My girlfriend at the time …" and quickly got the impression he never spent much time, if any, without a woman in his life.

"I enjoy having a muse," he said to me. "A person to inspire me."

Not sure I want to audition for that part, I thought. I couldn't help but sense the weight of the role and made a mental note of the fact for future reference.

As he continued talking about his life, my mind wandered a bit. I thought of how remarkably different he was compared to the men of my past and wondered just what might be in store for me if we courted further. *Hmm, I've never dated a free-spirited, artistic type. This could be an interesting adventure or a total crash and burn.* Knowing it was too soon to tell, I elected to continue the investigation.

As we walked out of the restaurant, Boulder held out his arm for me to embrace. I took a deep breath, wrapped my arm around his, and we stepped into the night.

During our brief walk to the theater, Boulder told me of his love for live theater and how he'd been reserving box seats for all the Broadway touring shows for years. He'd discovered a way to secure the best seats in the house for particular performances and was able to offer his clients wholesale prices for premium seats. I envisioned a lot of live theater in my future.

Once in the venue, he handed me a ticket saying, "You go ahead to our seats, I'm going to get us a drink."

"Okay," I replied, thinking nothing of it.

I gave my ticket to the usher. He looked at it then motioned his flashlight toward the stage indicating the need to walk towards it. Halfway down the aisle, I was met by another attendant. She looked at my ticket and said, "You're at the front. Your seat is front row center."

No wonder he'd sent me on alone—greater impact. He's definitely a showman. Must do this for all his dates. I know I would. He's gonna be trouble, I thought with a smile.

The night couldn't have gone better, and the show didn't disappoint. It was very much the sultry, sexy masterpiece I'd known it to be. I remember calling my friend, Christina, at intermission to tell her I was sitting front row center for *Chicago*. It'd been a long time since I'd been on a proper date, one that made me feel special. I was on cloud nine.

In the weeks that followed, we'd talk on the phone regularly and sometimes for hours. I found it refreshing to have another adult to share my thoughts with, and there was an air of comfort between us. I'd noticed it the first time we met. It was as if our souls knew each other from another era. I'd vent and he'd listen, then we'd swap, each offering the other perspective and support, something I really needed. My current roles of single parent and CEO were very lonely positions, so the novelty and excitement of our new friendship brought light to what was a very weighty time in my life.

Boulder and I met a couple of times for lunch or a movie. I'd go right from work or during times when the kids were otherwise engaged. I wasn't sure what this was to become and wanted them to have no part of my experimentation.

I'd learned long ago the benefits of compartmentalization and thought it made perfect sense to deploy the tactic for this situation. Compartmentalization is a coping mechanism that allows conflicting ideas or values to co-exist in one's mind to avoid mental discomfort, and that sounded good to me. I'm not endorsing it as an entirely healthy approach but must admit that I'm rather good at it. Besides, whatever this was needed to stay on the down-low. A mission that would prove easier said than done.

I felt Jackson would be relatively easy to elude, but Kate was another matter. Our souls were connected in ways neither of us completely understood. We'd often experience one another's emotions, sense each other's physical angst, and then there was the fact that she thought nothing of looking at my phone.

As you might have predicted, I did my best for a time but ultimately failed. I couldn't keep them in the dark for long, and during the time I tried, I did more damage than good. My plan to protect them imploded giving way to suspicion and distrust.

I came clean, atoned for the errors of my ways and vowed to never withhold such things again. Jackson accepted my apology, agreed to keep an open mind and moved on. Kate checked my phone for months, questioned my every move and made it crystal clear that she was not in agreement or at all happy with any of my ideas or decisions.

"How's it going with the man?" Nora asked while settling into one of the cozy porch chairs. Mark and Lorie, our close friends, had called a Friday afternoon porch party. We held these extended family gatherings frequently, they were a time to connect, relax and catch up.

"Oh, okay," I replied with a sheepish smile. "We've met for a few dates, but I haven't kissed him or anything. Not sure what side of the fence he's truly on. This might be more a friend thing."

"I call bullshit. You're just saying that because you're scared. You're interested," Lorie inserted. "Bethy, it's been three years, have some fun."

"Yeah, how about you plan something more intimate and see where it goes," Nora suggested.

"Say, dinner and a movie at the house."

"Whose house? Not mine. And I'm certainly not ready to go to his!" I replied.

"How about here?" Lorie offered. "Mark and I are headed out of town. You two can hang here."

"That's a great idea! And I'm right across the street if you need me," Nora added.

"Okay, I'll think about it," I said in a very defeated manner, all the while knowing I'd probably do it. They'd called me out and won. Curses!

Boulder met me at Mark and Lorie's the following Friday. I arrived early to prep food, turn on a few of the lights and most importantly, turn up the heat. Lorie, who often crossed the thin line between thrifty and cheap, was notorious for shutting off the heat or air conditioning whenever she left town.

I'm reminded of the time Nora and I house-sat for their family in late fall. There wasn't much to do. Bring in the mail, water a few plants and feed the fish Mark's daughters had given him for Father's Day, Oscar. He was a welcome addition to the tank, until he started eating all the other fish. Oscar appeared to actually be an oscar fish and not the breed the girls thought they were sold. At this point, he was solo in the tank and quite large.

Nora and I traded off days checking on their place. It was a pretty routine house-sitting gig, until an unexpected cold snap hit. Nora called me in a panic, "Beth, Oscar's not moving. Something's wrong. Can you come over here?"

"Be right there," I replied.

Upon entering the house, I was immediately met with frigid air. "Oh my, it's cold in here. I can see my breath." The house temperature read twenty-five degrees. I turned on the heat, cranked the thermostat then headed for the tank.

The water was ice cold and Oscar was lying at the bottom, frozen stiff. "The tank heater must have gone out," I said while looking about. "Nope, I see the problem. The heater's not plugged in. Mark must've forgotten to plug it in after cleaning the tank, and they didn't notice it before because the house was warm."

"Do you think if we turn the heater back on, he'll defrost and revive?" Nora asked out of desperation. Her track record with neighborhood animal care was a bit grim, and she really wanted to avoid another black mark.

"Doubt it, but won't hurt to try," I offered. "Let's meet back here tomorrow morning to see what we have. I'll look up Fish CPR on YouTube."

Sadly, there was to be no such luck for Nora, or divine intervention for Oscar. We were unable to revive him. He'd met his demise.

"What do I do with him?" Nora asked.

"I don't know. You can't flush him, he's huge. You can bury him or just put him in the trash," I responded.

"They might want to say goodbye. Let's wrap him in plastic and put him in the freezer," she said.

"Sure, it's as good a plan as any," I replied.

I told the fish story to Boulder within minutes of his arrival. It's become a family classic.

Boulder was sharply dressed, which appeared to be his chosen style. He had on one of those buttoned cardigans immortalized by university professors, a dress shirt, slacks and a tie. I wondered if he owned a pair of jeans but didn't actually ask. I can't remember what we made for dinner or what type of wine we drank, but what I do remember is that I had my first kiss by another man in front of Lorie's open refrigerator. Boulder swooped behind me, placed his hand on the small of my back and pivoted me towards him. His other hand cradled my head as he kissed me gently but fully. I was present in the moment but then again, not. My brain was asking, *Are you honestly doing this?* while my body happily played along. *Guess that's a hard no on the gay best friend theory*, I thought.

Later, he inquired about the kiss and wondered what my thoughts were around the idea of having more of them. I talked honestly about my insecurities, the uncomfortable nature of it all and he was gracious and understanding. We cuddled a bit while watching *Doctor Strange*, then later danced to a few tunes by way of Alexa and at the end of the evening we parted ways, but not without a goodnight kiss. One that felt much more delightful than the first. *Baby steps*, I said to myself.

Boulder invited me to brunch in his town before we attended a matinee performance of *On Your Feet*. I agreed to the arrangement mainly on the premise that seeing how someone lives can be insightful regarding their nature. *This is part date and part recon mission.*

His home was located in the mountains west of town. While scenic, the drive was more of a twisted alpine experience than I'd anticipated. *Hate to drive this in the winter*, I thought. His home was positioned at the end of a dirt road that hosted a handful of homes. Most were tucked away within the pines and sported mountain rustic exteriors. All except Boulder's that is. His home stood out and not in a good way.

The 1960s split-level sported a pinky-tan-colored façade and Kelly-green trim. Neither color complimented the other, nor did they belong on a house in the Colorado mountains. The front door was formal and colonial in design making the whale tail door knocker that adorned it seem out of place. There was an overgrown fairy garden and a few planted pots, otherwise the landscape was natural. I took it all in and swore to reserve my comments and potential suggestions for a time when they were solicited or when I just couldn't keep my mouth shut anymore.

Boulder met me on the front porch. He had on a T-shirt, khaki pants and a Micky Mouse baseball cap. *Yep, dresses up better than down*, I internally confirmed. After a hello hug, he gave me a tour of the house that confirmed my initial impression of good bones and potential but appears dated and confused. There were too many conflicting ideas going on and an overall lack of direction. I wondered how many of those sentiments could be said about him.

He explained the mismatched décor was purely bachelor-related, but the odd color schemes were compliments of his ex-wife. "She had eclectic taste," he stated. "I'm waiting for my next special someone to do with it what she desires."

I ignored his second comment.

After a lovely brunch in town, Boulder popped into his local barbershop for a haircut. One he sought my opinion on. "I don't have to look at it. You do," he said to me several times. Tony, the barber, had been cutting his hair for over thirty years, and by the looks of the shop, nothing had changed much over that time, including the style of Boulder's hair. I offered my suggestions as requested and each time I did, sensed Tony's hesitation. He'd look to Boulder for confirmation before moving forward, and in the end, Boulder walked away with a slightly shorter version of his usual. I made a mental note, *Creature of habit. Not as keen on change as he thinks.*

On Valentine's Day, we met for an early dinner at one of our favorite spots, The Bentfork Grill. They had a nice wine list, buffalo cauliflower wings and a seared salmon that was to die for. When I arrived, Boulder was waiting for me at the entrance. The host gave me a cheeky smile before showing us to a booth at the back of the restaurant. In what I was beginning to appreciate as Boulder's typical modus operandi, he'd gotten there early and dressed the table with flowers and valentine décor.

We exchanged gifts over dessert and being that we were both geeky, I opted to stay in that lane giving him heart nebula cufflinks, handmade by a local artisan, in a Captain America tin with dark chocolates.

My gift was hidden in a large chest filled with layers of notes and treats. Each one revealed a hint regarding the final gift. All clues pointed to jewelry, or more accurately, a ring. *He wouldn't do anything like that*, I thought to myself while reaching for the final container.

I hesitantly removed the lid and peered into the box. Sitting on a bed of pillowy satin was The One Ring: the ring of power, the ring of doom, the one ring to rule them all. Boulder had given me a replica of Sauron's ring from *Lord of the Rings*. I was simultaneously thrilled and relieved. He sat across from me sporting a prideful grin.

Yep, gonna be trouble, I thought.

I'm not sure where we were going to or coming from, just that the subject came up. Boulder and I talked about most things with ease, but this particular topic made me cringe. What subject, you ask? Physical intimacy, or more precisely, sex. He inquired if that would ever be something I might be interested in exploring. "I don't know," was the gist of my reply. I have nothing against it and feel it can be a beautiful way for two people to connect, I just didn't understand what my current relationship with the act was.

After Greg died, I figured that part of my life was over. *Sex was something other people did*, I'd say to myself. There was no place or time for such things in my life and that was just fine by me. I happily chose celibacy and coined my state of being "my wiginity."

In truth, Grief was my bedfellow. He'd clung to me like a ball and chain, clouded my mind and padlocked my heart.

I told Boulder I'd think about it and would get back to him, but planned to avoid the subject at all costs. I mentioned that if we were to ever go there, he would need to show me a clean STD test prior—it's the responsible adult thing to do. Besides, it threw a wrench in things, which was all good to me.

Over the coming weeks, I ran the topic by a few close friends who were supportive, and some gave me the "it's time to get back on the horse," speech.

"The thought of being naked with someone new horrifies me," I explained. "Greg and I understood the life scars our bodies had accepted." I remember he used to say to me, "My six-pack abs are still there. I'm just protecting them with fat."

They offered assurances like, "He's going to be nervous too," or, "He's older as well," and, "It's just like putting on a pair of jeans, except this time you're trying on a new pair."

A few Sundays later, Boulder and I went hiking and to brunch. On the ride back to his place he handed me an envelope and said, "Here, you asked for this." I looked at him a bit puzzled then opened the letter. He'd gone to a clinic and his clean bill of health was recorded on the paper before me. I chuckled a bit then thanked him. He replied with, "I don't need one from you. I know where you've been the past twenty-five years."

I'm a child of logic, a Virgo, and full disclosure, quite an over-thinker; therefore, the next phase of contemplating sex was a pros and cons list. The pros included things like, I'm in a comfortable trusting relationship, a safe place to explore new things, and I'm an adult with free will to do what I choose. The cons spoke directly to my biggest fear: vulnerability. Giving up my "wiginity" would require letting go of the sense of control I'd relied on to battle grief.

I elected to take those scary steps toward living a few weeks later. I was young and the idea of spending another thirty years or so without physical intimacy seemed highly illogical. I'm not going to go into the details of it all because it's my private affair and more importantly, my mother's going to read this book. What I will tell you, is neither one of us expected the emotional onslaught that followed. Every feeling one could ever know consumed me. I was traumatized and shattered.

I recognized that my reaction wasn't about Boulder or what we shared, it was clearly all about me. I'd had an emotional litmus test and the results indicated, not ready.

If Boulder wanted to remain in my life, it would have to be as a friend with no benefits. He valued our intellectual bond and synchronicity, and for those reasons agreed to my parameters, but not before offering the caveat of if or when I was ready to alter the boundaries, he'd be all in.

We spent the next six months cultivating our friendship. We'd get together for movies, meals and help each other with minor home projects or vexing business issues. He welcomed my home design consultation services, and together we completed several projects that made his home more cohesive and modern. In the process, I learned that Boulder's a "measure once cut twice" kind of guy and that it was best for us to leave the heavy lifting to professionals.

What Boulder excelled at was creating magical moments. Birthdays and holidays were filled with elaborate scavenger hunts and way too many gifts—a propensity he engaged in often and at times struggled to restrain. "Too much of a good thing isn't good," I'd tell him. He'd acknowledge my point of view but did whatever he wanted anyway.

The kids were somewhat appreciative of his efforts but remained hesitant about our friendship. Jackson enjoyed the fact they shared geeky gaming interests and welcomed having another male around once in a while. Kate, like Boulder, was a lover of theater, but she was not a fan of our association. She was too young to appreciate or understand my position. She just wanted her father back. Who could blame her? So did I.

A series of chance encounters and conversations with a male friend I highly respected gave me the courage to consider moving my relationship with Boulder out of the friend zone and into the fun zone. He challenged me to shift my perspective and more importantly, told me to get over myself. Sometimes when you gaze through the eyes of others you see things in ways you hadn't before.

What are you waiting for? You play so well together, why not give this another shot? I asked myself. *It's time to let go and have a bit of fun.*

And that's exactly what we did.

Over the next year, Boulder and I played, danced and even traveled together. Our live theater tally included *Hamilton, Wicked, Beautiful, Aladdin, The Book of Mormon, Come from Away, The Play That Goes Wrong* and *The Santaland Diaries*. We attended numerous concerts in big and small venues, with Elton John and Cyndi Lauper being two of our stand-out favorites. The Monet exhibit at the Denver Art Museum was to die for and dancing the night away at benefits and New Year's Eve events was a dream come true.

We were that couple: the pair everyone else watches and wishes they could emulate. I remember looking at all the women sitting next to their dates who didn't dance thinking, *They wish they were me right now*. I wished that for them too because it felt fabulous.

I joined Boulder on a few of his business trips. I'd write while he attended conferences, then after we'd enjoy all the area had to offer. Our trip to Orlando included a visit to Star Wars: Galaxy's Edge, EPCOT's food and wine fest and a rousting day at Universal Studios. There's nothing better than a little Harry Potter action followed by massive roller coasters to round out a theme park vacation.

I mentioned I was writing on these trips; an act that began to throw some anxiety into the mix. My first book, *Tragically Beautiful*, is a series of essays based around my fiftieth year and the loss of my husband, Greg. In the telling of the tales, I was reliving so many profound and painful moments it literally felt like I was having a love affair with Greg while simultaneously cheating on him with Boulder, and to add more emotional fuel to the blaze, my father was actively dying. I was torn and began to wonder where I truly belonged, what I wanted and who needed to be my priorities now.

Boulder was hoping to move beyond friends with benefits to a deeper association, and in his hopeless romantic, not-so-subtle nature was giving it the full-court press. His actions drove the growing wedge between us further into the ground.

He longed for a soulmate to partner in life and grow old with and, being that he was nine years my senior, felt his clock was ticking. I'd sensed the tug between his desires and mine months before and told him if that's what he truly wanted, he needed to move on because I'm not the one. He told me not to worry and assured me he was capable of taking care of his emotional needs, but in truth he was hoping to change my mind. That would never happen. For where I was in life, Boulder was simply a guilty pleasure.

A few days after our excursion to Ojai, Boulder drove me to the airport for my trip home to my dying father. It was there we shared our final romantic goodbye. I knew what I was about to face would forever change me and once again, priorities would be realigned. Ready or not, it was time to travel separate roads. Our fellowship had come to its end.

Boulder needed to be free to discover his special someone, a muse to light his path. I didn't have the bandwidth to be that for anyone, nor did I want to. I'd been through so much and wasn't yet the me I wanted to be, and with that in mind, I made what I felt was the right decision for me, my family and our future.

Early in our relationship Boulder sent me flowers with a card that read,

Spock –
Be careful what you wish for …
J.T.K.
(James Tiberius Kirk for all you non-Trekkies)

Since that time, I've thought a lot about the differences between what we wish for and what we truly need, and while I don't have all the answers, I've come to believe we wish for many things in life and if we're lucky, will be granted only what we actually need.

Sandwiched

My Hero

I took a seat at the bar, ordered a glass of wine and stared at it. I rotated the stem and studied the golden elixir as it swirled about the vessel. My connecting flight was delayed rendering me stuck in the Charlotte airport, but my thoughts, they were already home with my dad. I wondered how his day went, what he'd managed to eat and if he would be asleep when I finally arrived? I was overwhelmed to the point of feeling nothing and consumed with my mission. *I hope I make it ... I have to make it*, was the mantra in my mind.

"You gonna drink that?" a low-toned voice questioned from beside me.

I rejoined my body and formulated a reply. "I think so," was all I managed to come up with.

"Traveling for work or pleasure?" the gentleman to my left asked.

"Neither."

His puzzled look beckoned for clarity. I complied. "I'm going home to be with my father. He's dying."

His demeanor softened, and he shifted in his seat lessening the distance between us. I continued, "My flight's delayed. I hope I make it."

"You will," he stated as if he knew something I didn't.

We talked about the mundane but repeatedly circled back to stories of our fathers. Another gentleman, seated to my right, joined the conversation a few tales in. He talked of his father's passing and how life didn't afford him the opportunity to say goodbye. "That's not going to be your experience," he offered in support. Both men were fathers and happily shared endearing stories about their families. When the time came to board my flight, I paid the bill, thanked my bar mates for their company and headed to the gate. It was time to go home.

We'd moved to North Carolina in the summer of seventy-three. I was almost eight, which meant I'd be spending my formative years in Winston-Salem. My first day of school, or more specifically my first bus ride, taught me a few things about my new home.

As I made my way onto the bus, the driver, a stout middle-aged woman with most of her teeth, extended a warm welcome then firmly explained the rules of the road. I nodded my head in affirmation and at the end of her lecture, she dismissed me by saying, "Take the first seat you come to."

I looked for an open seat amidst the sea of prying eyes before me. They were curiously checking out the new girl, a.k.a. me, no doubt formulating if I was friend I or foe. The driver watched me move down the aisle in the massive rearview mirror above her head, and after I settled into a middle row, she asked me one final question. "Hey hon, where'd y'all move from?"

"New York," I offered.

With those words, my fate was sealed. The boys in the back of the bus took up imagined arms, declared war against the north and began firing. It was then I realized I was a Yankee in rebel territory. An unwelcome historical adversary. I chose not to engage, which ended the battle before it began. Oh, and the driver yelling at them to quit acting foolish and sit down aided my position. As the bus rolled on, I wondered if those boys even knew that we "Yankees" actually won that war.

Thankfully, the Winston of my youth has evolved into a vibrantly diverse community. Healthcare, medical research and nano-technology have eclipsed the textile and tobacco industries, attracting transplants from all over the country and beyond. So much so that Winston-Salem's city council officially dubbed their beloved town, "The city of Arts and Innovation."

I began my healthcare career at the city's largest teaching hospital over thirty years ago, and now I was back to navigate those same walls but from a different vantage point. My background in healthcare made me the obvious choice for medical power of attorney for my father, and knowing my parents had access to state-of-the-art healthcare made living fifteen hundred miles away a bit easier. I wasn't always able to be there in person, but I'd been with them every step of the way: talking to healthcare providers, reviewing records and helping to make treatment decisions that respected the quality of life they both desired.

It's often thought that one doesn't die from prostate cancer alone and that it's more likely for some other disease process to claim a life first; however, in my father's case prostate cancer was the sole culprit. It took away certain abilities, limited his freedoms, and when the medications were causing more harm than good, we said enough. What quality is there in life when you can't put two words together or stay awake long enough to engage with those you love?

The rapid decline started in early January. Dad was in severe pain and struggling to walk. His urologist graciously stopped by the house to see him and felt a round of radiation as a palliative measure for pain control was in order. My brother, Todd, and I traveled to Winston to help Mom bring Dad home from the hospital for the last time.

Mom was overwhelmed, sleep-deprived and barely putting thoughts together. It felt like we had two patients on our hands. I wished she'd called sooner.

Dad was a bit ornery—which to me was a good thing. He wanted to brush his teeth, swish with Listerine and use his own toilet. *Fair enough*, I thought while helping him with all three. Dry mouth is a side effect of radiation, and as a result Dad couldn't be without his Blistex, so I bought a value pack and made sure one was always within reach. With the pain under control, he was able to walk short distances and get in and out of a chair or the bed with coaching and minor physical help. I understood his current physical abilities would be short-lived, and our primary task was to prepare for the decline. To arrange for the inevitable.

I spent two weeks coordinating a plan for his needs while Todd waded through the mountain of paperwork that had accumulated on Dad's desk. Todd paid bills and organized documents while I made calls to hospice, private caregivers, medical equipment companies, and activated Dad's long-term care policy. I knew how to navigate the system and spoke the lingo, but I still struggled to pull it all together. I couldn't help but think that as a medical community, government regulators and the insurance sector included, we've not made it easy for those who need care to access it. We've tied our hands so tight that we struggle to get out of our own way much less find avenues to collaborate on behalf of those we serve. I wondered if one day I might want to be part of the team that discovers the solution.

Todd and I made a quick trip to the La-Z-Boy Gallery to look for a chair that would suit Dad's current status and meet Mom's decor requirements. As luck would have it, we found a floor model quite similar in size and color to their current chair with the now needed power recline. I immediately asked for the manager, explained our situation and pleaded with him to sell us the floor model. We picked it up the next day.

Dad enjoyed the chair for about a month before he was resigned to the hospital bed we neatly positioned in the master bedroom. I'd returned to Colorado to be with my children but kept tabs on his status, ready to travel at a moment's notice. That notice came a mere two weeks later.

My flight landed in Greensboro at nine-thirty on the night of February twelfth. Mom arranged for a neighbor to bring me to the house, and when I arrived my brother, Bryan, who'd come a few days before, greeted me in the driveway. "How is he?" I asked while hugging him.

"It was a rough day," he answered. "He's struggling to breathe."

Mom was waiting at the door and gave me a quick hug before we locked arms and headed to the bedroom. "They dropped off oxygen today." She pointed to the equipment as we entered the room.

"Hi, Dad … I'm here," I said while giving him a hug and kiss on the forehead. He was alert and aware of my presence. He could move his arm and head but the rest of him was puffy and immobile. I put my cheek next to his so he could kiss it. His breathing was labored, which made it difficult for him to speak, managing only one or two words.

I asked Mom a few questions about the day while surveying the medical equipment in the room. "Did anyone teach you how to use this?" I pointed to the nebulizer kit on the dresser. She had no idea, but fortunately I did and immediately gave Dad a breathing treatment, which seemed to calm him slightly.

We made it through the night with only one episode of distress. I helped him through it with another nebulizer treatment then stood by his bedside for a time, watching and listening to him breathe. I grabbed my iPad and Googled Cheyne Stokes Breathing, an abnormal breathing pattern associated with death. I studied his breathing for about an hour before I went back to my room to sleep. *It's not going to be long now*, I told myself.

When I woke a few hours later, I saw Mom bustling around the house, Bryan working in the office, and Dad awake watching TV. I was amazed he was still with us. I spent the next half hour telling him silly stories, holding his hand and watching him struggle to breathe. His body was dying. I felt powerless.

He's essentially drowning, I thought to myself. *He shouldn't have to be awake for this. I'm going to talk to Mom about giving him some morphine.* Dad's coughing brought me back from my internal thoughts. I helped him sit up a bit and wiped the fluid from his mouth. Once settled, he shook his head, rolled his eyes sarcastically, looked at me and said, "This is shit." I smiled, laughed and agreed with him. Seconds later, Dad was released from his physical form.

I called out to Bryan and Mom saying, "This is it. He's dying. Get in here."

We held him and talked to him as he passed. I encouraged him to go toward the light and told him I was happy he was free.

"Time of death, nine twenty-four," Bryan proclaimed.

I paused, looked at him and offered a cheeky reply, "You've watched too much *Grey's Anatomy.*"

Mom's tears were those of sorrow and relief. She'd been saying goodbye to aspects of her husband for some time and was happy to see him free from the burden his body had become.

She told me to call Todd feeling we ought to be together as a unit of five one last time. He'd recently lost his spouse to heart disease and needed to stay on the periphery for this one. We all understood.

"Don't call the funeral home yet!" Mom shouted in a panic. "I'm not ready for him to go."

I assured her. "There's no rush. We'll call them when you're ready." I did, however, call our hospice nurse as she needed to confirm his death. Her proclamation would be the official time of death. Sorry, Bryan, or should I say Doctor McDreamy.

Over the next hour, we walked around the house with occasional purpose, but most of the time aimlessly. We took turns calling family and spending private time with Dad's body, and when Mom was ready, I phoned the funeral home.

When they arrived, I told them of his military service and that I was going to help prepare the body. I couldn't think of a better way to honor my hero than to care for his fallen form. After we were done, the men draped an American flag over his body in honor of his service to our country, but I reflected on his dedication to our family.

My father had held on to life for me. I'm sure there were several times he could have just let go, yet he chose to endure, to hang on to life until I could be there to hold his hand as he passed from this world onto the next.

We spent the rest of the day canceling support services and arranging for the removal of medical equipment. I sensed an uneasiness between Mom and the mountain of medical supplies that had accumulated in the bedroom. The once tools were now merely objects, unwelcome reminders of difficult days filled with decline and loss. Moments that no longer mattered and were better yet forgotten. Bryan and I made quick work of organizing, removing and returning the bedroom to a space that spoke of happier times.

The next morning over breakfast we began to discuss funeral arrangements. "You're going to have to give the eulogy," Mom said to me as if it was assumed.

Unbeknownst to me, I'd become a death expert. Our family's appointed end of life specialist. My background offered insights into the field, but my proficiency came from on-the-job training. I was bestowed the honor of being the first to experience loss, becoming the family's original widow.

"Okay," was my only reply. I wasn't surprised. I'd felt compelled to tell the world of the man that was my husband, the special person he was for me. I delivered a flawless tribute to Greg during his funeral, which appears to have earned me professional eulogist status. I hoped I could do the same for Dad.

In between the must-dos of the coming days, I began to think about the type of eulogy I wanted to deliver. I flipped through photo albums, dug deep into file cabinets and visited with a couple of Dad's lifelong friends.

I learned that he'd taken an effective speaking course and received the best speech award for his uniform, humorous and informative final presentation. He even had a letter of recommendation from the instructor in the file. Those who've had the pleasure of knowing my father are probably laughing right now, and my response to them can only be … I know, right? Who knew?

Mom and Dad had lived in the south for well over forty years, yet he never lost the New England accent. Dad tended to mumble, often confused people's names and at times, when excited, struggled to finish his statements. I can't begin to tell you how often I functioned as a translator for his unique dialect.

I uncovered a company newsletter with an article titled, "Burleigh builds his own abode." Home is where the heart is, especially if you build it yourself, the article boasted. It went on to talk about the countless nights and weekends Dad spent building a home for his young family, and next to the article was a picture of us standing in front of the Spanish-styled two-story house complete with hand-carved mahogany doors imported from Mexico. I was three at the time but can remember that home as if it was yesterday. We slept in the living room until the upstairs was finished. They fashioned a playhouse for me in the basement, and on cold winter nights Dad would reach out my bedroom window and break off an icicle from the eave for me to enjoy during story time.

My trip down memory lane was one of reflection and revelation. I'd visited past experiences with the wisdom and perspective of my present and marveled at nuances that were unapparent to my younger self. It was with this richer understanding of the man who was my father that I formulated his eulogy.

◆ ◆ ◆

It fills our hearts with joy to see you all today. On behalf of our entire family, thank you for being here to honor and celebrate my father. It's often said, actions speak louder than words and that the choices we make in life shape and define us. With those thoughts in mind, I want to share three lessons I learned from my father.

In the end, we only regret the chances we didn't take.
- Lewis Carroll

Dad was in finance, a numbers man. He enjoyed the black and white of things and was a lover of routine and consistency; however, many of his actions spoke differently.

He was the first in his family to leave the small mill town in Maine to pursue his goals. Breaking the mold by going to college and later earning a master's degree.

He turned down job opportunities that weren't in the best interest of his family. Trusting and knowing a better path would appear, and one of the gutsiest moves he made was asking out his roommate's ex-girlfriend, Peg. They danced the night away and well, the rest is history.

The harder you work, the luckier you are. - Gary Player

In addition to his day job, Dad, alongside my godfather, Dick, built homes for their families. They worked every evening; every weekend and every hammer strike was theirs. I had a chance to talk with Dick a few days ago and he told me, "Beth, he never shied away from hard work. He was a great partner in business and life."

Dad loved the game of golf. He pursued the sport with great passion and commitment. Many times it got the better of him, but he found great joy and lasting memories playing the game with many of you.

Where there is love, there is life. - Gandhi

Underneath that thin, sarcastic crust was one of the biggest hearts you will ever find. He was a loyal supportive friend, husband and father. Dad loved animals but more importantly, animals loved him.

If you asked my father, what's the best thing he ever did, he would say marrying my mother. From their first date, he swept her off her feet, and together they danced seamlessly for fifty-nine years.

The definition of a funeral is preserving the memory of, to reflect and celebrate. Let's take this moment today, to share our memories and more importantly, create new ones.

◆ ◆ ◆

One of the best things about funerals is that you get to see so many people you haven't in ages. My daughter, Kate, flew in to join me and was having the time of her life hanging out with her cousins and a local friend. Bryan and I caught up with childhood pals and neighbors, and Mom's friends stopped by with homemade goodies. We told stories, played games, took walks and watched movies. Once again, the house was bustling with life. A state of being I knew Dad would be very happy about. He confirmed my assessment later that evening.

"I'm going to lay down for a little while," Mom informed us as she crossed the den making her way toward the bedroom.

"Okay, sounds like a good idea," I offered. "Rest well."

The day's events had concluded, and we were all ready for a little downtime. Bryan and his boys were seated around the table playing games, talking and snacking on the array of sweet treats that filled the kitchen. Kate and I elected to snuggle on the couch and binge-watch our latest obsession, *The Great British Baking Show*. I'm not sure how many episodes we'd watched before it happened, just that it did. The lights in the den and the kitchen flashed three times in a purposeful pattern. Bryan and I shot out of our seats simultaneously.

"Did one of you do that?" I asked.

"Nope, not us," they replied.

I glanced outside to see if the weather might have been the cause and then in the doorway of Mom's bedroom. Crystal clear outside and she was sound asleep.

"Are you thinking what I am?" I said to Bryan. We'd experienced numerous electrical phenomena in the days, weeks and even months after Greg died. Purposeful experiences that pointed to only one conclusion.

"Yep, we're not alone," he replied.

Then, as if on cue, the lights once again flashed three times in the identical pattern. We smiled in wonder, joy filled our hearts and laughter entered the room; all welcome companions for this difficult journey.

"Hi Dad," I said. "Glad to know you made it … love you."

Margaret

On the day I was born the Yankees shut out the Red Socks nine to nothing, a fact my father frequently reported when reminiscing about my entry into the world. He'd brought a radio to the hospital knowing his wait could be long, and there'd only be *Reader's Digest* and outdated newspapers to occupy his time. I arrived at the top of the sixth, and while he was thrilled, the rest of the anxiously waiting fathers-to-be were disappointed the only guy wise enough to bring a radio was leaving first.

In those days, fathers weren't part of the birth experience, and as it happened, my mother wasn't either. They'd sedated her and delivered me with forceps—a common practice at the time. When she gained consciousness, the nurses brought me to her bedside and informed my father of the good news. He entered the room only to find his newborn baby girl upside down and stripped of all clothing. "She was counting your fingers and toes. She wanted to make sure you were all there," he'd say as an explanation for her unusual actions.

Truth is, her behavior was far from peculiar given the last experience my mother had at the hospital. Three years earlier, she carried to term and delivered a baby girl with significant deformities and health issues, who lived for about two hours and was laid to rest beside my grandparents intended plots. Mom elected not to name the baby as she'd chosen only one girl's name, and God willing there'd be cause to use it in the future. I was that cause. Their final child and only daughter whose pre-determined destiny was to be baptized, Elizabeth.

My mother earned a home economics degree from Saint Mary's College in Notre Dame, Indiana, and was a genius homemaker. She took pride in exhibiting her mastery of the domestic arts by regularly sewing outfits for me with the remnants of her latest looks. I was a mini-me, or better yet, a mini-her, and have images to support my claim along with a photo of me in my first Halloween costume. She'd tied a scarf around my head, handed me a toy broom and declared me a housewife. Given her flair for presentation, I can only assume she spent way too much time on my brother's getups and had to improvise mine. By the looks of the photo, I didn't care.

Over the years, Mom made sure I was exposed to all things thought to be girl. Ballet, piano, cheerleading, tumbling, Brownies, and later, Girl Scouts. For some reason, she got the notion to sign my brothers up for tumbling as well. An idea that went over like a lead balloon and something they remind her of and laugh about to this day.

When our Girl Scout troop was absent a leader, she assumed the helm, and during her tenure, Troop 412 hiked, camped, and crafted their way through the Smokey Mountains and performed a less than stellar flag dance to "The Yankee Doodle Boy" at the bicentennial jamboree. A few of us singed our bangs learning how to fashion a Buddy Burner, but it was worth it. Mastering that skill was the only thing standing between me and the Adventure Camper Badge.

Mom was always there for me, even when I didn't want her to be. What teenage girl does? During my adolescence, she weathered many not-so-nice days, rude remarks and even a few "I Hate You!" moments. Wise to what a young me was incapable of comprehending, Mom remained positive and consistent no matter what I hurled her way. She knew her presence in my life was vital, and someday I'd be grateful for it.

That someday came when I was in my mid-twenties. I don't recall the catalyst of the epiphany, just that it occurred. The blinders of youth vanished, and my perception of the world's depth and dimension became tenfold. I promptly called her to apologize for my behavior.

When I moved west to Colorado she said, "It'll be good to put some miles between us … otherwise I might get too involved in your life."

"I hope fifteen hundred is enough," I said with a smile, knowing we'd stay close regardless.

Our family just rolled that way. It didn't matter where you were in the world or how long you'd been apart, we'd picked up as if it were yesterday and openly shared our lives. We celebrated the good, shouldered the bad and called out the ugly. You never had to wonder or worry about what another of us thought, because we'd already told you.

Mom could take one look at any of us and immediately diagnose our mood, stress level, and annoyingly, exactly how much weight we'd gained. She would make suggestions that felt like directives indicating how to remedy our current woes and trimming off a few pounds was frequently on the list, or at least it felt like that to me and my brother, Todd. We'd inherited my father's stature and slow metabolism. "I just look at food and gain weight," he'd often say. Sadly, I've discovered his perception to be quite true.

When the grandchildren began arriving, Mom was in her element. She schooled each of us on the needs of our children. It was slightly trickier for her to intervene with my brothers, fearing she'd upset their wives, but when it came to me, all gloves were off. I didn't mind as the perks were well worth it. She and my father flew out countless times to give two tired, working parents some respite. They walked dogs, fed cats, and ferried kids to school and extracurricular activities. The bonus being, upon our return, numerous home maintenance projects would be completed as well. "We washed all your windows inside and out," she reported. And look! I reorganized your linen closet." I opened the door to discover a structural masterpiece. Labeled bins neatly lined the shelves indicating their contents, and the towels and sheets were color-coded and folded to perfection.

My mother's ability to fold is sheer brilliance. The clothes she launders are museum quality. Their neatness, compression and symmetry are exquisite. "I wish you could fold like your mom," Greg would say to me. I agreed, then suggested he give

it try. We were always saddened when the last article of clothing she'd folded was put to use.

The pandemic arrived three weeks after my father passed
away. Mom, who had barely begun to adjust to life without her
partner of fifty-nine years, was forced into solitary confine-
ment. We hoped she would be able to get back to the many
social engagements she'd missed while caring for Dad. Book
club, the gym, and dining with friends were staples in her life,
and now more than ever she needed them to help her navigate
grief. Our world had other plans.

We checked in regularly, but phone calls and Zoom chats
don't compare to in-person interactions and the gift of human
touch. A squeeze of a knowing hand or, better yet, a big hug
is what she needed, and there would be none of it for quite
some time. She took to walking her neighborhood twice a day.
"I'm getting my three miles in every day," she'd report, along
with the happenings of those who crossed her path. A wave,
a thumbs-up, and at times a distant conversation highlighted
her strolls, and a trip to Chick-fil-A's drive-through for a sand-
wich and a milkshake became the social event of the season.
Enough! I thought.

I picked Mom up from Denver International Airport
in early December to spend the holiday season with us. The
woman who got in my car was a shell of the person I'd left nine
months earlier. Social isolation, known to increase anxiety and
depression, coupled with a newly grieving widow status and
pandemic paranoia was an inescapable trifecta of terribleness.
I wished she'd agreed to come sooner.

In the weeks that followed, I learned details about my mother I'd failed to fully appreciate. She was the social chair and marketing director in the family and had little to no interest in the details of finance as well as an aversion to technology. Those had been Dad's areas of expertise. Their two halves made for a seamlessly beautiful whole that was no longer complete, and at eighty-two, Mom possessed neither the desire nor capability to assume the other half. The Shift, as I've come to call it, had arrived, and it was time for her children to become the rock that she leans on.

The Year of The Rat

January 25, 2020, marked the inauguration of a new era: the start of both the twelve-year and sixty-year Chinese zodiac cycles coupled with the dawn of a new decade. The trifecta of new beginnings was upon us and suggested 2020 would be a year for ushering in innovation—new ideas, new opportunities, new possibilities. A time for reinvention and starting over. It was to be a year of change.

Chinese astrology is closely related to Taoism, a sixth century Chinese philosophy advocating for simplicity, patience, compassion and harmony. The principles of Chinese medicine, divinity, astrology and alchemy were formalized by these concepts. A person's destiny was thought to be determined by the time of their birth, the position of the sun, moon and planets, and their zodiac sign.

The sixty-year lunar cycle's ten heavenly stems are constructed from the five elements: metal, wood, water, fire and earth in their yin and yang forms. Yin, the feminine, the dark side, is associated with hard, cold, wet, while Yang represents masculinity, light, warmth, and dry. The twelve-year lunar cycle's earthly branches are identified and defined by the attributes of zodiac animal signs.

Kimberly, one of my besties, is famous for her Chinese New Year cards. She's an acupuncturist and sends the cards out on behalf of her practice. I enjoyed the notion of foreseeing what the future held for me. Well, potentially, as I'm a believer in free will. I typically keep the card by my bedside and review it several times throughout the year comparing predictions to current affairs.

2020's card didn't disappoint. It anticipated the new astrological cycle would spark major shifts in the way things currently were and promised a quite different ending to what would be a combative year of change. The year of the Yang Metal Rat was upon us.

Buckle-up, I thought.

The winds of change came early for my family. My sister-in-law, Heidi, succumbed to her long battle with cancer and heart disease in November. She'd been like a cat with nine lives, bouncing back more times than one could ever imagine. My brother, Todd, stood beside her every step of the way. Their strength and commitment to one another was inspirational. Together they endured a very twisted journey, all the while knowing there'd be only one inevitable outcome.

My father's two-year battle with prostate cancer was also coming to an end. He'd weathered two years of illness with more grace, courage and acceptance than I ever imagined. At eighty-six, he was content and just wanted to cross the finish line with the least amount of angst possible. He was gifted that fate in mid-February. I'll never forget his final words, "This is shit" and often applied the sentiment during tumultuous times.

◆ ◆ ◆

Promises and Predictions from the Metal Rat
by Lillian Pearl Bridges

People may find themselves vacillating between being alone due to the metal element and sometimes too close to others from the water element. Mother nature will be temperamental, and the winds of change will blow for years to come. People will want to refine their image, dress and take charge of their health. The earth element is weak, which may mean some areas of the world will experience famine or food insecurity. Stock up on emergency supplies.

In March, the World Health Organization declared the COVID-19 outbreak a pandemic, and we were plunged into an alternate reality for which there was no escape. Our world suddenly became very small, and we found ourselves united in a war against a common foe. A microscopic enemy, one we didn't understand, weren't at all prepared for and had no identified strategy to defeat. Conflicting reports and recommendations fed the growing panic. Store shelves were cleared of food, cleaning supplies and for some crazy reason, toilet paper. *If we're in a pinch, I can think of several substitutes for that,* I thought. *Baby wipes, napkins, maxi-pads and shop cloths came to mind. Besides, this is a respiratory virus.*

Our classification of essential personnel was quickly redefined. Hospital workers, truck drivers and grocery store employees found themselves on the front lines. I remember texting the administrator and marketing director at my former hospital saying, "You both have very big jobs at a time like this. Stay strong. Support each other and most of all, take care of yourselves. My heart is with you." I couldn't help feeling grateful and appreciative about the timing of my departure. I'd watch this one from the sidelines.

The world as we'd known it had ended and we found ourselves thrust into an uncertain future. Schools, stores, restaurants and gyms closed their doors and scrambled to identify and implement alternative operations. I remember telling the kids, "You're witnessing history in the making. This is a first for all of us." At one point, the governor of Colorado mandated the closure of liquor stores. All hell must have broken loose, because thirty minutes after his address they retracted the directive. *Whew, now that's a finger you don't want to take out of the dike*, I thought.

Being "socially distant" wasn't much of a stretch for us. Jackson's current lifestyle was already in keeping with the mandates. He wasn't much of a socialite and preferred to connect with others through online gaming platforms and apps. Kate is not much of a morning person, so getting her out of bed to get to school on time was a daily battle, one we were both happy to set aside for a while. I was close to having the manuscript for my first book ready for editing eyes, and the mandate was a welcome catalyst for me to focus solely on writing.

Most days we'd set up shop on the patio. I'd write, the kids did schoolwork and the dogs happily lounged in the sun. After lunch we'd take a walk along the irrigation canal that bordered our property before getting back to it. I often thought of those who were isolated indoors with no room to roam and felt ever so grateful for country living.

After accomplishing each day's to-do list, we turned our attention to our heart's desires. Jackson usually chose to immerse himself in the world of *Assassin's Creed*. He appreciated the historical accuracy of the games and spent hours pillaging and conquering foreign lands while simultaneously watching Minecraft and political satire videos on his phone.

Jackson's a knowledge sponge with an astonishing capacity. I'm reminded of the time the three of us were driving home swaying to the sounds of Bob Marley's *Buffalo Soldier*. Jackson interrupted the jam session to school us on the facts surrounding the soldiers. Kate and I learned that in 1866, six all-Black cavalry regiments were formed by congress to protect settlers, stagecoaches and wagon trains from the Native Americans of the Plains, cattle rustlers and thieves. The regiments patrolled the frontier, built roads and were instrumental in the Civil War. Popular belief is that the nickname, Buffalo Soldiers, was given to them by the Native Americans they encountered.

Kate opted for more typical teenage leisure pursuits. She connected with friends via Snapchat while binge-watching *Grey's Anatomy* and make-up or hair tutorials posted by her preferred beauty influencers. Like most her age, Kate wrestled with acne and pined for clear skin. She quickly embraced the mandatory mask directive as it hid her blemishes and offered her style points among her peers who'd declared them the hot new fashion trend. She bought several in a variety of colors and patterns as it was believed to be a fashion violation not to coordinate your mask with your ensemble. In late summer, we elected to go with the Accutane regimen knowing that our timing offered her an opportunity to beat teen acne before the mask mandate would be lifted.

I'd like to tell you that I used my alone time to engage in personal growth activities or home improvement projects, but I'm not fond of lying. If it's on Netflix, I've probably seen it. That goes for Hulu, Prime Video, HBO Max and Disney+ as well. There's a cushion on my sofa that pretty much has an imprint of my backside in it. I can't tell you the number of hours I spent binge-watching or napping to whatever tripped my fancy, just that it was a lot! To be fair, I did multitask, often. There are those shows that don't require your complete atten-tion to stay with the storyline. Besides, you can always pause or back-up. I'd stream those while cleaning, cooking, working in the girl garage or during my favorite task, clearing-out and organizing. Those girls on *The Home Edit* have nothing on me. I've been color-coding, labeling and bin organizing for decades. My mother has a master's in home economics. The domestic arts are my blood.

On clear, still nights, Jackson often took the lead by an-nouncing, "I'm going to make a fire," which was code for meet me at the fire pit in fifteen minutes with s'mores makings in tow. We'd sit around the fire revisiting stories from the past while trying to toast the ideal marshmallow. Many didn't make the cut. They'd get too close to the flame and ignite, becoming torches at the end of our skewers. Others softened too quickly and slipped into the fire. Only a few would achieve the crusty, brown exterior, which when bitten revealed the decadent creamy interior we coveted so.

Once our bellies were full, we'd sit back and take in all that surrounded us. We'd watch the bats circle overhead feasting on mosquitos, and listen for the hoots of our resident owls. Coyotes cried in the distance and deer crossed the pasture making their way to water and a resting place. Jackson regaled us with all he'd learned from astronomy class, pointing out planets, constellations, and noting lights that were most likely planes.

I cherished our fireside chats, for all too soon my babies would be venturing out on their own. I'd often make a wish on the brightest star hoping for their safe and secure future.

We fell into a simple, peaceful routine. One that felt very novel until it didn't.

By August, pandemic fatigue consumed us. There was nowhere to go, nothing new to do and we were over it! Sick of each other and the same four walls. Our once healthy habits were led down sinister paths by boredom and frustration. We thirsted for normalcy and found it at the drive-through. "It won't hurt if we go once in a while," I said to the kids. We quickly became regulars at Chick-fil-A and Starbucks with Dairy Queen and Dutch Bros. closing in fast. You had to time it right, because around any given meal hour the cars would be at least thirty deep. Apparently, we weren't the only ones seeking escape and comfort in food. Little did we know, the flambé was about to be served.

On August thirteenth, the mountains west of us erupted in flames. Sparking the start of what would be a catastrophic wildfire season. Once again, we were witnessing history in the making and not in a good way. Whole towns were evacuated and hundreds of thousands of acres burned. We were engulfed in smoke for months and the air quality was so poor you couldn't be outside for more than a few minutes. Masks became necessary for a different purpose. Colorado's signature big, blue skies were replaced by smog, ash and a glowing red sun. *We've just taken up residence on Tatooine*, I thought.

◆ ◆ ◆

There may be up-risings of like-minded people standing for important causes such as civil rights. Massive shifts in public opinion or politics. Protests and demonstrations about repressive and unfair policies aimed at the government calling for change. People will want stronger boundaries and a desire for personal freedom, equality and fairness. Skepticism will be common and a slowdown in economic growth will continue until 2025.

I'm not one to delve into politics, but I felt the Metal Rat's predictions in this arena were spot on, making them worth a mention. It was an election year and our country never seemed more divided. The extreme lefts and rights were playing tug-of-war while many in our nation took to the streets standing up for social justice, calling for change. This year brought to the forefront the inequities that have existed in our nation since its conception.

I found it hard to evade the negativity and nervous uncertainty that lingered in the air. The events of this remarkable year of change created a breeding ground for fear. An emotion that should never be the basis of one's decisions. Fear in its most general term implies anxiety and the loss of courage. I couldn't help but think a little courage would be a good thing right now. *To bravely go where no other man has gone before*, I thought, channeling Star Trek. *To step out of the box, welcome new possibilities and write our own history.*

We're all entitled to our opinions, but some struggled to maintain perspective, often pressing their beliefs on others. This behavior typically revealed itself via a Facebook rant. Those who took the bait would fire back with opposing positions. Sometimes the discussion took on a life of its own, and other times you'd see a subsequent apology from the poster after they'd had a chance to settle down.

I minimized my time on social media and had long since gotten rid of the newspaper and network television. Decisions I felt served me well during this politically charged chaotic year. I turned my focus to weathering the storm with as much grace and integrity as I could muster. I remember telling the kids, "Treat others as you would want to be treated and hold onto hope for humanity. This too shall pass."

◆ ◆ ◆

A major facet of this year is going to be difficulty in interpersonal relationships, especially those of a romantic or intimate nature. Old friendships will be broken, new ones formed and by the end of the whirlwind that is 2020, things will look very different.

The Bullards ended up three for three on this prediction. Jackson's relationship with an old high school flame fizzled out three months after it started, but not without offering a few milestone moments. The first being the fact that it happened at all. If you've seen the movie, *The 40-year-old Virgin*, then you've met Jackson. He's the living definition of a late bloomer.

He started talking to said girl via Snapchat. She liked something he posted and the conversation sparked from there. Jackson summoned the courage to ask her out a few days later and surprisingly she said, "Yes!" Well, that's how Kate and I felt about it.

"Mom, I'm going on a date tomorrow," he announced matter-of-factly.

"You're what?" was my shocked response. "Seriously?" I was waiting for the punchline. It never came. He wasn't joking.

"Yeah, it's with this girl I knew in high school. She had a crush on me back then. We're meeting for lunch and to walk around the shops at Centerra," he explained.

"Oh, okay," I answered while thinking, *I wonder if she'll show?*

After my shock wore off, I began the questioning: "Who is this girl? Where are you meeting for lunch? You might want to shower, shave and actually comb your hair. Oh, and most of all, what are you going to wear?"

"Don't worry, Mom. I got this," was his only answer.

At noon the next day, Jackson left for his very first date. I was nervous and unsure. It felt much like the first day of kindergarten or when your child pulls out of the driveway for the first time. I wondered if I should just happen to go shopping but quickly thought better of it. I turned my thoughts to what I was going to do to console him if she doesn't show. About that time, Kate surfaced from the basement.

"Where'd Jackson go?" she asked while rubbing her eyes and surveying the refrigerator for breakfast options. I filled with delight and held my response in order to position myself for this ever-so-sweet mic-drop moment.

"Your brother's on a date," I said casually.

"What!" she said, twirling around to meet me eye to eye. "You've gotta be kidding me."

"Nope, true that. He's on his very first date," I replied with a big smile.

"Do you think she'll show?" she asked. "Oh God, what did he wear?"

"I wondered the same thing. Oh, and jeans and a black shirt. Not sure she'll show, but we need to be ready either way," I answered.

We talked more about the particulars of his chosen ensemble and the few facts I knew about her and the date. Kate wondered if we should text him to see if it was going okay, but I said no, thinking we should let things play out naturally. About five hours later, Jackson sauntered into my bedroom. He was floating on air.

"So how'd it go? I asked.

"It was good," was his simple reply.

"Tell me more about it? What did you guys do?" I queried.

He gave me one or two details but not much else. *Looks like I am going to need to go in for the kill*, I thought. "Did you kiss her?"

"Yes, I did. We cuddled in the back of her car," he answered while sporting a Cheshire grin.

"Wow, your first date, your first kiss and now your first official girlfriend. I gotta tell you, I don't know how I feel about all this. I'm not sure I'm ready?" I told him.

"Mom, I'm twenty. It's about time," he replied before leaving the room.

A few decades sooner than I ever imagined, I thought.

After Kate realized Jackson was home, she rushed to my room for the skinny on the date. I filled her in on the minor details Jackson offered.

"I don't know what I think about all this?" she said.

"I know, right. I feel the same way," I replied. "Guess Jackson's gonna have a life beyond the four walls of his bedroom."

"Consider me mind-blown," Kate said while making gestures with her hands as if her head was exploding.

Jackson and said girlfriend went out a handful of times over the coming months before the relationship went south.

Sadly, he broke up with her on his birthday. The two were supposed to have dinner together to celebrate but she bailed on him at the last minute. It wasn't the first time she'd done it, more like the third or fourth. When we heard the news, Kate and I quickly rallied in an effort to salvage the birthday. Over dinner at one of Jackson's favorite spots, we surveyed text conversations, talked about their lack of compatibility and addressed the elephant in the room: she wanted out but was too chicken to do it. Jackson absorbed all we discussed and on our way home from dinner, respectfully let her off the hook.

Kate ended an almost two-year bond with her boyfriend over the holidays. I'd seen it coming for quite a while, but she needed to get there. They'd hang out from time to time but rarely went on what one would consider a proper date. To me, they had more of a friend versus romance connection, and Mom was all good with that. I remember telling them early on, "You both are very young and the chances of you two staying together long term are not likely, so your friendship is the most important thing you have. Respect that."

I'm all for keeping things real. In a multitude of ways, they'd grown in different directions and wanted different things. Kate knew it but held on because she respected their friendship. Then one day out of the blue she casually said, "Oh, by the way, I broke up with my boyfriend."

"Okay," was my only reply while thinking, *It's about time, glad you finally got there.*

"Yeah, I'm enjoying being with friends and working. I don't have time for a boyfriend anymore," she said.

Music to my ears, I said to myself and gave her a thumbs-up.

My relationship with Boulder shifted back to that of a respected friendship. I felt it coming for a while, but much like Kate, held on because of my admiration for our serendipity. I realized she and I may look different, but we are far more alike than either of us will ever want to admit. Looking in the mirror isn't always easy. *No wonder we knock heads so much*, I said to myself.

Once again two people recognized they were at different junctures of life and wanted different things. He was hoping to find that special someone, a life partner to play and grow old with. I wasn't interested. I had two children at crucial stages in life and aging parents to care for. My dance card was full. It was time to part ways.

One of the nice things about being in an emotionally intelligent adult relationship is that you want what's best for the other person, and although decisions like these aren't easy or without loss, you accept them knowing they're what's right.

◆ ◆ ◆

Too much of anything is never good, and we'd definitely had too much of a lot of things in 2020. I was more than eager to turn the page. On February 12, 2021, we bid a fond farewell to the tumultuous Rat and happily welcomed the Year of the Metal Ox.

In discovering I wanted to base this essay around the Chinese zodiac, I happily invited myself to Alan and Nora's annual Chinese New Year festivities. They made it a point to celebrate this special holiday with their daughter, Lily. They adopted her from the Jiangxi province of China when she was just over a year old. The paperwork stated she lived in an orphanage, The Yujiang Social Welfare Institute, near the small town of Jin Jiang, but Nora later discovered she'd never spent a day there. A local woman who's paid by the orphanage to take in infants cared for her until her adoption was final. When Lily arrived in Colorado, it was obvious she'd been constantly carried as she had no idea what her legs were for or capable of. The therapist in me took over and with the help of our bestie, Lorie, we had that girl motoring around in no time. As the African proverb indicates, "It takes a village to raise a child." We were Lily's village now.

We gathered around the table to enjoy our favorite Asian dishes and beverages. Nora decorated the table with traditional Chinese colors and symbols and had a plate of sauces and a basket of sweet treats in the center to accompany the main dishes. For my contribution, I asked Kimberly to send me Lillian's predictions for the Metal Ox year early so I'd have them for the evening. I read her thoughts out loud as we dined.

> The Ox is respected and valued for its ability to work hard and endure. It's predicted to bring peace, stability and inspiration. The earth element is harmonious with metal making way for calmer waters. It will be a time for many "re" actions. Regroup, rebuild, reform, revitalize, and the not so fabulous, recession. The year will require patience and trust. The ox is slow-moving, therefore many of the positive shifts are forecast to come in summer or fall.

Over dessert, we read our fortunes and the individual zodiac predictions for all present. My fortune cookie stated, "Your mind is creative, original and alert … a pleasant surprise is coming." Sounded good to me. *Bring it on!* I thought.

My Chinese zodiac animal is the Snake, and with any luck this is what's in store for me:

> This is a good year for snakes. The Yin nature of the year is empowering. There will be financial rewards and opportunities for the snake that others won't get, so snakes need to take them without hesitating. This is also a beneficial year for romance and friendship.

Sounds promising … I'll keep you posted.

Our Seven Deadly Sins

The battle of wills that lies within the heart of man is a universal part of the human condition. Scholars have contemplated the concept of Good and Evil within individuals or ideologies for centuries, and the dichotomy is a recurrent theme in ethics, philosophy, religion and literature. Evil can be defined as the absence of that which is considered good. An ambiguous definition with ample room for interpretation. For what is truly good? Oxford Languages definition of the term is to be desired or approved of, and that which is moral, is equally nebulous to me. Seventeenth-century English philosopher, Thomas Hobbes, offered the following on the matter:

> Moral philosophy is nothing else but the science of what is 'good,' and 'evil,' in the conversation and society of mankind. 'Good' and 'evil' are names that signify our appetites and aversions, which in different tempers, customs, and doctrines of men, are different....

Now let's flash forward to the twenty-first century to read American writer, George R.R. Martin's, take on the subject:

> In real life, the hardest aspect of the battle between good and evil is determining which is which.

Their quotes caused me to question how much humanity has truly evolved and wonder if we're traveling in more of a circular pattern. A causality loop. Continually looping back around to relive the blunders of the past but with modern amenities.

Over two thousand years ago, Greek philosopher and scientist, Aristotle, studied and presented character traits he believed enhanced human well-being: virtues. He considered the lack or excess of a trait a vice, and our modern theory of the seven deadly sins is thought to have originated from his work on ethics.

Subsequent scholars, such as Dante, a fourteenth-century poet, political thinker and moral philosopher, further defined and characterized cardinal sin. His poem, *The Divine Comedy*, is a three-part epic that follows a man, thought to be Dante, as he visits Hell, Purgatory and Paradise.

Over the centuries, mankind has adopted and adapted these philosophies for their own social or political advantage by creating external incentives and sanctions to guide others away from the vices that rulers or religions deemed undesirable, claiming it would be in society's best interest for individuals to master their passions rather than being enslaved by them, when in truth it was more often about power and control.

I wondered if I could use this same tactic with the menagerie currently residing on my farm. They're a hedonistic group who strive for virtue but are more often ruled by their vices. In an attempt to create what I dubbed as "harmony" over my domain, I began to compare the character traits of our heathens to those of the seven deadly sins; Pride, Greed, Lust, Envy, Gluttony, Wrath, and Sloth. If I hoped to become their supreme leader, I required a greater understanding of the virtues and vices that influenced their behavior.

First up is Harley, our gorgeous harlequin-faced calico kitty. She takes great pleasure in herself and is a shining example of Pride, the original and most serious of the seven sins. She's head of the shop pack and has made it clear to the rest of us that she's above all others as well—canine and human included. If there's excitement to be had, you can bet Harley will be front and center. Well, only when she wants to be. When my Girl Garage was on a local tour, Harley made it a point to sprawl herself across the welcome table for all to admire. "No need to see the garage folks, the best is on display right here," she declared.

She moves with great confidence and little care about anything or anyone in her path. She's an exceptional hunter, scales trees with ease, often surveys the farm from her throne on the roof of the shop and lounges in my window boxes. She stands at the back door when in need of our services or feels we must admire her. She's also classic for jumping into cars when you're not looking and has spent several hours locked in mine a few times.

The neighbors regularly send me pictures of her sunbathing on their decks or lounging on their furniture. It pains me to know she travels so far, and watching her cross the road is never easy, but Harley does whatever she wants and does it well. She's been crossing the road almost daily for over seven years, looking both ways at least twice before stepping out to cross.

The virtue associated with Pride is humility, a trait Harley knows nothing of but instills in others. We're humbled by her confidence, beauty, talent and amazingly cool vibe.

Next up is Finnley, Kate's pandemic pup. Our neighbor fosters pregnant dogs and usually has a litter or two at any given time. Kate and I regularly stop by for a puppy fix and once in a while she lobbies for a pup, but I never seriously consider it. That all changed when we met Crow, an adorable black and white border collie mix. He was super chill for a puppy, preferred lounging to playing, and bonded to Kate in record time. She immediately fell in love, and I wasn't far behind. He had a kindness in his eyes that was endearing and a docile nature that was unique among his siblings. On subsequent visits, he'd be waiting for us at the gate and always whimpered when we put him down or left the kennel.

Long story short, I gave in and said yes. Given we were now in an official pandemic, the kids and I were going to be home all summer long to train and love our new family member. *As good a time as any*, I thought. Crow became Finnley and a part of our family two weeks later.

Finn's love for his toys and selfish desire to hoard everyone else's makes him the epitome of Greed. Being the youngest of our canine threesome, his place in the pack was clearly at the bottom, but what he lacked in age he quickly made up for in size. The DNA test came back a week after we brought him home and the results revealed his mother was a border collie lab mix as suspected, but his father was a Great Dane. Our pandemic pup was to become a horse!

Finn's excess went beyond material goods. He desired to go everywhere and do everything his considerably smaller pack members could. When we brought him home, I declared Finn banned from any of the furniture. My directive failed. He whined his way into our laps then onto the couch and now full-grown, takes up the entire thing. You can carve a space for yourself provided you're willing to have his head in your lap. "Finn thinks he's a ninety-pound Yorkie," a friend said to me. I never thought of it that way, but he was spot-on.

Finn's not one for being left behind. If anyone goes outside, he's going too. The trouble is, in his eagerness to join the fun, he unknowingly forces the little ones to flee for fear of being stepped on, and once out, wants to play, which can be very annoying when needing to potty or hoping to lounge. I've added seasoned doorman to my résumé, as much of my day is spent staggering the ins and outs of three dogs to meet the needs of all.

Charity, the quality of being open or giving freely, is Greed's complementary virtue. From the first day we met our gentle giant, he's given his heart freely to all creatures on the farm. His easygoing and moderately lazy nature tempers his youthfulness and size, and the joy he's brought to our family is immeasurable.

The ruling monarch of our animal kingdom is a seven-pound Yorkie-poo named Izzy. She's my rival for supreme ruler, but fortunately I have an asset that should sway things in my favor. Queen Izzy's vice is a lustful heart that craves power and devotion. All who enter her kingdom are greeted with a demand for attention that won't end until she's acknowledged. She's skilled in the art of persuasion and uses her charms to coax her subjects into willingly submitting to her every desire.

What she lacks in stature, Izzy makes up for in tenacity and has yet to be defeated in battle or have her reign doubted. She backs ninety-pound Finn into his bed with merely a look and a few suggestive barks. Our other dog, Lucy, is passive by nature and flees at the first sign of conflict. The cats respect her authority and tolerate her advances when unable to avoid them. She often attempts to hump my leg, which is an inherent behavior that's thought to be either a display of supremacy or an invitation to play. In our case, the first hypothesis is most likely the reason.

I'm pretty certain I'm to blame for creating such a dominant sovereign. Izzy thinks everyone should love her as much as she loves herself, and why wouldn't she? From the moment she entered our lives, she's been doted on, and if she ever did something amiss, we'd just pick her up, which further endorsed her actions. If you likened Izzy to a Disney princess, she would be Merida from the movie, *Brave*: an impetuous, independent and courageous lass.

Purity, the virtue that combats Lust, can be described as a state of innocence or freedom from corruption. Queen Izzy's rule is just that, pure and true. One will never doubt their place in her kingdom, nor will they fear treachery or revenge. For her heart is full of love and her ultimate desire is to safeguard those she holds dear, and that's my trump card. Izzy will forever bow to my will because I'm her bonded person: the one she trusts and loves most of all.

Shakespeare's thought to have coined the idiom 'green with envy.' In *Othello*, Iago warns his lord to beware of the green-eyed monster known as jealousy, a vice that brings discontent to those who fall prey to passion, and as it happens, our coincidently green-eyed tortie, Rafter, is no exception. She desires the attributes her siblings so easily exhibit. Those of confidence, bravery and trust.

Rafter's insecurities impede her from receiving the human affection she so longs for. We often see her hiding in the shadows just out of reach, watching and pining for the love she wished she had the nerve to know. There are glorious moments when she summons the courage to interact with us. They mainly come in the evening and involve the wet cat food she adores. We'll caress her while she eats, and at times she'll hop in a lap for a cuddle session after.

If Rafter sleeps in or welcomes our advances, it's usually an indication that something's up and she needs our help. Trapping her for vet checks can be quite the challenge, but when unwell she embraces envy's opposing virtue, gratitude. Rafter accepts our love and care with no objections but once mended, she'll withdraw from human contact even further. Retreating to the shadows of the shop until she's ready to start trusting again.

About three months after our beloved Paisley passed away, the kids and I agreed that while the barn kitties were wonderful, we missed a feline presence inside our home. We understood there was no replacing such an extraordinary cat but sensed there might be room for another. I took our collective feelings as a mutual thumbs-up and began combing the available adoption lists on local shelter and rescue websites.

Two weeks later, a three-year-old mackerel tabby, named Em, entered our lives. I likened her name to that of the character, M, played by Dame Judi Dench in some of the more recent James Bond movies, and felt we should keep it.

"Let's call her Ember, and Em for short," Kate suggested.

"Perfect," I replied. We were in the midst of a historically horrendous fire season, so the name seemed fitting on several fronts.

We learned that Ember's past wasn't full of sunshine and daisies. She'd been a stray living in the back alleys of Rome, Georgia. A local rescue, Floyd Felines, found her hungry, pregnant and in need of medical care. They took her in, and when she was stable, transferred her to our local rescue where she gave birth to seven kittens. Once all the kittens were adopted, Em was spayed and prepared for her new home.

Ember's rough start is most likely the reason for her vice, Gluttony. The term means to over-indulge or consume more than one requires. I can't think it was easy growing up as a street rat. Always having to be on alert and at the same time wondering where your next meal would come from. Enduring the elements, evading predators and surviving on whatever scraps you could beg or steal.

It's not enough for Ember to have her bowl filled twice daily. Once she polishes off her saucer, she's on to any others that may have a few pieces of kibble left in or around them. She cleans the floor of any random edible items and scouts the house for empty food wrappers or plates that may contain a crumb or two.

If I'm preparing a meal, she's close by watching and waiting for me to turn my back so she can swoop in and steal a sample. I found her in the kitchen sink lapping up the remnants of a drained tuna can then turned on the water to see what she would do. She didn't move. Living a hard-knock life has made Ember stealth, swift and rather fearless.

All good traits to have when living with three dogs, I thought to myself.

I'm reminded of the time I turned my head to grab the salt and she made off with an entire chicken thigh. I chased her into the laundry room, but she ate most of it before I could get to her. After that altercation, I determined it was time to get a bit more serious about boundaries and work on self-restraint. In an effort to defend our food, we strategically positioned spray bottles filled with water around the kitchen and posted a sentry when hosting visitors. She wasn't keen at first, but in time surrendered to my will, as I am the hand that feeds her, and in the weeks and months that followed, her gluttonous desires were lessened by the virtue of abstinence.

In most dynamic duos, the sidekick often possesses qualities that balance the protagonist. SpongeBob had Patrick, Harry Potter had Ron Weasley and our Izzy has Lucy, a slightly overweight submissive Yorkie mix. Lucy's a docile girl who's quite content to play second fiddle to her alpha. She prefers belly rubs to roughhousing, fears the lawn sprinklers and loves riding shotgun in the car. Patience is the virtue Lucy possesses in spades. She's easy-going and when confronted, typically responds by removing herself from the situation. However, the addition of Finn shifted the dynamic.

His unpredictable puppy behavior and constant desire to play has exposed Lucy's hidden vice, Wrath. She does her best to tolerate his provocations, but at times he gets the best of her. She'll bare her teeth and offer him a fair warning growl before unleashing her inner warrior. The fury that ensues is typically short-lived and frequently a calculated effort on her part to move him out of the way so she can retreat under a bed. I've seen her egg him on a bit, and there are moments she appears to be enjoying the sparring sessions, but those are short-lived.

Izzy often joins the skirmish in an effort to control her pack, which causes further chaos. I find the whole thing rather annoying and have taken to planning walks and playdates with Finn's big dog friends to curb his enthusiasm. An endeavor I think Lucy genuinely appreciates.

The last of our seven sinners is Cali, a rather large, or more accurately extra-large, calico kitty, who resides in the shop and is the poster-child for Sloth. She's long given up hunting, as that requires physical effort. Something she uses her virtue of diligence to avoid. Lounging has become her primary occupation, and she's a master.

If Cali leaves the shop at all, it's to sun herself in the backyard. She'll lie just about anywhere there's sun and a cool surface, and when she gets too hot, she'll seek shade under a parked car or the old wagon outback. She's a rather neutral gal who's known for being more slow-then-go. The dogs will run up and sniff her and she'll meow in return but never move an inch. Cali's become a fixture in the backyard when the weather's good and in the shop when it's not. Jackson describes her status as officially retired.

My Supreme Ruler aspirations are often thwarted by small uprisings that frequently occur an hour before dinner or treat time, in an attempt to overthrow my decree of "dinner at five" and "bones at seven." Lucy will position herself in the middle of the den, look me straight in the eye and howl in a repetitive pattern as if she's chanting. In the meantime, Ember sits on the banister swatting Finn in the face causing him to bounce about and whine. Izzy then spins around the two of them barking.

The orchestrated dramatic production is their way of infuriating me to a breaking point. Achieving a level of frustration that will cause me to give in to their demands. This battle of wills is a recurrent skirmish where my victories only slightly outweigh my defeats. Some nights, I stand my ground enforcing the established laws or even lengthen the wait as penance for their actions. Other times, my desire for peace, or our schedule, results in feeding them early.

Oh, and the country's need for Daylight Saving Time causes tremendous strife in our realm. I'm all for reconsidering that phenomenon.

Scholars and theologians thought sin to be the cause of unhappiness, but from my perspective our seven little demons seem quite content. Maybe it's because they live in the moment. Seeking only what is presently required and accepting life exactly as it is today. A rather simple approach we humans tend to overcomplicate with scars from the past or my favorite, future tripping.

My foray into the perils of Good and Evil has resulted in a fresh perspective and greater respect and appreciation for the duality that lives within a soulful heart. Darkness is necessary for our survival and evolution while light presents us an opportunity to explore meaning and purpose, and with that in mind, I've reconsidered my approach to the menagerie that resides on the farm. There will be no supreme leader among us. Our kingdom will be more of a corporative existence that dwells in the present and ebbs and flows as needs and circumstances dictate.

> Those who teach us the most about humanity aren't always human. – Donald Hicks

The Oppressed

Since the dawn of man, we've been considered sub-human. Looked upon by many as sinister, unlucky, and for some, downright evil. Our so-called "affliction" was believed to be spawned from Lucifer himself, and as a result we were cast out and persecuted for centuries. Cursed simply for being unique.

Some cultures thought better of us. In 750 BC, the Celts worshiped our kind, believing we were a source of femininity and life. The Incas also embraced our rarity, feeling we possessed magical powers and healing abilities, a belief the indigenous people of the Andes continue to respect today.

Unfortunately, the prejudice against us knew no bounds and the voices of our supporters were swiftly silenced. We took to the shadows and when necessary hid our uniqueness from others for fear of being converted, beaten until our actions aligned with their beliefs. Disapproval of our kind grew as Christianity and Islam spread throughout the world. It spanned the globe, weaving through cultures and eras, and sadly, remains present today.

Ten percent of humans bear the mark. A percentage, which by research standards, has been consistent for over five hundred thousand years. Why no change you ask? It's hypothesized that we were talented competitors as our uniqueness was an advantage over others. In that world we reigned, but alas, over time, cultures gave up fighting and adopted a more cooperative existence, operating on behalf of the many versus the few. Those principles required us to conform to the norm, which put us at a disadvantage. The opposing concepts of competition versus cooperation are thought to be the reasoning behind our stagnant numbers.

The origin of our uniqueness is epigenetic, a variation caused by gene expression rather than alteration of DNA. Genetic markers, biology and environmental influences are all factors that hardwire a human's preferences before birth. Yes, this unique characteristic is determined in the womb, long before we take our first breath.

Have you figured it out yet?

The human trait that's oppressed ten percent of the world's population for hundreds of thousands of centuries. Oppression that has known no bounds. It's universal, manifesting in a variety of discriminatory practices and damaging attitudes throughout the known world. Oh, and of note, race, sexuality, religious beliefs, level of education, and financial or societal status have no influence over the downtrodden. We are equally persecuted by all. My son, Jackson, is also a member of this subjugated group, an ancient minority who have been tormented through the ages for merely being left-handed.

The term left, obtained its sinister roots from the Latin word, *sinistra*. Anglo-Saxons coined the term *lyft*, which meant weak or broken. Religion further divided the body into ideals of good and evil. In Christian teachings, Jesus sits at the right hand of God, making it the favorable hand. Right became a symbol of all that is pure, correct, lucky and angelic, while left was believed to be the hand of judgment. Those who fell from God's favor were sent to the left, and traveling the left-hand path meant you were entering into deception, darkness, black magic and Satanism.

The Islamic concept of purity calls for men to use their right hand for pure actions such as eating and shaking hands, while the left hand is used to perform the impure actions of personal hygiene and taking off clothes. In Arabic cultures, the left hand has been dubbed "the unclean" or "dirty" hand. I can't help but wonder if this concept was more of a well-crafted public health initiative disguised as a religious directive, but regardless, the belief has been ingrained for centuries.

Numerous other cultures consider the use of the left hand for pointing, gesturing, or greeting another as rude or unlucky. So much so, individuals regularly placed their left hands behind their backs when greeting or interacting with others.

The fifteenth and sixteenth centuries brought the height of the witch hunts and trials. During this time, left-handers were strongly oppressed throughout medieval Europe and beyond. Their handedness was commonly judged as sufficient proof of consorting with the devil, and they'd be condemned and later executed. I'm glad I wasn't around to experience those turbulent times.

The eighteenth and nineteenth centuries were no better for we lefties. Discrimination against us became socially ingrained and attempts to suppress us were downright brutal. We were seen as savage, corrupt criminals with pathological behaviors. In school, children's left hands were tied behind their chairs to promote right hand use, and those who didn't comply were often subject to corporal punishment. If a child was caught using his left hand in some African cultures, his hand would be submerged in a bucket of boiling water as a lesson to one and all.

Thankfully, lefties gained a few allies in the mid-twentieth century and our left-handedness became merely perverse or impish behavior. Being no longer considered the spawn of the devil himself, opened the door for further contemplation and study. In the 1960s and 1970s, educators and researchers determined that forcing children to become right-handed was leading to increased incidences of stammering, dyslexia and emotional distress, but regrettably, their findings fell upon deaf ears. Religious school teachers continued to inflict corporal punishment on left-handed students, often accusing them of being in cahoots with the Devil or strangely enough, Communists. Many European countries enforced anti-left policies forbidding the use of one's left hand for writing in school, and the country of Albania took it a step further, declaring left dominance a crime.

Education reformer, John Dewey, and psychologist, Marian Annett, gave lefties their biggest break yet. Dewey argued for tolerance toward hand preference while Annett's research revealed numerous fundamental flaws in prior studies.

Her work debunked the myth that left-handed individuals were stubborn, clumsy losers destined for a life of crime, and that their risk of mental illness and early death was no greater than that of their right-handed classmates.

I entered kindergarten in the 1970s and am grateful for the acceptance I received from my teachers as I progressed through the elementary years. Unfortunately, my uncle was among those forced to change his natural handedness to conform to the established norm. An act that fostered learning disabilities and ultimately, shaped the trajectory of his life. I recall needing extra support with writing in cursive as my penmanship was atrocious. A fact that wouldn't matter in the long run as I chose to enter the world of medicine—a place where professionals abbreviate just about everything, use an incredible number of symbols, and legibility is optional.

I'm all for owning my part in things and will do so regarding handwriting, but I'd like it noted that being instructed by right-handed teachers and sitting at a right-handed desk probably had an impact on the quality of my penmanship. At the time, lefties weren't taught to shift their paper in the opposing direction to match their handiness. As a result, many had to contort their wrist to be able to see what they were writing and to avoid the dreaded smudge. All too often the side of our hand brushed the paper, smearing our work and worse, staining our hand. Let's not forget to mention that binders' and spiral notebooks' spines, made for the majority (right-handed people), are on the left. An obstacle we lefties must continually navigate over when using them. And don't even get me started on scissors! No wonder my cut and paste projects were regularly deemed less than ideal. That's what you get when you're asked to do something backward.

I think it's the reason why I tend to read magazines and newspapers backward, and at times transpose my numbers. I'm not sure if most lefties have a touch of dyslexia, but I know I do. Double-checking my work and spell check is a must!

In thinking about handedness, it makes perfect sense that our world's tailored for the majority. Ninety percent of humans on our planet are right-handed, making it highly likely that developers, architects, engineers and manufacturers who create all we use in the world do so from a right-handed perspective. Why wouldn't they?

When you go to an ATM or gas up your car. Which side are the credit card readers and keypads on? Look at your toaster oven or microwave. I hazard a guess the control buttons are on the right. Pay attention to the tray table on your next flight. I bet the cup holder indentation is on the right. Manual and power tools, musical instruments, cooking utensils, cameras, sporting equipment, and even firearms are all made with the majority in mind. Manufacturers have fashioned left-handed compatible counterparts for some of the aforementioned items, but more often than not we lefties just use what's readily available and never give it much of a thought. We've been conditioned to live in a world of right-hand privilege.

There are those who have risen above, thriving in the face of oppression. Michelangelo, Raphael and Leonardo da Vinci evaded persecution becoming Italian masters. Da Vinci was known for his mirror writing in which he wrote his text backward. Maybe because he knew moving from left to right would be too messy! Julius Caesar and Napoleon both ruled with a left hand. Napoleon objected to the tradition of marching on the left side of the road with weapons ready at the right because it put him at a disadvantage.

Mozart shaped classical music, and Renoir mastered French impressionism from the left. Lewis Carrol wrote famous novels about a quirky girl named Alice, while Marie and Pierre Curie captured the Nobel prize. Of note, their daughter, also a lefty, earned her Noble prize for radioactivity.

Lefties are thought to possess a wider scope of thinking, excel at complex reasoning, creativity, intuition, rhythm, and visualization. Presidents Barack Obama, Bill Clinton, George H.W. Bush, Ronald Reagan, Gerald Ford, Harry Truman, Herbert Hoover and James Garfield are all part of the lefty ten percent. As is Bill Gates, Steve Jobs, Mark Zuckerberg and Michael Bloomberg. Mother Teresa and Ruth Bader Ginsburg were among the eight percent of women lefties. Media executive and billionaire philanthropist, Oprah Winfrey, is also a member of the left-handed faction. I'm honored to share this unique trait with these accomplished ladies.

Lefties are thought to have an advantage in sports such as boxing, tennis and baseball, as their dominance offers an unexpected edge over the competition. Ty Cobb, Ted Williams, Sandy Kofax, Barry Bonds and Babe Ruth confirmed that theory. Successful southpaws like Marvelous Marvin Hagler, Manny Pacquiao and Pernell "Sweet Pea" Whitaker dominated their opponents in the ring, and John McEnroe, Martina

Navratilova, Rafael Nadal, Phil Mickelson and Wayne Gretzky are proof that lefties can not only hold their own but excel in sports.

Hollywood's seen its share of lefty leading men and ladies. Charlie Chaplin, Marilyn Monroe, Judy Garland, Morgan Freeman, Julia Roberts, Robert De Niro, Nicole Kidman, Mark Hamill, and my favorite, Keanu Reeves, are a few of many talented ten percenters. Keanu and I also share a birthday, 2 September. He's extra special in my book.

The music world is saturated with lefty creatives: David Bowie, Annie Lennox, Sting, Celine Dion, Paul McCartney, Jimi Hendrix, Adam Levine, Lady Gaga, and my girl, Pink, to name a few.

Writing this essay has made it clear to me that while being left-handed does have its disadvantages, it also comes with blessings, and like most things in life, it's all about mindset. Do you allow yourself to become defeated, assuming the stagnant role of victim, or do you accept yourself as a whole and meet, or better yet, rise above the challenges life offers you? I chose the latter.

We lefties may be a minority but we're mighty, and more importantly worthy. Fear not the differences in others, but welcome their unique individualities and the gifts a diverse society provides.

Viva la difference … Celebrate the Lefties in your life!

Vallarta

"Hey, you doing anything tonight?" Nora asked.

"Nope, I'm currently without a social life," I said as we rounded the final corner on our Friday morning stroll.

"Why don't you come over for a cocktail this evening," she suggested.

"Sure, that works. Hey, maybe we can video chat with Mark and Lorie."

"Yeah, let's. I haven't talked to them in a while."

"It'll be like old times," I declared. "Be over about six."

"Okay, see ya tonight."

I settled into a chair at the kitchen table and flipped through the newspaper while Nora opened a bottle of chardonnay. She'd prepared a few appetizers to accompany our wine, and they were neatly displayed about the table. We reviewed the tedious details of our day and potential plans for the weekend.

"Hey, let's try Lorie." I grabbed the iPad, pulled up Messenger and hit the phone icon. Lorie answered after a couple of rings.

"Well, hello from Bend, and happy Friday," she said as she raised her glass of wine in celebration. We spent the next hour piecing together the timeline of life events since our last conversation. Mark popped on the screen once he arrived home from work, and soon after, Alan, Nora's husband, commandeered the iPad for a bit of male bonding time. Hour two of our virtual Friday Afternoon Club was when the bright ideas and plans started hatching.

"Okay, when are we going to see each other again physically?" I asked.

"Nora, you need to come to Bend. Beth's been out since we moved, but you haven't," Lorie pointed out.

"Yeah, I know. We've just been so busy with Lily's volleyball and Tru's baseball. It's hard to carve out time to get away."

"Hey, we have extra timeshare weeks, how about we meet up in Mexico?" I proposed. That suggestion started the wheels turning, and after a few calls and emails between ourselves and the vacation club, we secured two condos for two weeks in Puerto Vallarta in late April. Mark and Lorie planned to be there the entire time, while Nora and I felt we'd each take one of the weeks. That plan fell apart after Tru's baseball schedule came out.

"Tru, and Alan for that matter, don't want to miss any practices," Nora annoyingly explained.

"Seriously, it's only a few practices." My frustration with Tru's adolescent logic and perspective spilled into our Chinese New Year celebration.

"Tru, I can't believe you're going to give up a trip to Mexico for two baseball practices," I said to him as we dined on orange chicken.

"I can't believe you planned a trip during my baseball season. I missed out on the Spain trip, and now this one. It's not fair," he replied.

I think of Tru as one of my own, thus had no reservations about continuing our button-pushing banter. "You're a sophomore, and we're in the middle of a pandemic. If any scouts come to your practice, which I doubt by the way, they'll be eyeing the upperclassmen not you. Besides, who knows if the practices will even happen."

"I think you and Mom are being selfish and need to change the dates to after baseball season."

"I think you're being ridiculous, and I can't wait for the day you grow up enough to realize it too," I said, then promptly changed the subject. Tru was having the time of his life vexing me, and I no longer wanted to give him the satisfaction.

Alan and Tru were now out of the travel picture, and so was Jackson. He was a junior at Colorado State University, and his spring break didn't match up with our plans—plus, he wasn't interested as we'd made this same trip before. Kate, on the other hand, was another story. When she realized the men were out, she jumped on the girls' trip train and worked it hard.

"Mom, you know it's my birthday month, and I didn't get a sweet sixteen party due to COVID, so how about we celebrate in Mexico this year?"

"Yeah, but it's not your spring break week, and your grades are less than stellar," I pointed out.

Kate wasted no time telling her best friend, Kaitlin, about the possibility, and together they produced a PowerPoint presentation detailing their plan for academic success despite the missed school days, and the work hours they'd scheduled to secure funds for the trip. I said I would think about it and get back to them by the end of the week. I knew I would most likely say yes but wanted to see them initiate the plan first. I ran the idea past Nora the next day.

"If they each have someone to pal around with, then we're off the hook," Nora suggested. "Lily's birthday is two days after Kate's, so we could celebrate both."

"It would definitely make up for last year's bust of a birthday. And instead of a senior trip, she'll just have a junior trip," I offered.

Against our better judgment, Nora and I agreed to a birthday girls' trip for Kate and Lily, complete with a friend of their choice, provided the friend buys their own plane ticket and brings money for daily expenses.

I booked myself and the girls on the same flight Mark and Lorie were connecting to in Denver so that we could pick up the rental car and travel to the condos together. I retained some sense of sanity and extended my trip four days beyond the girls. I said it was for uninterrupted writing time but knew I'd likely need downtime after a week with two teenagers. I gave Nora our itinerary and told her to get on it, which she didn't do.

Nora's always been a bit of a procrastinator, which this time resulted in her having to pay the extra sixty bucks to expedite Lily's passport. "I'm using flight points on another airline for our tickets. We'll arrive the day after you and return on the same day as your girls," she explained.

"So, we're all there at the same time?" I asked hesitantly.

"Yep, we wanted to be there with you guys."

"Okay, the younger girls will have to take the sofa bed, and I guess you're bunking with me." *I'm certainly gonna need those four extra days*, I thought to myself.

A couple of days before we were set to leave, Nora called me in a panic, "I just got a call from Lily's school. She's had a COVID exposure."

"Oh no, what are you going to do?"

"I don't know."

"They don't require a COVID test to enter Mexico."

"Yeah, but they do to leave. I don't want to take a chance on getting stuck there with Lily."

"You gonna come anyway?"

"I don't know. Let me talk to Alan."

Just before boarding, the girls and I met up with Mark and Lorie at the gate. I seated the girls several rows behind me, figuring we'd have enough bonding time in the days to come, but neglected to consider the customs and immigration documents.

"Did you two have any trouble filling out the forms on the flight?" I asked as we showed our health documents to the agent and passed the temperature screening area.

"Yeah, we're good," Kate informed me. We slowly worked our way through the long switchback line that led to the customs agent, and when we were a few rows from the front, I asked, "Do you have your passport out and ready?"

"Oh no, I put mine away," Kaitlin reported. We stepped aside to let others by us until she could locate it and then stepped back in line.

"We're up soon. Put your customs and immigration forms in your passport," I informed them.

"Wait, you don't have it? I didn't get one from the flight attendant. I told her you would fill it out for me," Kate stated. Once again, I moved the girls aside, asked the agent at the front of the cue for the form and handed Kate a pen. When she was done, we stepped back in line and waited to be directed to an agent station.

"Number two," the line agent said as she pointed at a handsome young gentleman two stations down. The girls giggled with excitement and anticipation. I handed my documents to Miguel with an "*Hola*" and a smile. Kate was next as families share a customs form, and Kaitlin, who seemed more interested in flirting, followed.

"*Hola*," she said with a smile and a flip of her hair.

Miguel played along until he discovered her error. "You need a separate customs form since you are not related to them," he explained as he handed the form across the counter. Once again, we moved to the side so others could pass.

"I can't believe you two. We're never gonna get out of the airport," I said with a hint of sarcasm and mounting frustration.

"Mom, get over it. We're on vacation," Kate reminded me.

Next stop, the button of destiny: the final hurdle that stood between us and paradise. One by one, we stepped forward to discover our fate. If a green light appeared on the screen, you were free to exit the airport, but if a red light flashed, your bags were subject to a thorough search. Thankfully the travel gods blessed us with three green lights, and we sauntered through the glass doors and into the timeshare madness tunnel. "Keep your head down, don't make eye contact, and just keep walking," I said to the girls. Lorie was waiting for us on the other side.

"Where have you been?" she asked.

"Ever go through customs with two teenagers. It's a miracle we made it out at all," I offered.

Lorie laughed. "I figured it was something like that. I sent Mark to get the car. He'll swing around and pick us up." Ten minutes later, a small grey sedan stopped next to us.

"What happened to the van we reserved?" Lorie asked.

"No *más* vans," Mark replied. "The guy told me to check back tomorrow."

"Well, we have to come back to pick up Nora anyway, so it might be worth a shot," I proposed. After Mark played suitcase Tetris, we loaded into the car and headed to Alta Vista.

Our vacation club had three different properties in Puerto Vallarta, but we stayed at Alta Vista more often than not. The condos are more spacious and the pool is larger than Casa de La Playa, the property right on the beach just north of the Malecón, and it's only a short walk to the beach or old town, which the largest of the three properties, Conchas Chinas, is not. "I like each for a different reason but think Alta Vista best suits our needs," Lorie confirmed as we pulled up to the building.

Upon check-in, our hosts welcomed us with bright smiles, a temperature check and instructions regarding the departure COVID screening they set up for residents. Masks were required indoors but optional elsewhere.

"What happens if one of us tests positive and can't leave the country?" I asked.

"We confine you to your condo and bring you anything you need until your isolation is over."

"Sounds divine. We'll see if any of us get so lucky," I said, and headed to the condo to settle in.

I told Mark and Lorie I'd meet them at the car to go shopping after we unpacked, but when I passed by their condo, the door was open, so I went there instead. Lorie, pacing about franticly and mumbling to herself, never acknowledged my existence. I saw Mark on the patio and decided it was best to join him. "What's up?" I asked.

"Lorie can't find her passport."

"She just had it a few hours ago."

"Yeah, I know, but she thinks it may have fallen out of her bag at the airport."

When Lorie wasn't pacing, she was digging through her luggage, checking and rechecking the pocket she swore she put the passport in. "It's not in my bag, and I know I put it in my bag," she chanted. Mark, being the calm problem-solving engineer that he is was proactively looking up how to get a temporary passport on the computer and trying his best to soothe Lorie's anxiety. I joined his offensive. "I think you need to step away, get some food and regroup. Lets' go to town for a drink and groceries. You can look again later." Thankfully, Lorie agreed to my suggestion, and we headed to town.

The following morning during breakfast, I asked, "What's the passport plan."

"Oh, I found it," Lorie said rather nonchalantly. "It was in my bag all along, just a different pocket." Mark rolled his eyes ever so slightly, smiled but said nothing. *Wise man*, I thought.

"Great news. I was thinking we'd be visiting an embassy today," I countered.

"Nope, we just need to pick up Nora and swap the rental car," Lorie indicated.

Mark and the girls left for the airport around noon. They'd made a welcome sign for Nora and wanted to be the ones to greet her outside of customs. She and Alan decided not to take any chances with Lily's possible COVID exposure. "I promised her a do-over once school is out," Nora explained while we drank mimosas by the pool. "I feel a bit guilty saying this, but I'm happy it turned out the way it did. I don't know what I was thinking. Entertaining and monitoring two twelve-year-old girls would have been exhausting."

"Not my idea of a vacation," I proposed.

"Cheers to COVID," Nora said as she raised her glass. Lorie, Mark, and I followed suit.

Mark never exchanged the rental car, which was probably a good thing. The streets in Puerto Vallarta are narrow, and we would've struggled to find a parking space large enough for a van.

"What do you want to do today?" Mark asked the girls during breakfast.

"I want to go to the beach," Kaitlin announced.

"Me too," Kate concurred.

"I'm game," Nora added.

"Okay, the beach it is," Mark declared. We four girls went back to our condo to prepare for a day by the sea.

"I didn't bring any sunscreen. Do you have some I can use?" Kaitlin asked me.

"You're kidding me, right? You're as fair-skinned as Kate, and you didn't think to pack a single ounce of sunscreen for a trip to the beach?"

"You brought six bathing suits but no sunscreen?" Kate questioned.

"Yeah, probably didn't think that through very well," Kaitlin said with a giggle and a smile.

"Here, use this. You can buy more if we run out," I said.

Waiting for the girls felt like an eternity. Choosing a swimsuit for the day required a fashion show with almost as many garment changes as a Victoria's Secret runway event. Bikini tops, bottoms, cover-ups, and even sandals were swapped around to achieve the ideal ensemble. Hair needed to be braided, twisted and pinned back, and packing their beach bags required an act of congress. While I feebly attempted to speed up their process, Nora, tired of waiting, settled on the patio with a book.

When the girls declared themselves ready, our entourage of ladies left for the beach. Mark and Lorie, who'd long since given up on waiting, secured us a couple of *palapas* and lounge chairs at a seaside bar. "Local peddlers aren't allowed to push their goods to bar customers," Lorie explained. "Makes for a more relaxing experience."

White-clothed merchants, hoping to sell their trinkets, lined the beach for a far as the eye could see. "Good call Lorie. What other tips do you have?"

"Oh, Mark and I have a lot of travel hacks."

"Let's hear a few."

"Most people have a pedicure before they come to Mexico, but we wait and do it here. It's cheaper. Nine dollars for a deluxe pedicure with a massage," she explained. "Show them your wallet, Mark." He leaned over and pulled a slender wallet from his back pocket.

"I carry a fake wallet with bogus cards in my back pocket," he placed the wallet on the table for our review. "My real wallet's in the front one," he said while tapping his front thigh.

"Pickpockets are more apt to steal from the back." Lorie added. "Oh, and we have a dedicated travel debit card and only keep four hundred dollars in the account at any given time."

"I would never have thought to do that," Nora offered. Lorie moved on to packing.

"I always pack spices I know I may not easily find where I'm going, extra baggies, and an insulated cup to keep my beverages cool. Oh, and as far as clothes, I only take one set of jewelry and pack light clothes that don't wrinkle easily and can be hand washed."

"I remembered the spice trick and brought some this trip," I reported.

"Another is that we often pack older underwear and just throw them out after they're worn. I do the same thing with my treadmill sneakers, but since they're usually in good shape I leave those in the condo for housekeeping. I can live out of a carry-on for at least a month," she stated with pride.

Mark changed the subject. "What do we want to see and do over the next week?"

"I want to go to Yelapa. The first chapter of my book is dedicated to the people and experiences I had there years ago. I want to give Judith at Sky Temple a signed copy," I said.

"I want more beach time," Kaitlin declared.

"Me too," Nora added.

"I want to shop on the Malecón," Kate told the group.

"We can do all of those things," Mark stated.

The following day, we drove to Mismaloya Beach and boarded a boat bound for Yelapa. I gave the group a quick tour of the town, which was as I remembered but also different. Buildings once inhabited were now either abandoned or repurposed, and a new school as well as a Museum of History, Art and Culture had been erected where the old school once stood. We hiked to the town's signature waterfall before settling in at Domingo's restaurant on the beach. Yelapa offered something for everyone, and to this day is one of the highlights of our time in Mexico.

"I'm gonna walk to Sky Temple to see if I can find Judith," I said.

"I'll go with you," Nora offered.

"We're good here," Kate stated, and Kaitlin concurred.

Nora and I waded across the river then worked our way through the jungle and onto the cobblestone path that headed east into the forest. The narrow, winding path felt familiar, but the landscape and foliage looked dusty and broken. "I wonder what happened here?" I said to Nora.

I stopped at the gate that, from memory, led me to Sky Temple, but the jungle looked overgrown, and the path beyond it, abandoned. "Maybe I have it wrong. Let's walk a little further east." It didn't take me long to realize the gate I first chose was probably it. Nora and I circled back, opened the gate, and started to make our way up the mountain.

"I don't think anyone lives here anymore," I said to her.

"It does look a bit sketchy," Nora replied.

A moment later, we came upon three rather giant iguanas sprawled across the path. They appeared to be less than thrilled by our presence, and the hissing and clicking sounds they began making confirmed it.

"Welp, that's it. We're outta here."

"Yeah, they don't look pleased," Nora suggested.

Once back on the path, two girls with green and purple eyeshadow and matching Pokémon T-shirts rode past us on horseback. My curiosity got the better of me.

"Hey girls, can I ask you a few questions?"

"Sure," The older of the two offered.

"Is that the path to Sky Temple? And why does the jungle look so dusty?"

"Mudslides wiped out this area two years ago. It's not safe. Most people have moved across the river," she explained.

"Are you from here?" I asked.

"Yeah, we live here six months out of the year, and the other six months in the Yukon. We're leaving tomorrow."

"We're riding to town to return these books," the youngest girl added while pointing to the bag hooked on the saddle horn. We talked a bit more about living in the Yukon, and I thanked them for their time and wished them a safe journey. Nora and I watched the horse trot out of sight then made our way back to the beach.

"Did you get the book dropped off?" Lorie inquired.

"Nope, but we met two girls with crazy eyeshadow and an extraordinary off-the-grid life that Alan would be totally jealous of," Nora offered.

As luck would have it, the bartender at Domingo's knew Judith and told me he'd be honored to give her the book. *Bartenders know everyone. I shoulda gone that route first*, I thought.

By day three, the girls felt comfortable venturing out on their own, which gave the adults time to catch up or chill. Mark put in some remote work hours before meeting up with Los Muertos owner and brewmaster at their new location. Lorie caught up on her telenovelas, washed her hair and talked with family in the States. Nora soaked in the sun at the pool, and I began mapping out book two, *Sandwiched*.

"Let's grill dinner by the pool around six," Mark announced before we scattered for the day. The girls returned from the Malecón around four and joined Nora at the pool for a dip. Lorie and I came down around five to set up and join them. They told us of their adventures at the beach and on the Malecón, and Kaitlin proudly flashed around the jewelry she bought off a beach vendor.

"I like bartering," she announced.

"I don't," Kate added.

After dinner, we moved the party to our patio, and that's when things got silly.

"I'm good with driving to Sayulita, but I don't want to leave until I've had my morning poo," Lorie clarified. "I don't want to chance it or use a public bathroom for that."

"Ever gamble on a fart and lose?" I asked the group.

"No, but I'm a regular at crop-dusting," Kate declared.

"I can attest to that. She does it at work all the time," Kaitlin explained.

"Ah, the dreaded dirty squirty," Nora added.

Our laughter filled the patio and echoed into the night.

"I think we've all been there or come dangerously close," Mark suggested.

"I pooped my pants on a date," Nora divulged.

Once again, laughter filled the night air.

"Oh, do tell," I said, and the girls concurred.

"Well, it really wasn't a date. I was with a boy, but he was just a friend. Anyway, we'd gone to the movies, and after, he suggested we drive over to another friend's house to hang out. She lived way up in the hills, and during the winding drive up the mountain, I got that feeling in my stomach. You know the one where you say this isn't going to end well, and you look for the nearest bathroom? I held it together in the car, but when I got out and stood up, the dam broke, and it all started coming out. I rushed upstairs to the bedroom, burst open the door and said, 'I shit my pants.' It was after that I noticed her room was full of other girls. 'Get my zebra boots off. You're getting poop in them,' she said as I rushed across her room and into the bathroom. I'd borrowed her boots to wear to the movies. I was so embarrassed and upset that it took them over two hours to convince me to come out. The stomach flu and too much popcorn. What a deadly combination. I was traumatized for years."

After everyone's morning poo, we headed north to Litibú Beach, a remote, pristine, mile-long stretch of sand way off the beaten path. We traversed a dry creek bed and bottomed out the car several times on the precarious drive to the access. We shared the beach with a handful of others who had braved the journey. Mark noticed a rundown shade hut fashioned out of sticks and palm strands and set up camp there. The girls frolicked in the ocean, and my adult companions read while I walked the sand and hiked the hills capturing shots of this majestic area.

"Hey, you know the yellow house I showed you in the real estate book?"

"Yeah, the one we talked about buying?" Mark replied.

"I think it's right behind us. Up that hill," I said.

"Cool, Let's drive up there on our way out," he suggested.

We only spent a few hours at the beach as there were no facilities, and by then we'd all had too much sun.

"Where are we going?" Kate asked.

"On an adventure," I answered.

"House hunting," Mark offered as he gunned the engine to make the hill. We leaned forward, hoping it would help the sedan make the climb. The homes in the area seemed nicer than their surroundings, and the neighborhood had an ex-pat air about it.

The yellow house was just beyond the crest of the hill. We walked the exterior, peeked in windows and imagined what it would be like to stay somewhere so remote. "Look, they have a cistern and a generator," I pointed out.

"That says volumes," Nora suggested.

"You wouldn't want to have to go to town very often," Mark offered.

"Yeah, definitely more of a retreat vibe," I said.

On our way out, we talked to the neighbor, an ex-pat who'd lived there for decades. He gave us a rundown on life in Litibú past and present and said he thought the yellow house was sold. "Developers are knocking at the door of this small town, and home prices are skyrocketing," he told us in a tone that indicated he wasn't thrilled about the idea.

"I think I'll take a pass on living in Litibú," I said as we made our way back to Vallarta.

"Yep. Too remote. Besides, when I come down here, I want amenities," Nora proclaimed, and Mark concurred.

The following evening, we celebrated Kate's birthday in style. Hamburger Mary's, in the romance zone, had their grand opening party on our first night in town. We watched the spectacle, visited with a few staff members then hatched our birthday plan. Mark bought a cake with seventeen candles and delivered it to the restaurant while the rest of us primped and pre-gamed. We walked down to Mary's around six.

"Their sign says Sassy-Juicy-Sexy. Shouldn't it say Saucy-Juicy-Sexy? It's a burger joint," I asked.

"Who cares," Nora answered. "Bring on the drag queens."

"Birthday burgers with a side of drag. Might be the best one yet," Kate said.

Over dinner, a gorgeous queen dressed in a flashy, purple frock performed a few classic diva numbers and worked the crowd. Participation is highly encouraged at Mary's, so Lorie and I joined her on stage for the Whitney number.

"I've never seen a queen rock a full beard," Nora said.

"I've never seen a drag queen," Kaitlin stated.

"Come on. You've seen Ru Paul, right?" I asked.

"Who's that?" she answered.

I shook my head in disbelief. "You have much to learn, my young Padawan."

A few moments later, the jumbo screen behind the drag queen flashed, Happy Birthday Kate, and the girls were summoned to the stage. Kate was roasted and celebrated by the performers, and after the show, they presented her cake, complete with fireworks streaming out the top, to our table and sang the birthday song in English and Spanish.

"I think that makes up for last year," I said to Kate as we made our way out of the restaurant.

"Yeah, that was so much fun."

"Don't tell Lily," Nora said. "I don't want to have to try and top it."

After Nora and the girls left, I had sex on the beach twice and then got screwed. Lorie saw the two for one drink-special earlier in the day and suggested we return after our airport run to partake and watch the sunset.

"I'm so putting the drink pun in my Vallarta essay," I said.

"Don't forget travel hacks," Lorie suggested.

"Or the drag queen birthday party," Mark offered.

"And poop stories," I decreed.

On the way to my mandatory COVID exit test, I dropped two signed copies of my book at the front desk before heading to the hospital, one for the library at Alta Vista and the other for mailing to Coral Mar in Cancún. I'd written about our vacation club and my travels to both in the book, so leaving a signed copy, just as I did in Yelapa, felt right. A full-circle moment of sorts for me.

Regrettably, I received a negative test result email the next day. "My hopes for an extended vacation have just been dashed. Looks like I'll be leaving on Wednesday as planned."

"Guess we better make the most of our final two days," Lorie suggested. And that's just what we did. We packed a champagne picnic and traveled up the coast to San Francisco. Did you know there was a town in Nayarit, Mexico, with that name? I didn't. It's situated along the pacific coast just north of Sayulita. San Pancho, as it's also called, is a quaint village known for its sense of community, laid-back vibe and surfing. We picnicked on the beach and after, strolled through the town's sleepy streets, taking in the art and culture of the area. I preferred it over Sayulita, which was our next stop. Sayulita was so overrun with tourists that we stayed only long enough to say we'd been there.

"I can't believe how many people are packed on the beach," Lorie remarked.

"It's crazy here. I'm dodging bodies left and right," I offered.

"So much for social distancing," Mark commented.

"I know, and no one's wearing masks," Loire pointed out.

"Maybe they didn't get the memo, or more likely, they don't care," I suspected.

"I've seen enough. Let's move on to Bucerías," Mark suggested.

We spent the rest of the day slowly making our way back to Vallarta, pausing when curiosity or desire called us to do so.

On my final morning, I rose early to capture the sunrise as it washed over the vibrant art and architecture of *la zona romántica* and after, sat on a bench by the sea cataloging the precious memories we'd made. Life-altering experiences for the girls that were life-affirming for the rest of us. We'd chosen connection and family over the uncertainty and fear fueled pandemic, and for that, I am forever grateful.

I left Vallarta with a rejuvenated perspective and a renewed conviction for my life. I reaffirmed my vows to embrace risk, grow from failure and never make decisions based on fear. To trust my gut and march into the unknown knowing a life well lived is how I hope to be remembered.

Becoming A Writer

Three days after my husband died, I was compelled to write a book. I didn't know when or how I'd accomplish it, just that amid the chaos of family, funeral plans and flowers, a voice in the back of my head kept chanting, *Watch, listen, remember.* So I did.

I bought several small journals and set one at my bedside for dream catching, a second in the kitchen, because that's where all the action happens, and another at work for the thoughts that distract me from the day. I placed the tiniest of the four in my purse so I'd always have one with me. I recorded moments, comments, occurrences and feelings. I became a voyeur of my own life.

The role of observer came quickly to me as it required little to no emotion, which due to the shock of trauma, I'd yet to summon. The position placed me safely outside of myself, away from the devastating existence I was living.

My best friend, Kristen, gifted me the title of my yet-to-be manuscript within the first week. She was on the phone with a friend who must have asked about the funeral. Her response was, "Tragically Beautiful." *That's it*, I thought. I picked up the kitchen journal and recorded the words.

In the month and years to follow, I documented my walk along the twisted path of grief, noting highlights, hazards and detours I encountered on the treacherous trail. Then, on a wintry evening in early 2019, I became a writer.

I didn't know it at the time. My definition of a writer was a well-read individual who studied their craft and published libraries of works. I possessed none of those qualities. I've read, and do read, but am nowhere close to being thought of as an avid reader. Many of my friends fit the profile, which explains the bewildered looks when I revealed my intentions. "But you don't really read," or, "You know most writers are robust readers," often accompanied their puzzled expressions. I deserved the uncertainty.

Years earlier, I agreed to join the neighborhood book club. I read some of the books, but most of the time I'd have my friend, Lorie, give me a synopsis on the walk over, then work the room like an Oscar-winning actress. I was good at listening and crafting a conversation that incorporated plot lines, pivotal moments and characters. Those who weren't in on the charade were none the wiser. "You were more believable than me, and I actually read the book," Lorie would often say after.

Spending thirty years in health care didn't help me either. That sector's philosophy on written communication could be summed up as less is more. I was instructed to keep it brief and objective, to employ a host of acronyms, and spelling was optional. All points that worked for this naturally dyslexic southpaw.

I studied the sciences versus literature, which meant my acumen of grammar, punctuation, and style was limited at best. I did, however, receive high marks in a freshman English course, a fact that wholly astonished my mother.

"I can't believe you got an A," she offered at the end of term.

"Me either, but I'll take it," was my response at the time. But I've come to appreciate the aspect of the class that connected with me: storytelling. It was creative in nature, emphasizing weaving a tale and connecting to your readers, and I respected and adored both.

During my medical career, I was asked by a nonprofit group to write an article for their newsletter on assistive devices for self-care. I turned the piece into a David Letterman-inspired top ten device list that was not only informative but engaging and funny. "This has your stamp all over it, Beth. Great job."

A month after the article ran, I received a call from the national association asking to run it in their upcoming publication. I'd become a published author but hadn't thought of myself as a writer yet.

Let's start with something light, I said to myself as I glanced through the outline of topics before me. I landed on Paisley, the kitty we brought home two weeks post-loss. I stared at the blank screen thinking, *Once you open this door, there's no going back.* I acknowledged the thought, turned the knob and stepped through anyway.

The first few paragraphs moved from thought to page with fluidity, but a roadblock was waiting for me as I rounded the corner. *Oh crap, I've gotta write dialogue. How do I do that?* I considered breaking from the piece to review the guidelines but didn't want to lose momentum, so I opted to wing it and clean up the details later. I finished the story in a few hours and, years later, adapted my debut work for consideration in a book about grief, loss, and healing. Paisley was selected and published in the Chicken Soup for the Soul series in early 2022.

Feeling compelled to do something can be a gift, as it removes doubt. I never worried or questioned my ability, because I had to write the book. My soul demanded it. The pain that lived within me needed to reside somewhere else before I could begin to let it go. For that reason, I retreated into the past, spending weeks and, at times, months reliving the moments, embracing the pain, and making peace with the horror that had upended our lives. Writing that manuscript was a cathartic journey, my destiny, and I realized during the process that once you accept fate, the world gets a lot lighter.

By November of that year, the manuscript was nearing completion. I began to turn my thoughts toward editing and publishing. I wasn't sure who might be interested in taking on a fledgling writer or when they might have the time for me, so I figured getting started sooner than later was a safe bet. I knew self-publishing was the only route for me and, fortunately, had a person in my life who was a master at it.

Kristen and I sat on the balcony of her luxury condominium, sipping champagne and catching up. I'd flown down to Phoenix that morning to see her new place before we embarked on a road trip to San Diego the next day. She'd booked us into the Del for a weekend of spa treatments, yoga on the beach and cocktails by the sea. We also had plans to catch up with our longtime friend, Carl, who we'd not seen in decades.

Kristen and I were piecing together the time puzzle since our last visit when I dropped the book bomb. "I'm writing a book," I said. I stared at her blank expression for a brief moment, then went on to talk about the content and my hopeful timeline for publishing. Kristen listened intently, but I could tell she was a bit surprised at the declaration. No doubt, due to my lack of reading prowess, and that the comment might have been a bit out of left-field. We sat in silence as she carefully formulated a response.

"Why do you want to write the book, and how do you define success?" she queried.

I'd thought a lot about the answer to her question over the previous two years but never put words to it until that moment. "If one person can feel less alone because I've shared my story, because I've given a voice to those things often lived but never talked about, then I've won. That's the reason."

"Good answer," she said. She went on to impart pearls of wisdom and truths she'd learned from twenty years in the author's chair, and throughout the weekend we touched on writing and publishing but didn't dwell. Our time on Coronado

Island was meant for relaxation and rejuvenation, and it was sublime.

Dinners with Carl were equal parts catching up and reminiscing about our twentysomething days in Denver. We both especially enjoyed the small-town Christmas parade that marched by the Del one evening. Locals decorated their bikes, cars, wagons, and even strollers in miles of garland and twinkling lights. The high school band played holiday tunes while dance groups sashayed down the main street. It was the epitome of small-town America, and just what we needed to ignite our holiday spirit.

Once back in the writer's chair, I split my time between essay revisions and schooling myself on self-publishing. I joined BookBub, Goodreads, and SmashWords and listened intently to Mark Coker's entire *Smart Author* podcast series. I interviewed and hired a local company to assist me with branding, website development, cover design, editing and publishing. I had an advanced release copy I could send to Kristen for her review and comment by June. She gave me tremendous insights, sparking an additional round of edits, and wrote a beautiful forward.

"I think I could edit the book forever," I said to her.

"Yeah, I know, Bethy, but at some point it just has to be done," she offered.

Tragically Beautiful Essays of Love, Loss, and Hope was released on 8 November, 2020. Thanks to friends and family, the book earned Amazon's hot new release ribbon for western U.S biographies. I'd done it. Completed the mission my soul demanded, but in doing so, I discovered I'd never be done.

My book was one among millions, and if I had any hope of getting the title into the multitude of hands that needed to read it, I was going to have to become her champion. I was instructed that twenty percent of my time should be spent writing, and the other eighty marketing. And there are no overnight sensations.

These facts were later validated by the author instructors of Master Class, an online educational platform I gifted myself for Christmas. Malcolm Gladwell spent two years in his car with a trunk full of books, traveling and talking to anyone willing to listen. David Sedaris gained notoriety through his public readings and storytelling. Roxanne Gay and David Baldacci advised me not to quit my day job, because very few authors make a living solely from book sales.

I joined the regional writers' guild, upped my social media presence and applied for the author's program at my public library. After networking with fellow writers, I felt I might have done things a bit backward. Most join writers' groups, take advantage of conferences and training, then pitch their manuscripts to agents or eventually self-publish. I never even considered an agent, and from the few I talked with during a conference, I was probably better off on my own. You see, I was a nobody, and to get your memoir picked up by an agent, you needed to be a somebody.

"Why do people want to read your book? What makes you credible?"

"Well, I lived it, for starters."

"Yeah, that's not enough. But I like your energy. Good luck. I hope you do well."

I quickly learned promoting my book would be a long, uphill battle. Still, I didn't anticipate the hesitation I'd have in my own backyard.

"Mom, have you read the book yet? Did you add it to your book club's list for next year?"

"No, I want to read it first."

"Do you have a copy?"

"No, not yet."

I ordered one from Amazon and had it shipped to her. Two weeks later, she cracked the cover, and that's when the phone calls began.

"I can't believe you remembered so many details. Oh, and your language. I'm impressed with your vocabulary," she said with a note of pride in her voice. I felt like a twelve-year-old.

A few days later she called to say she had finished it and gave the book to her friend, Jo, to read.

"I want to talk with you about it but want Jo to read it first so I have more to share," she offered.

"Okay, mom, whatever you need to do," I replied, thinking, *I guess Jo's going to be the deciding vote.*

The next week, Mom called me all flustered. "Oh Beth, I just had to call you as soon as I heard. Jo read your book in one day and said she really enjoyed it, but that's not the best part. She gave it to her husband, Skip, and he read it cover to cover yesterday. Can you believe it! He was so taken by it that he gave up Sunday football to read it. Oh, Beth, this is amazing!"

"I'm glad you're finally on board, Mom."

"I thought your book was only for widows or women in general, but now I know men can relate to it too. Please order me ten copies so I can give them to the neighbors."

Skip's approval transformed my mother from a cautious supporter into a self-appointed literary agent. She kept a stack of books on hand for gifting and called me regularly with the latest feedback from my readers in the south. *One down, millions to go*, I thought.

Another of my Master Class instructors, Walter Mosely, taught me that you can become a writer at any age and the older the better, for with age comes wisdom and experience. "A sixty-four-year-old man can write about being seventeen, but a seventeen-year-old knows nothing about being sixty-four." He also noted that reading and writing are two different processes; therefore, you don't have to be a big reader to be a good writer. I felt support and validation and swiftly worked my way through the site's entire author instructor series within months.

David Sedaris inspired me to let go of perfection and just be myself. To ask good questions, say yes to everything, and that anything is funny, eventually. He sighted boredom as the reason he prefers to write in essay format. I chose it because it felt approachable. I know what it's like to be intimidated by the size of a book and wanted to write works that were accessible for non-readers as well as avid ones.

Neil Gaiman's rules for writers were simple: you have to write, you have to finish, and you have to put it out into the world. He felt that perfect is an aspiration that doesn't exist and wisely pointed out that you can't fix a blank piece of paper. "Be brave, start writing and have faith in the process. Some will sing, and others will hum."

Most people read non-fiction because they're searching for something. They want to understand the world and often themselves more profoundly. Most of us write non-fiction for the same reason. We tell stories to dissect, analyze and explore our truths. Writing allows us to examine ourselves and the context of our lives from a reflective lens. We're able to say things we may not have said or understood at the time, and with any luck, utilize a richer perspective when doing so. We celebrate the real and the broken and welcome failure, as it provides an avenue for growth.

When I walked away from healthcare in the fall of 2018, I said to myself, you don't know what you're meant to do next, but if you follow your heart you'll find it, or it will find you. Writing has been a quiet companion of mine for decades. A steadfast friend who waited patiently for me to appreciate the possibilities our alliance could create. My "it" had been there all the time, watching and waiting for me to discover the depth and beauty of our association. I have a profound respect for the act of putting pen to paper and believe all who do are writers, including me.

I think of writing as my legacy project. An endeavor crafted by me, cultivated by many, and hopefully enjoyed by all who take a chance and turn the page.

The End

I highly doubt it.
Feels like I'm just getting started.

It's been an honor to share these essays on life with you. Thank you for spending time with my book. The journey from heart to page is a soulful adventure, and I'm forever grateful to all who inspired and supported me and to those who keep the conversation going.

If you enjoyed your time with me, please consider recommending my book to others or writing a review at your chosen retailer.

Want to know more about my other books, what's coming next, life on the farm, or see snapshots from the photography studio?
Visit my website and subscribe to my newsletter: **bethbullard.com**
And follow me on:
Facebook/Meta: **www.facebook.com/bethbullardauthor**
Instagram: **@bethbullardauthor**

In a book club? Consider contacting me to join the discussion: bethbullard.com. I've crafted a variety of questions to encourage spirited conversation. Enjoy!

1. Are you, or have you ever felt, sandwiched by life? Which parts, if any, of Beth's experience could you relate to?
2. Was there any one line, essay or passage that stood out to you? Why?
3. What feelings or emotions does the book, or a specific chapter evoke for you?
4. Do you have a memorable animal or travel story? How about an incident that might not have seemed funny at the time but on reflection, is hilarious? Please share.
5. Is Beth someone you could see yourself spending time with in real life? What adventures might you take together?